CAPTAIN WILLIAM DAMPIER

BUCCANEER-AUTHOR

CAPTAIN WILLIAM DAMPIER

BUCCANEER-AUTHOR

By WILLARD HALLAM BONNER

---

*Some Account
of a Modest Buccaneer and
of English Travel Literature in the
Early Eighteenth Century*

STANFORD UNIVERSITY PRESS
STANFORD UNIVERSITY, CALIFORNIA
LONDON: HUMPHREY MILFORD
OXFORD UNIVERSITY PRESS

STANFORD UNIVERSITY PRESS
STANFORD UNIVERSITY, CALIFORNIA

LONDON: HUMPHREY MILFORD
OXFORD UNIVERSITY PRESS

———

ROBERT M. MC BRIDE & COMPANY
4 WEST SIXTEENTH STREET, NEW YORK

MARTINUS NIJHOFF
9 LANGE VOORHOUT, THE HAGUE

THE MARUZEN COMPANY
TOKYO, OSAKA, KYOTO, SENDAI

———

To K. C. B.
W. H. B., Jr.
A. C. B.

I speake not against Travell, so usefull to usefull men . . . . at no great charge I offer a World of Travellers to their domesticke entertainment.

—*Purchas his Pilgrimes*

It is a strange thing, that in sea voyages, where there is nothing to be seen but sky and sea, men should make diaries.

—BACON, *Of Travel*

Our true sea epics are written in prose rather than in verse.

—JOHN MASEFIELD, *A Sailor's Garland*

TO THE READER

THE following pages are intended for anyone who may be interested to see how a modest mariner's simple journals, kept scrupulously in the midst of the greatest hardships, sometimes sealed in a bamboo cane, made their author famous, stimulated a rage for travel books, and penetrated English prose in several conspicuous places. They are for armchair voyagers who have not forgotten their *Robinson Crusoe* and *Gulliver's Travels,* and who still unashamedly believe that fortitude greatly maketh a man.

Certain parts of this book may reveal its origin, a dissertation submitted a few years ago to the Yale English Faculty. It has suffered a sea change since, however, with the sloughing off of much matter, certain bibliographical niceties, and many notes. What is left is an effort to round out the figure of Dampier, whose adventurous life has been done very well recently by Clennel Wilkinson. Dampier has formerly been chronicled as buccaneer, explorer, sea adventurer, with an occasional dark hint by such a person as Sir Walter Scott about his influence upon Defoe and Swift. It is this undetermined extent of his literary influence, the success and value of his four books of voyages, their precise relations with prose fiction and the publishing world of their day, and some final estimate of his rightful place in our literature that have been my particular concern. Unwittingly he carved a niche for himself. In illuminating it for a moment, I revive an all-but-slighted part of everyday life in England from 1697 to 1729. Dampier, who played so many actual rôles, I would present as a Baedeker, a Holinshed, and a very definite leaven in the loaf.

Acknowledgments are due the following:

Professor Chauncey Brewster Tinker, under whose guidance the work began.

My Family, who languished awhile in New Haven's Grub Street.

Those who have preceded me, whose work is duly acknowledged in my notes.

Certain libraries which were used freely through the courtesy of attendants, officials, and friends, including those of Yale and Harvard, the New York Public Library, the Boston Public Library, the Boston Athenaeum, the Explorers Club, the American Geographical Society, Grosvenor Library (Buffalo), and the British Museum.

N. M. Penzer, Esq., who has kindly given me permission to reprint with alterations his table of editions of Dampier's *Voyages* that appeared in Dampier's *New Voyage Round the World*, 1927, in the Argonaut Press Series.

The editors of *The Bookman* (now *The American Review*), who have given permission to reprint portions of my article, "The Man Who Was Friday."

Professors Arthur W. Secord, William A. Eddy, Henry Ten Eyck Perry, and Robert W. Seitz, who read and criticized portions of the manuscript.

W. H. B.

Buffalo, New York
April 1934

CONTENTS

PAGE

I. THE SEA: AN INTRODUCTION · · · · · · · I

II. THE FAR WANDERER · · · · · · · · 6

III. A LITERARY BUCCANEER · · · · · · · 31

IV. THE SILVER AGE OF TRAVEL · · · · · · 50

V. THE STRANGE SURPRISING ADVENTURES OF A YORK
MARINER · · · · · · · · · · 68

VI. PIRATES · · · · · · · · · · · 93

VII. A JOURNALIST DREAMS · · · · · · · 115

VIII. DAMPIER AND DEFOE · · · · · · · 148

IX. COUSIN GULLIVER · · · · · · · · 156

X. HONEST COMPLIMENT · · · · · · · 182

XI. UNWITTINGLY HE CARVED A NICHE · · · · 197

APPENDIX · · · · · · · · · · · 207

BIBLIOGRAPHY · · · · · · · · · · 215

INDEX · · · · · · · · · · · 225

I

THE SEA: AN INTRODUCTION

It is therefore a very happy Circumstance in this kind of Reading, that it charms us by a perpetual Variety, and keeps alive that Thirst of Inquiry, which we are apt to lose, when too closely confined to severer Studies.

—JOHN HARRIS, *Navigantium*

THE long swells of northern seas have moaned for centuries on England's shores. Ceaselessly the irresistible procession has washed over bars, pulsated in rocky channels, pounded cliffs into sands, and shaped the lives of Englishmen. Seafaring but sea-weary peoples, if our histories speak truly, first gave entity to the nation: Danes, Angles, Saxons, and others, melancholy marsh-dwellers from the Baltic's shores. Part of her civilizing was accomplished by far-voyaging spirits who crossed over water on two sides of the island to bring Christian hope and teaching to stalwart but gloomy hearts. Conquerors of England declared themselves by landing on the seashore. England herself, grown to nationhood through domestic strife and through defense of the common cause, asserted herself finally and triumphantly by ruling the wave. The embracing arm of ocean not only called up her adventurers sometimes to destroy them cruelly, but isolated her and often destroyed, or discouraged, her enemies. The sea is writ large in the history of England, and English mariners have filled a broad and interesting page in the history of the world. Englishmen have from the beginning been inveterate travelers, and necessarily travelers by sea. Yet with all this heritage of waters, the sea itself has washed its way but slowly into the hard strata of English literature.

It was not till the eighteenth century that its stirring spirit touched inner fibers of literature and produced a succession of great works in prose and verse. The sea as a fact had always existed, but the sea as matter for the shaping spirit of imagination did not wet many printed pages till late. Certain reflections of seafaring life are naturally to be found before 1700. The whole melancholy background of Anglo-Saxon epic and lyric poetry is of the sea. Chaucer pictures a shipman among those congenial companions en route to Canterbury. Many ballads like "Sir Patrick Spens" tell of marine catastrophes. The death of Celtic King Arthur harks back to the sea-burial of the Norsemen. Spenser breathed the spirit of the sea into "Colin Clout's Come Home Again."

Shakespeare paid passing homage to the great Elizabethan voyagers in *The Tempest*, in which he wrote a good sea-dirge. John Donne, at sea with Essex, wrote "The Storme" and "The Calme." Andrew Marvel sang a lotos-song of Bermuda to the rhythm of English oars. Milton's Satan displays amazing knowledge of geography. But these are strewn over a long period of time and form no large body of literature. No period was rich in the poetry of the sea except perhaps the very earliest, which is doubtfully called English. Few sang of its beauty and grandeur; of its joy, mystery, horror; of its austere force and magic power.

Dryden lamented in the preface to *Annus Mirabilis* that he had never read a nautical description couched in proper nautical terms. No one romantically pictured the nautical life or entertained with stories of its sailors. It remained for the nineteenth century to do this. Before Coleridge and the Romantic poets, scarcely anyone, with the possible exception of William Falconer, who in 1762 described a shipwreck and dolphins at play, wrote poetry filled with the beauty and mystery of the sea. Before Defoe and Swift and Smollett few had written prose romances of the sea, none with the atmosphere, the language, the characters of the sea. Before Congreve's *Love for Love* few nautical characters trod the stage. Only with the eighteenth century does the sea occupy a place in English literature at all comparable with its place in English life. A good French scholar has said that the memory of sailors good and bad and their doings, from Benbow to Nelson, has perished for lack of poets to sing them.[1] One might extend the time back to Drake. The late eighteenth and early nineteenth centuries brought this poetry. The early eighteenth century brought the prose.

In the time of town-dwellers like Addison, Pope, and Samuel Johnson, the sea, it has been said,[2] was too far away, too deserted, too cold, to draw the world of letters far from home. Though Thomson wrote "Rule Britannia," he and his followers were not truly at ease close to the elements. Whereas this is partly true of poetry, it does not hold for the world of letters *in toto* and must even be modified in its narrower application if we examine a strong undercurrent of feeling revealed in the substantial list of titles of poems of second and third rate.[3] The eighteenth century was a great

[1] Jules Douady, *La Mer et les poètes Anglais*, 1912.

[2] *Ibid.*, pp. 152–53.

[3] Impressive in a list but often individually unimportant are the following: John Hughes, "The Court of Neptune" (1699); William Walsh, "The Golden Age" (1703); Daniel Defoe, "The Storm" (1704); Ned Ward, "The Wars of the Elements: or, A Description of a Sea-Storm" (1709); William Diaper, "Nereides: or, Sea-Eclogues" (1712); John Gay, "Black-Eyed Susan" (1715), and " 'Twas When the Sea Was Roaring" (1715); James Thomson, passages in *The Seasons* (1730), and "Rule Britannia" (1740); Edward Young, "Ocean: An Ode, to which is prefixed an Ode to the King and a Discourse on Ode" (1728), and also "Imperium Pelagi: A Naval Lyric" (1730), and "Foreign Address in the Character of a Sailor" (1734); Charles Dibdin, many sailor songs and ballads (1745–1814); David Garrick, "Heart of Oak" (1757); William

marine epoch, and its manifold activities made their impression on English letters. Explorers of the century were penetrating the South Seas more and more, often continuing on around the world. Thus the Falkland Islands, the Hawaiian Islands, Tahiti, and many places in the archipelagoes of the East Indies were made known to the world for the first time. Scientific expeditions were sent into both the Arctic and the Antarctic regions. Thus the supposed land lying south of the Straits of Magellan was shown to be an island, not a continent; and Behring Strait, the Aleutian Islands, and the Arctic Ocean were added to the map. The Northwest Passage was diligently sought. The art of making maps was greatly perfected by the French early in the century, and England had great map-makers like Herman Moll. Land near the poles was proved by actual measurement to be flattened. England perfected her navy to a degree of sailing efficiency that was surpassed only by the performance of later clipper ships. She carried on a tremendous military expedition against Spain in America, a thing that could be done, of course, only with the aid of great naval strength. England, France, and Spain pursued an eager competition in discovering new lands and colonizing them. Africa, Asia, Australia, and America were during this century wrested finally from the clouds of mystery and myth and the totally unknown. And the men of England, seafaring from time out of mind, were foremost in the work. It was the age of Dampier, Anson, and Cook, when seven of the twelve important voyages around the world were accomplished by Englishmen.

London flourished as a great center of commerce, with Bristol, Liverpool, Newcastle, and Hull soon offering competition. Fishing was pursued to Greenland and the Grand

---

Falconer, "The Shipwreck" (1762); George Crabbe, passages in *The Village* (1783); William Cowper, "Verses Supposed to Have Been Written by Alexander Selkirk" (1782), and also "On the Loss of the Royal George" (*ca.* 1786), and "The Castaway" (1800).

Banks. Great trading organizations like the South Sea Company rose—and fell. Lloyd's still great commercial house took root in a coffee house of the same name. Many tales of shipwreck were current.

People's minds were on the sea, even if poetry was not their best medium of expression. If we examine at leisure many departments of literature—prose as well as poetry; plays, novels, romances, essays, and journals; the everyday reading and gossip of the everyday world—we shall find that the sea is really no insignificant part of the great body of eighteenth-century literature. Its rôle is greatest in the early years, where it soon surged into a flow of things nautical. And it is partly to reveal some of the fresh sources of this stream of interest that this book has been written.

From 1700 to 1750 there appeared not only the celebrated narratives of Robinson Crusoe and Lemuel Gulliver but a host of other tales in imitation of them. They in turn had been preceded by the printing and reprinting of hundreds of accounts of actual voyages and travels, so many that reading them was a rage. A number of celebrated voyages by Englishmen aided and abetted this reading fever. Dampier, Woodes Rogers, and Admiral Anson touched the public imagination by their circumnavigatory adventures. Both great and small were caught in the wild speculation of the South Sea Bubble in 1720. Sea fever raged and took its toll. Its marks may yet be seen upon the sands of those times. There was calamity and a sapping of energies, but there were also deep impressions that sink in upon the mind, which, if it be the mind of genius, become sublimated and transformed into something strange and new.

II

THE FAR WANDERER

Friend, if a man should sail round the world, and anchor in
every harbour of it, without learning, he would return home
as ignorant as he went out.

—Parson Adams

William Dampier was England's greatest buccaneer.
He was not the most cruel, the most desperate, the
richest, the most romantic, or the most successful. But he
was the most feared, the most refined, the most scientifically
minded, and, being the most skilful navigator and recorder,
the most useful to the world. He wrote three matchless accounts of his travels. "A man of exquisite mind," sighed
Coleridge in *Table Talk,* and advised contemporary writers
of travels to "read and imitate the old captains and admirals,
as Dampier, &c."[1] Andrew Lang, who cast reproaches on
West Indian buccaneers in an essay on the subject, made
Dampier his single exception.[2] Sir Walter Scott lingered
wistfully over Dampier's passages and felt sure Defoe must
have known him personally. The present poet laureate has
declared Dampier's *Voyages* to be "the best books of voyages
in the language."[3] Quiet, modest, gentle of manner, his head
full of new knowledge of distant seas and seacoasts, and in
his pocket a new map of the Pacific, he pleasantly surprised

[1] Oxford edition (1917), pp. 168, 280.

[2] "Adventures of Buccaneers," in the forepart of Esquemeling's *History of the Buccaneers of America* (1923), p. xiv.

[3] John Masefield, *On the Spanish Main* (1906), p. 234.

6

the antiquarian John Evelyn. A literary buccaneer is indeed something of a novelty, and the pursuit of information about him never loses the freshness and interest of its initial promise.

Dampier's life is told best in his books. One may find the story in official places and in popular travel series, but these only repeat what he himself has written in his four interesting volumes: *A New Voyage Round the World* (1697), *Voyages and Descriptions* (1699), and *A Voyage to New Holland* (1703) with its *Continuation* (1709). From these, chiefly, I have extracted the principal events in order that we may proceed more clearly in later chapters.

Like the hero of an old romance, perhaps Robinson Crusoe, Dampier early had longings to see the world. Orphaned at the age of sixteen, he was the next year (1669) sent down from his native Somersetshire, nurse of many literary souls, across the moors to Weymouth, where he was apprenticed to the master of a ship.

He then engaged in several trading voyages: to France, to Newfoundland, and to Java. He was so pinched with the rigor of the cold climate of Newfoundland that he determined never to venture thereafter in those parts but to consider only a warm voyage. Accordingly, he shipped as a foremast hand on the "John and Martha" in 1671, bound for Bantam in the East Indies. This voyage took a little more than a year. Although he gained more experience in navigation, he as yet kept no journal.

Because of the outbreak of the second Dutch war, he retired to his brother's home in Somersetshire in 1672 but soon grew weary of life ashore. He next enlisted in the Navy and served on board the "Royal Prince" under Sir Edward Spragge the last year of the war, 1673. During this time he had fallen sick, and, after some time on board a hospital ship and ashore at Harwich, he retired once more to his brother's house to recover his health.

THE CAMPEACHY VOYAGES

With the return of his health came back his great longing for the sea. He therefore accepted the offer of a gentleman of his native village to go to Jamaica to manage a plantation for him, and set out in 1674, being twenty-two years old. As a plantation manager, however, he was not happy or successful, being clearly out of his element. In something over six months he had disengaged himself from plantation life and joined a trading sloop that took coasting voyages along the shore of Jamaica between the plantations and Port Royal. A half-year of this made him acquainted with all the ports and bays about Jamaica, their manufactures, and how to navigate to and fro.

Leaving this employment, he sailed in August 1675 to the Bay of Campeachy in Honduras to cut and load logwood, a reddish-colored dye wood. Except for short interruptions, Dampier spent the next three years in and about the Bay of Campeachy with the logwood cutters, unblushingly poaching on Spanish preserves. Because of it he has left the most detailed account of the life of those men and the character of the country known to voyage-literature. The following are fair samples, taken from chapters one and two of *Voyages and Descriptions*, Part II.

It was not long after our Arrival at Port-Royal, before we were paid off, and discharged. Now Captain Johnson of New England, being bound again into the Bay of Campeachy, I took the Opportunity of going a Passenger with him, being resolved to spend some time at the Logwood Trade; and accordingly provided such Necessaries as were required about it (viz.) Hatchets, Axes, Macheats, (i.e. Long Knives) Saws, Wedges, &c. a Pavilion to sleep in, a Gun with Powder and Shot, &c. and leaving a Letter of Attorney with Mr. Fleming, a Merchant of Port-Royal, as well to dispose of any thing that I should send to him, as to remit to me what I should order, I took leave of my Friends and imbarked. . . . .

In a little time I settled my self in the West Creek of the West

Lagune with some old Logwood-Cutters, to follow the Employment with them. But I shall proceed no farther with the Relation of my own affairs, till I have given a Description of the Country, and Product, with some Particulars of the Logwood-Cutters; their hunting for Beef, and making Hides, &c. . . . .

He then enters into his detailed description of the coast and products of the Bay of Campeachy. Continuing on the subject of logwood, he writes:

The Native Indians that lived hereabouts, were hired to cut it for a Ryal a Day, it being then worth 90, 100, or 111 l. per Tun.

After the English had taken Jamaica, and began to cruise in this Bay, they found many Barks laden with it, but not knowing its value then, they either set them adrift or burned them, saving only the Nails and Iron work; a thing now usual among the Privateers, taking no notice at all of the Cargo, till Capt. James, having taken a great Ship laden with it, and brought her home to England, to fit her for a Privateer, beyond his Expectation, sold his Wood at a great rate; tho' before he valued it so little that he burned of it all his Passage home. After his return to Jamaica, the English visiting this Bay, found out the place where it grew, and if they met no Prize at Sea, they would go to Champeton River, where they were certain to find large Piles cut to their Hand, and brought to the Seaside ready to be shipp'd off. This was their Common Practice; till at last the Spaniards sent Soldiers thither to prevent their Depredations.

But by this time the English knew the Trees, as growing; and understanding their value, began to rummage other Coasts of the Main, in search of it, till, according to their desire, they found large Groves of it, first at Cape Catoch; (which, as I have said before, was the first Place where they settled to Logwood-cutting) and loaded many Vessels from thence to Jamaica, and other Places. But it growing scarce there, they found out the Lagune of Trist in the Bay of Campeachy; where they followed the same Trade, and have ever since continued it, even to the time of my being here.

From another place:

Our Cargo to purchase Log-wood was Rum and Sugar; a very good Commodity for the Log-wood-cutters, who were then about

250 Men, most English, that had settled themselves hereabouts; Neither was it long before we had these Merchants come aboard to visit us; we were but 6 Men and a Boy in the Ship, and all little enough to entertain them: for besides what Rum we sold by the Gallon or Firkin, we sold it made into Punch, wherewith they grew Frolicksome. We had none but small Arms to fire at their drinking Healths, and therefore the Noise was not very great at a Distance; but on Board the Vessels we were loud enough till all our Liquor was spent; We took no money for it, nor expected any; for Logwood was what we came hither for, and we had of that in lieu of our Commodities after the Rate of five Pound per Ton, to be paid at the Place where they cut it. . . . . I made two or three Trips to their Huts, where I and those with me were always very kindly entertain'd with Pig and Pork, and Pease, or Beef and Dough-Boys. . . . . I saw great Prospect of getting Money here, if Men would be but diligent and frugal.

But the buccaneers were not noted for this. Some of their more sober members came,

yet thought it a dry Business to toil at Cutting Wood. They were good Marks-Men, and so took more delight in Hunting; but neither of those Employments affected them so much as Privateering; therefore they often made Sallies out in small Parties among the nearest Indian Towns; where they plundered and brought away the Indian Women to serve them at their Huts, and sent their Husbands to be sold at Jamaica; besides they had not forgot their old Drinking-bouts, and would still spend 30 or 40 l. at a sitting aboard the Ships that came thither from Jamaica; carousing and firing of Guns three or four Days together.

The Spaniards caught them rioting sooner or later and captured them, "a thing I ever feared, and that was the reason that moved me at last to come away, although a Place where a Man might have gotten an Estate."

In 1678 Dampier returned to England, married a woman by the name of Judith of the household of the Duchess of Grafton, but returned to Jamaica in 1679, intending to go again to the Bay of Campeachy.

BUCCANEER LIFE

Instead, he was concerned with other business, and before the year was up was about to return to England, presumably to settle upon an estate in Dorsetshire purchased while he was at Jamaica. However, he went off on a trading voyage to the mainland with a Captain Hobby. But, meeting with the famous buccaneers under Coxon, Sawkins, Sharp, and others, he deserted Captain Hobby along with the rest of the crew and joined the buccaneers.

Thus from Christmas 1679 to September 1691 Dampier was one of a large number of West Indian buccaneers, under first one captain then another, attacking Porto Bello, crossing and recrossing the Isthmus of America on foot, living in Virginia for thirteen months, rounding the Horn and cruising in the South Sea along the coast of Peru and Chile and Mexico, sailing away to the Philippines, Formosa, the Celebes, Australia, and the Nicobar Islands (northwest of Sumatra). Here, properly speaking, Dampier's career as a buccaneer ended; for, tired of buccaneers and their ways, he left them, after piratical escapades of eight and a half years.

In chapter five of the *New Voyage* stands this account of cruising off the island of Lobos near the coast of Peru:

Here we scrubbed our Ships, and being in a readiness to sail, the Prisoners were examined, to know if any of them could conduct us to some Town where we might make some Attempt; for they had before informed us, that we were descried by the *Spaniards*, and by that we knew that they would send no Riches by Sea so long as we were here. Many Towns were considered on, as *Guiaquil*, *Zana*, *Truxillo*, and others: At last Truxillo was pitched on, as the most important; therefore the likeliest to make us a Voyage if we could conquer it: Which we did not much question, tho' we knew it to be a very populous City. But the greatest difficulty was in Landing: for *Guanchaquo*, which is the nearest Sea-Port to it, but six Miles off, is an ill place to Land, since sometimes the very Fishermen that live there, are not able to go in three or four Days. However, the

17th of *May* in the Afternoon, our Men were mustered of both Ships Companies, and their Arms proved. We were in all 108 Men fit for Service, besides the sick: and the next Day we intended to sail and take the *Wood* Prize with us. But the next Day, one of our Men being ashore betimes on the Island, descried three sail bound to the Northward; two of them without the Island to the Westward, the other between it and the Continent.

We soon got our Anchors up and chased: and Captain *Eaton*, who drew the least draught of Water, put through between the Westermost Island and the Rocks, and went after those two that were without the Islands. We in Captain *Cook's* Ship went after the other, which stood in for the Main Land, but we soon fetched her up, and having taken her, stood in again with her to the Island; for we saw that Captain *Eaton* wanted no help, having taken both those that he went after. He came in with one of his Prizes; but the other was so far to Leeward, and so deep, that he could not then get her in, but he hoped to get her in the next Day: but being deep laden, as designed to go down before the Wind to *Panama*, she would not bear sail.

The 19th Day she turned all Day, but got nothing nearer the Island. Our *Moskito*-strikers, according to their Custom, went and struck six Turtles; for here are indifferent plenty of them. These Ships that we took the Day before we came from *Guanchaquo*, all three laden with Flour, bound for *Panama*. Two of them were laden as deep as they could swim, the other was not half laden, but was ordered by the Vice-Roy of *Lima* to sail with the other two, or else she should not sail till we were gone out of the Seas; for he hoped they might escape us by setting out early. In the biggest Ship was a Letter to the President of *Panama* from the Vice-Roy of *Lima;* assuring him that there were Enemies come into that Sea; for which reason he had dispatched these three Ships with Flour, that they might not want; (for *Panama* is supplied from *Peru;*) and desired him to be frugal of it, for he knew not when he should send more. In this Ship were likewise 7 or 8 Tuns of Marmalate of Quinces, and a stately Mule sent to the President, and a very large Image of the Virgin *Mary* in Wood, carved and painted to adorn a new Church at *Panama*, and sent from *Lima* by the Vice-Roy; for this great Ship came from thence not long before. She

brought also from *Lima* 800000 Pieces of Eight, to carry with her
to *Panama:* but while she lay at *Guanchaco,* taking in her lading
of Flour, the Merchants hearing of Capt. Swan's being in *Baldivia,*
order'd the Money ashoar again. These Prisoners likewise informed
us, that the Gentlemen (Inhabitants of *Truxillo*) were building a
Fort at Guanchaquo (which is the Sea-Port for *Truxillo*) close by
the Sea, purposely to hinder the designs of any that should attempt
to land there. Upon this News we altered our former Resolutions,
and resolved to go with our three Prizes to the *Gallapagos;* which
are a great many large Islands, lying some under the Equator, others
on each side of it.

A fine early chapter (chapter two) recalls in his simple,
mariner's style the gaunt days of crossing the Darien country
from the Pacific to the Atlantic. With no display of emotion,
he sets down the facts of that tattered anabasis through the
rain-soaked wilderness. They were forty-four desperate buccaneers, dissenters, who had left Captain Sharp in the Pacific
and struck out for the shore in a launch, a longboat, and two
canoes. They were going home—to Jamaica. The specter
of the Spaniard haunted them, and at least three Spanish
men-of-war prowled along the coast looking for them. One
hundred fifty Spanish soldiers and seamen awaited them at
the very point where they first landed. But they evaded
them. Solemnly agreeing to shoot to death the man who
faltered, they sank their little craft and took to the woods
and swamps. The passages to follow give a taste of the bitter
perseverance and shrewd devices of this strange company.

Most of the Indians were friendly, but one whom they
needed as a guide was hostile.

At first he seemed to be very dubious of entertaining any Discourse with us, and gave impertinent Answers to the Questions that
we demanded of him; he told us he knew no way to the North-side
of the Country . . . . We could get no other Answer from him,
and all his Discourse was in such an angry Tone, as plainly declared
he was not our Friend. However, we were forced to make a Virtue

of Necessity, and humour him. . . . . We tempted him with Beads, Money, Hatchets, Matcheats, or long Knives; but nothing could work on him, till one of our Men took a Sky-coloured Petticoat out of his Bag and put it on his Wife; who was so much pleased with the Present, that she immediately began to chatter to her Husband, and soon brought him into a better Humour. He could then tell us that he knew the Way to the North-side, and would have gone with us, but that he cut his Foot two Days before.

They set forth in the rain.

The 4th Day we began our March betimes, for the Forenoons were commonly fair; but much Rain Afternoon: tho' whether it rained or shined it was much at one with us, for I verily believe we crost the Rivers 30 times this Day: the *Indians* having no Paths to travel from one part of the Country to another; and therefore guided themselves by the Rivers. . . . .

We had much ado to kindle a Fire this Evening: our Hutts were but very mean or ordinary, and our Fire small, so that we could not dry our Cloaths, scarce warm our selves, and no sort of Food for the Belly; all which made it very hard with us. . . . .

Foreseeing a Necessity of wading through Rivers frequently in our Land-march, I took care before I left the Ship to provide my self a large Joint of Bambo, which I stopt at both Ends, closing it with Wax, so as to keep out any Water. In this I preserved my Journal and other Writings from being wet, tho' I was often forced to swim. When we were over this River, we sat down to wait the coming of our Consorts who were left behind, and in a half an Hour they came. But the River by that time was so high, that they could not get over it, neither could we help them over, but bid them be of good comfort, and stay till the River did fall: But we marched two Miles farther by the Side of the River, and there built our Hutts, having gone this Day six Miles. We had scarce finished our Hutts, before the River rose much higher, and overflowing the Banks, obliged us to remove into higher ground: But the next Night came on before we could build more Hutts, so we lay straggling in the Woods, some under one Tree, some under another, as we could find conveniency, which might have been indifferent comfortable if the Weather had been fair; but the greatest Part of the Night we had extraordinary hard Rain, with much Lightning, and terrible Claps of Thunder.

All but one slave ran away in the night, taking the Chirurgeon's gun and money.

The next Morning being the 8th Day, we went to the River's side, and found it much fallen. . . . . Then we contrived to swim over . . . . But this was not so feisable: for we should not be able to get all our Things over. At length we concluded to send one Man over with a Line, who should hale over all our Things first, and then get the Men over. This being agreed on, one *George Gayny* took the end of a Line and made it fast about his Neck, and left the other end ashore, and one Man stood by the Line, to clear it away to him. But when *Gayny* was in the midst of the Water, the Line in drawing after him chanced to kink or grow entangled; and he that stood by to clear it away, stopt the Line which turned *Gayny* on his back, and he that had the Line in his Hand threw it all into the River after him, thinking he might recover himself; but the Stream running very swift, and the Man having three Hundred Dollars at his back, was carried down, and never seen more by us. Those two Men whome we left behind the Day before, told us afterwards that they found him lying dead in a Creek, where the Eddy had driven him ashore, and the Money on his Back; but they meddled not with any of it, being only in Care how to work their way through a wild unknown Country.

On the tenth day they crossed the same river by Dampier's count twenty-two times, making nine miles.

Thus we finished our Journey from the *South-Sea* to the *North* in 23 Days: in which time by my Account we travelled 110 Miles, crossing some very high Mountains; but our common March was in the Valleys among deep and dangerous Rivers.

They lost but one man.

We travelled at least fifty Miles more than we need to have done, could we have gone up *Cheapo* River, or *Santa Maria* River: for at either of these Places a Man may pass from Sea to Sea in three Days time with ease. The *Indians* can do it in a Day and a half, by which you may see how easy it is for a Party of Men to travel over.

Dampier's time with the buccaneers ended, I have said, in 1688 at the Nicobar Islands not far from Sumatra. From here, with only a few companions, he made a hazardous, stormy journey in a native canoe to Achin on the island of Sumatra. Forty leagues' sail over the open tropical sea in a frail boat no larger than a London wherry is an enterprise either foolish or desperate. Quite calmly in chapter eighteen Dampier relates it in one of his best passages:

It was the 15th of May, 1688, about four a Clock in the Afternoon, when we left Nicobar Island, directing our Course towards Achin, being eight Men of us in Company, viz., three English, four Malayans, who were born at Achin, and the Mungrel Portuguese . . . . We had a good substantial Mast, and a Mat Sail, and good Outlagers lash'd very fast and firm on each side the Vessel, being made of strong Poles. . . . .

The 18th Day the Wind freshnd on us again, and the Sky began to be clouded. It was indifferent clear till Noon, and we thought to have had an Observation; but we were hindred by Clouds that covered the Face of the Sun, when it came on the Meridian. . . . .

We had then also a very ill Presage, by a great Circle about the Sun (5 or 6 times the Diameter of it) which seldom appears, but storms of Wind, or much Rain ensue. Such Circles about the Moon are more frequent, but of less import. We do commonly take great notice of these that are about the Sun, observing if there be any Breach in the Circle, and in what Quarter the Breach is; for from thence we commonly find the greatest stress of the Wind will come . . . .

The Wind continued increasing all Afternoon, and the Sea still swelled higher, and often broke, but did us no damage; for the Ends of the Vessel being very narrow, he that steered received and broke the Sea on his Back, and so kept it from coming in so much as to endanger the Vessel: Though much Water would come in, which we were forced to keep heaving out continually. And by this time we saw it was well that we had altered our Course, every Wave would else have filled and sunk us, taking the side of the Vessel: And though our Outlagers were well lash'd down to the Canoas Bottom with Rattans, yet they must probably have yielded to such a Sea as this; when even before they were plunged under Water, and bent like Twigs.

The Evening of this 18th Day was very dismal. The Sky look'd very black, being covered with dark Clouds, the Wind blew hard, and the Seas ran high. The Sea was already roaring in a white Foam about us; a dark Night coming on, and no Land in sight to shelter us, and our little Ark in danger to be swallowed by every Wave; and, what was worst of all, none of us thought our selves prepared for another World. The Reader may better guess than I can express, the Confusion that we were all in. I had been in many imminent Dangers before now, some of which I have already related, but the worst of them all was but a Play-game in comparison with this. I must confess that I was in great Conflicts of Mind at this time. Other Dangers came not upon me with such a leisurely and dreadful Solemnity. A sudden Skirmish or Engagement, or so, was nothing when one's Blood was up, and pushed forwards with eager Expectations. But here I had a lingring View of approaching Death, and little or no hopes of escaping it; and I must confess that my Courage, which I had hitherto kept up, failed me here; and I made very sad Reflections on my former Life, and looked back with Horrour and Detestation on Actions which before I disliked, but now I trembled at the remembrance of. I had long before this repented me of that roving Course of Life, but never with such Concern as now. I did also call to mind the many miraculous Acts of God's Providence towards me in the whole Course of my Life, of which kind I believe few Men have met with the like. For all these I returned Thanks in a peculiar Manner, and this once more desired God's Assistance, and composed my Mind as well as I could in the Hopes of it, and as the Event shew'd, I was not disappointed of my Hopes.

Submitting our selves therefore to God's good Providence, and taking all the Care we could to preserve our Lives, Mr. *Hall* and I took turns to steer, and the rest took turns to heave out the Water, and thus we provided to spend the most doleful Night I ever was in.

About Ten a-Clock it began to thunder, lighten and rain; but the Rain was very welcome to us, having drunk up all the water we brought from the Island.

The Wind at first blew harder than before, but within half an Hour it abated, and became more moderate; and the Sea also assuaged of its Fury; and then by a lighted Match, of which we kept a Piece burning on purpose, we looked on our Compass, to see how we steered, and found our Course to be still East. We had no occasion to look on the Compass before, for we steered right before the Wind, which if it shifted we had been obliged to have altered our Course accordingly. But now it being abated, we found our Vessel lively enough with that small Sail which was then aboard, to hale to our former Course S.S.E. which accordingly we did, being now in hopes again to get to the Island *Sumatra*.

But about Two a-Clock in the Morning of the 19th Day, we had another Gust of Wind, with much Thunder, Lightning and Rain, which lasted till Day, and obliged us to put before the Wind again, steering thus for several Hours. It was very dark, and the hard Rain soaked us so thoroughly, that we had not one dry Thread about us. The Rain chill'd us extreamly; for any fresh Water is much colder than that of the Sea. For even in the coldest Climates the Sea is warm, and in the hottest Climates the Rain is cold and unwholsome for Man's Body. In this wet starveling Plight we spent the tedious Night. Never did poor Mariners on a Lee-shore more earnestly long for the dawning Light than we did now. At length the Day appeared; but with such dark black Clouds near the Horizon, that the first Glimpse of the Dawn appeared 30 or 40 Degrees high; which was dreadful enough; for it is a common Saying among Seamen, and true, as I have experienc'd, that a *high Dawn* will have *high Winds*, and a *low Dawn small Winds*.

Serious tropical distempers did not prevent him from taking trading voyages then to India and Tonquin (in Indo-China). Finally he became a gunner in the English fort at Bencoulen (Sumatra) but escaped by stealth in 1691 from the rough treatment he received there. Taking passage for England in an English ship, he returned by way of the Cape of

Good Hope and Saint Helena, arriving in the Downs in September 1691. He had made a circumnavigation of the globe in a wandering, spasmodic fashion, taking in all twelve and a half years to do it.

It was while Dampier was cruising with the buccaneers that he began conscientiously to keep a journal, a devotion that British naval officers still point to with affection and pride.[4] Although his published account of this voyage around the world begins in the Pacific Ocean on April 17, 1681, with only a short introduction to summarize the events of the two years preceding, yet Dampier must have been carefully recording his observations and experiences for several years. For, in his second volume, he gives with great detail and accuracy his experiences in the Bay of Campeachy six years before.

No one can read his account of this voyage without perceiving that through all its variety of experience there is but one thing that impels Dampier: a desire to see the remote portions of the earth and to record his observations faithfully. While others caroused, he kept his journal. Long before he left the buccaneers he had this desire. "It was not from any dislike to my old Captain," he said once, giving his reason for going with Captain Swan instead of Captain Davis, "but to get some knowledge of the Northern Parts of this Continent of Mexico. And I knew that Captain Swan determined to coast it as far North, as he thought convenient, and then pass over for the East-Indies: which was a way very agreeable to my Inclination."[5] In the Philippines he is glad to get away from Captain Swan, being very dissatisfied with his

---

[4] Sir Clements Markham, in chapter xxv, *The Royal Navy* (edited by Clowes, 1898), II, 548.

[5] *Dampier's Voyages* (edited by Masefield, 1906), I, 242. All page references to Dampier hereafter made will be to this excellent edition of the *Voyages*.

actions. In other words, the first long voyage of Dampier shows him to be an experienced (though as yet obscure) seaman with a passion for geographical and topographical observations plus the determination to record his observations.[6]

Very noticeable in this part of Dampier's life is his seriousness of mind and purpose in the midst of events that would prompt the ordinary traveler to recount roaring tales of wild adventure. At the island of Saint Helena, for example, while his companions swarmed ashore to fill the punch houses, to treat their scorbutic distempers with fresh fruits and vegetables, or to make love to the shapely island maidens, Dampier strolled off with his "Painted Prince" to learn about the place. He took note of its history, its products, its wild life. By such sedate action he was able solemnly to record that the Saint Helena manatee are not manatee, but sea lions. Besides this, he placed on record important (because careful) descriptions of the coasts of Mexico, Peru, and Chile, of the Islands of Juan Fernandez with an account of the rescue of a Mosquito Indian left there three years before, of the routes of the Spanish galleons to Acapulco, and of the Philippines, the Spice Islands, Tonquin, and Achin.

THE VOYAGE IN THE "ROEBUCK"

There are two blanks in our knowledge of the active life of Dampier. One is his life and whereabouts during his thirteen months' stay in Virginia. The other is the six-year period from 1691 to 1697.

At some time during the 1691–1697 period he prepared his journals, with some assistance, for publication. In February 1697 James Knapton published Dampier's first volume,

---

[6] Attention has been called to the ingenious length to which Dampier went in order to preserve his journal from dampness by rolling it up and stuffing it in a hollow bamboo cane (*Dampier's Voyages*, I, 47).

A New Voyage Round the World. It was dedicated to Charles Montague, president of the Royal Society, and became tremendously popular. It is needless, perhaps, to add the corollary: it made Dampier famous, as I shall soon show. This was in February. In the midsummer Dampier was in line for a position in the Customs House which he later got. On the second of July he appeared before the Council of Trade and Plantations (along with Lionel Wafer) to describe the Isthmus of Darien and the country between it and Porto Bello, a description later to be put in writing. This was on account of the design of the Scotch East India Company under William Paterson to establish a colony at Golden Island near the Isthmus of Panama. In September of the next year (1698) he was consulted by the Council again, this time in regard to the best means of fitting out a squadron against the pirates to the east of the Cape of Good Hope (Madagascar). In August he dined with Samuel Pepys, Secretary of the Navy, and John Evelyn.

In the meantime he was busy preparing for a new voyage and writing his second volume. The success of his first book prompted him (and his publisher Knapton) to complete his account by publishing lengthy parts omitted for continuity's sake in the first. Thus the second volume of Dampier's *Voyages* contained material supplementary to the first ("Voyage to Tonquin"), two voyages to Campeachy (which properly preceded the voyage around the world), and a "Discourse of Trade-Winds." The book appeared in 1699 under the title, *Voyages and Descriptions.*

In the meantime, again, Dampier had drawn the attention of the Earl of Orford, First Lord of the Admiralty, who requested him to present a proposal for a voyage of exploration. He suggested New Holland and New Guinea. Accordingly, he was made a captain and given command of the "Roebuck," a nine-year-old fireship fitted out with twelve guns. The vessel was manned with fifty men and boys and was but poorly provisioned. In this ship Captain Dampier sailed for New Holland in January 1699, a troublesome voyage. He went away to the coast of Brazil first, then passed the Cape of Good Hope and struck the barren shore of western Australia. His crew was mutinous. His vessel was unseaworthy. Water was hard to find. Scurvy broke out. A series of discouragements handicapped Dampier so that he was forced to turn back earlier than he had planned, having skirted only the northwestern shore of New Holland for five weeks. He sailed to the Island of Timor for water, and then went on to New Guinea where he had thought of touching first. He circled the Island of New Britain, discovering it to be an island. The passage between it and New Guinea still bears his name. His task now was to get his vessel home safely. He touched at Timor again and at the Cape of Good Hope, but the "Roebuck" "founder'd thro' perfect Age near the Island of Ascension," February 22, 1701. The first week in April, Dampier and his men were picked up by three English men-of-war and carried home.

Dampier as before kept a careful journal, which he published as *A Voyage to New Holland* (Part I, 1703; Part II, 1709). He brought back a collection of plants and illustrated the two volumes with many plates of plants, fish, and animals. By the order of the Royal Society he deposited his collection of plants in the hands of Dr. John Woodward, geologist and physician. This collection is now preserved at Oxford.

The voyage was far from a complete success, however. Biographers differ widely on the subject, from Mr. Masefield's brief remark that it "effected little, nor did it add anything to his reputation,"[7] to that of Clements R. Markham (Secretary of the Royal Geographical Society), who writes that "Dampier commanded this expedition with distinguished

----

[7] *Dampier's Voyages*, I, 5.

ability and some success."[8] Geographers in general today regard it as far from fruitless. It was, at least, one of the earliest examples of a government expedition sent out purely for purposes of discovery. Dampier himself felt particularly that the loss of his ship hurt his reputation "extreamly." In this disaster, also, he lost many of his books and papers and a collection of shells. There was other trouble in store, too. In order to forestall a mutiny among a crew of grumbling men and boys only two of whom had ever crossed the equator before, Dampier had put his lieutenant in irons, had treated him with no gentleness, and had turned him over to the Portuguese officials at the Bay of All Saints in Brazil. Upon his return to England he had to face a court-martial on that account. In this proceeding he was found guilty of great cruelty, was demoted from the captaincy, and was fined all of his captain's pay.

Yet in spite of these serious checks to his reputation he did not lose favor. Ten months after the court-martial he was introduced to the Queen and kissed her hand. And with the reopening of the conflict with Spain (War of the Spanish Succession) his knowledge of the sea and his skill as a buccaneer were still respected enough to be in demand for further voyages. And in the midst of the disturbances of court-martial and preparations for another voyage, he hastily composed the first part of his *Voyage to New Holland*, promising more as soon as he should have time. The book appeared on February 25, 1703, two months before he departed upon his next voyage.

THE VOYAGE IN THE "SAINT GEORGE"

On April 30, 1703, Dampier sailed again for the South Seas. This time he was in command of a privateering expedition, sponsored by private individuals, and probably

[8] *Sea Fathers* (London, 1884), p. 182.

planned largely by himself. He sailed with a commission from the Queen to prey on the Spaniard. Two vessels were under his command, the "Saint George" and the "Cinque Ports," Dampier being on board the former.

Once more he had to put up with unruly officers and crews. The expedition sailed directly to the Pacific cruising grounds by way of the Horn, passing round it in January. By this time Captain Pickering of the "Cinque Ports" had died and Lieutenant Stradling had been put in his place. Stradling was something of a tyrant, so that his men mutinied at Juan Fernandez. Dampier, however, persuaded them to go back to their ship. They next engaged some French ships larger than their own near the island, but thought best to flee from them. On the coast of Peru they failed to surprise the town of Santa Maria, through lack of discipline. They took some small Spanish prizes, however, and one large provision ship.

Next, Dampier and Stradling quarreled, and Dampier sailed away from Taboga (in Panama Road) without Stradling. In an engagement with a Spanish ship of thirty-two guns, his men, who were drunken and insolent and would not obey orders, permitted the Spaniard to give him the slip over night. Dampier's vessel was now old and much eaten on the bottom. The recent failures, the discord, and the general gloomy prospects caused his mate to desert him. The mate seized provisions and powder and ran away with twenty-one followers in one of the Spanish prize barks (September 2, 1704). Three months later, off the coast of Mexico, Dampier, now with sixty-four mutinous and drunken men and boys, sighted and attacked the great Manila galleon, but was beaten off. This caused William Funnell, who calls himself on the title-page of his book, "Mate to Captain *Dampier*," to desert the expedition. With him went thirty-four more. They sailed away to the East Indies in the other prize ship (February 1, 1705). Dampier was now left with a rotten old ship and less than thirty men. His Spanish prisoners had been turned ashore by the deserters to warn the Spanish coast of his whereabouts. Furthermore, his men had already agreed to continue to cruise in those waters only upon the written guaranty that they would soon sail for India.

Dampier's movements from this point to his return to England are not perfectly clear, but he abandoned the old "Saint George" and sailed to the East Indies in a Spanish brigantine. Here he fell into the hands of the Dutch, who seized his vessel and goods and imprisoned him for a few months. He finally reached England late in 1707 without his ship and with only another disastrous voyage to his credit. "It is a Miracle in Nature how I did it," he said.[9]

William Funnell, one of the deserting officers, arrived home before Dampier and published immediately an account of the voyage.[10] It is cluttered with tedious descriptions and is damaging to Dampier's character as a commander. There are in it many sneers, if not downright lies, calculated to justify himself and to prejudice opinion against Dampier. He does this even though masquerading his book cleverly as the "Account of Captain *Dampier's* Expedition into the South-Seas in the Ship *St. George.*" It may be because of being forestalled in this fashion that Dampier published no account of it himself. It may be that he forebore giving a true account with his own pen knowing that it might do him no great credit.[11] He knew that the whole expedition (and

[9] *Dampier's Voyages*, II, 585.

[10] *A Voyage Round the World. Containing an Account of Captain Dampier's Expedition into the South-Seas in the Ship St. George, in the Years 1703 and 1704* (London, 1707).

[11] The whole business of placing the blame for the disasters of this voyage has never been clearly settled. A later editor of John Harris' ponderous collection of voyages, impressively titled *Navigantium atque Itinerantium Bibliotheca or, A Compleat Collection of Voyages and Travels* (London, 1705), lays the blame for the failure of the whole expedition

Mr. Funnell's account of it in particular) had seriously lowered his reputation. He did publish an angry reply to Funnell, entitled, *Captain Dampier's Vindication of His Voyage to the South Seas in the Ship "St. George,"* in which he protests against the harm done him by his enemies. Would they bereave him, he asks, "of my Good Name here, and stab my Reputation for ever?"

For all practical ends the expedition in the "Saint George" and the "Cinque Ports" was a failure. That it did not ruin Dampier we shall soon see. Another occurrence of importance while the vessels were in the South Sea was the abandoning of Alexander Selkirk (prototype of Robinson Crusoe) on the island of Juan Fernandez by Captain Stradling of the "Cinque Ports." Selkirk, who was according to Dampier a very good sailor, had chosen to stay there alone rather than go under a cruel captain in a leaky vessel. It was as a member of Dampier's expedition that he was left there in September 1704, and it was by Dampier, sailing as pilot for the Bristol privateers four years later, that he was rescued.

THE VOYAGE WITH THE BRISTOL PRIVATEERS

Dampier was now fifty-five years old, ripe in experience in all the Indies and the South Seas, but suffering from se-

---

chiefly on Dampier's "own odd Temper, which made him so self-sufficient and over-bearing, that few or none of his Officers could endure him" (*op. cit.* [ed. 1764], I, 149). Recent study of the case upholds editor John Campbell notably in this opinion and even further incriminates Dampier. A summary of an unpublished document concerning the legal action against Dampier (in the *Mariner's Mirror* for October 1924) indicates not only that he was largely responsible for the disputes of the voyage but that he was unfaithful to the trust placed in him by the owners of the expedition. He misapplied funds and even planned to ignore his obligations and turn pirate. (See the unsigned article, "New Light on Dampier's Voyages of 1703," in the *Geographical Journal*, LXV, 183, and the article in the *Mariner's Mirror*, by Dr. B. M. H. Rogers.)

rious reverses. He was by no means through, however. One
of his best voyages he was yet to make. Soon after his arrival
in England he was engaged as pilot for the South Sea in a
privateering expedition being fitted out by a group of Bristol
merchants. There seems to be reason for thinking that Dampier addressed himself to the merchants of Bristol with a
plan for the voyage. Two vessels, the "Duke" and the
"Dutchess," sailed on this expedition and became famous as
the "Bristol privateers." Dampier's prompt engagement in
this enterprise is proof that his reputation, despite all failures
and adverse criticism, was still great. It was perhaps the
most carefully planned and the best organized privateering
expedition that ever put to sea. Dampier could not have
been chosen hastily or inadvisedly.

In many ways his position on this voyage was appropriate
for one of his experience, for one making his last voyage. In
many ways it was a great tribute to him. He was carried
along in an advisory capacity, as expert navigator, but re-
lieved of the supreme responsibility. Captain Woodes Rogers, to whom it fell, was an extremely capable commander.
The whole expedition was carefully regulated from first to
last by written agreements and frequent councils of officers
(including Dampier) to prevent misunderstandings and dis-
orders. For Dampier it was a post of honor. In the Council
of Affairs, Dampier was "Pilot." Among the officers of the
"Duke" he was described as *"William Dampier,* Pilot for
the *South-Seas,* who had been already three times there, and
twice round the World." An unconscious tribute to Dampier,
and also a bit of consolation for his former misfortunes, is to
be noted in the list of officers for the "Duke." John Ballet
is described as having been "Captain *Dampier's* Doctor in
his last unfortunate Voyage round the World."[12]

[12] Woodes Rogers, *A Cruising Voyage Round the World* (London,
1712), pp. xvii, 6, 7. This is the authoritative account of this famous

Apparently, in the midst of preparations for this voyage, too, Dampier was busy writing. His *Voyage to New Holland* was not yet complete, although promised. He must have prepared Part II for the press at this time, for it appeared as *A Continuation of a Voyage to New Holland*, in 1709, when he had been several months at sea.

The voyage of the Bristol privateers was a romantic one. The "Duke" and the "Dutchess" left Bristol on August 2, 1708. In January 1709 they rounded the Horn and entered the Pacific. Dampier was consulted many times here regarding courses, winds, etc. At Juan Fernandez they picked up Alexander Selkirk, a long account of whom is given by Rogers in the official journal of the voyage. Upon Dampier's good recommendation, Selkirk was made mate on board the "Duke," later being made sailing-master of a Spanish prize.

The expedition next proceeded against Puná and Guayaquil on the coast and took several Spanish prizes. The Spaniards, however, on the whole coast had already been warned that Dampier was in the South Sea conducting a squadron of ships against them. "Bristol privateers" meant little to them. It was Dampier whom they knew and feared. No enemy, they said, had been in those parts since Captain Dampier was there four years before. Captain Rogers was shrewd enough to use this to his advantage, improving on "this Spanish story of a Squadron."

On December 22, 1709, the Bristol privateers took the lesser Manila galleon, a rich prize; but the greater ship, which they engaged four days later, the grand and golden prize of buccaneers' dreams, repulsed them easily. By a written agreement, on which stands Dampier's name, it was

_____

expedition and has furnished me my facts. It is interesting in itself, having been reprinted in 1928 in *The Seafarers' Library*.

decided not to attempt her again but to be satisfied with the lesser ship. Even this must have been a deal of satisfaction to Dampier, who then at last engaged in the taking of a prize he had been criticized for losing before. When the plunder was divided, Dampier, along with Selkirk and one other, was appointed judge "to promote the general Good with the utmost Sincerety and Dispatch."

With booty worth £170,000, the privateers went home by way of the East Indies and the Cape of Good Hope, arriving in the Thames famous and rich on October 14, 1711, having been out three years and two months.

This ended the active life of William Dampier. He was now fifty-nine years old. It is assumed that he retired to his position in the Customs House, living probably in London in Coleman Street, where he died early in March 1715. Whether or not he kept a journal of his last voyage is unknown. At least, nothing of his was published. The official account was written by the commander, Woodes Rogers, under the title, *A Cruising Voyage Round the World* . . . . *Begun in 1708, and finish'd in 1711* . . . . It appeared in 1712 and became the most popular book of voyages of the time. It deserves, better than some others, to be included between the covers of the set called, ten years later, *Dampier's Voyages*. His books went through many editions, and were illustrated with maps made by Herman Moll, the foremost geographer of the time.

Thus William Dampier was an extraordinarily engaging figure in his time: buccaneer, author, scientific observer, explorer, and master-mariner. He saw more wherever he went and he went oftener to the uncharted regions than anyone else in all England, perhaps in the whole world of that time. His narratives were rigorously plain, almost apologetic, but contained much more than bearings and soundings, harbors and headlands. His descriptions were something more than catalogues of observations. He was, furthermore, a quiet man of reserved manner who sat for his portrait with a book in his hand.

It is no wonder that Dampier is still a celebrated figure. He has dimmed but little with the passing of time and remains not only surrounded by the glamour of buccaneering beneath tropic skies but sufficiently compelling to warrant further serious study. In that study we shall have occasion to remember (1) his lifelong desire to see the world, (2) his fame as a buccaneer, (3) his fame as an author, (4) his knowledge of the sea, (5) his descriptions of logwood-cutting, of Brazil, the Philippines, Tonquin, and New Holland, and (6) his connection with Alexander Selkirk.

III

A LITERARY BUCCANEER

I have gone through it, [Dampier's *New Voyage*] and find it very well worth my time, being very delightsome, and I believe true.—Letter from CAPTAIN JOHN COVANT of Portbury to a gentleman in London

Others have a custome to bee always relating strange *things* and *wonders*, (of the humor of Sir *John Mandevile*) and they usually present them to the Hearers, through *multiplying glasses.*
—HOWELL, *Forraine Travell*

FIRST APPEARANCE OF THE "VOYAGES"

WHEN Dampier came home in 1691 he had nothing to show for his years of wandering but a tattooed East Indian from the Spice Islands, called Jeoly, Giolo, or Job, in whom he had part interest. Being without money, however, he was forced to sell his interest bit by bit and soon lost his sole source of income. Jeoly, he heard, was thereafter publicly exhibited for money, but died soon at Oxford of smallpox. What Dampier did until 1697 remains unknown. It is a safe conjecture that he haunted sailors' rendezvous along Thames bank, swapped yarns, and engaged himself to captains of ships for short voyages. Eventually he met someone who suggested that he write his adventures and who perhaps assisted him. With all his store of knowledge and experience he remained hidden as under a bushel until he published *A New Voyage Round the World* in February 1697.

It was an immediate success. Announced in the press as

early as the previous November, it found a public ready for it, so that a second edition had to be run off in May and a third in November. And early in 1699, when his second volume appeared, the *New Voyage* went to a fourth edition. Three editions in nine months indicate a brisk sale. The dizzy pace of modern printing and publishing was unknown then. *Robinson Crusoe*, one of the most popular books of the time, went to only four editions in eight months. Coming twenty years later, it had the further advantage of greeting a public bred to travel literature and eager for more, whereas Dampier's *Voyage* came with little impetus from similar books immediately preceding it.

The *New Voyage* was Dampier's introduction to the proper people. He dedicated it to the Right Honorable Charles Montague, Esq., President of the Royal Society, whom it apparently pleased. Montague recommended Dampier to the Treasurer of the Navy, the Earl of Orford, and got him a position in the Customs House at eight pounds fifteen shillings a quarter. The Royal Society recognized the contribution the *New Voyage* made to scientific knowledge by digesting its contents in the *Philosophical Transactions* immediately (February). From the start Dampier was known, not as just another Esquemeling, historian of the buccaneers, but as a man of dependable knowledge gained from varied experience. Because of this he was summoned to attend the Council of Trade and Plantations on July 2 and again on September 22, 1698, to answer various questions as already noted.[1] In a short time he became a famous man. Members of certain great families took pleasure in conversing with him.

Charles Hatton, writing to Christopher, First Viscount Hatton, late in May 1697, says with an obvious air of being in the midst of things: "I have discoursed wth Dampier. He

---

[1] *Dampier's Voyages,* I, 3, 4, 550.

is a blunt fellow, but of better understanding than wou'd be exspected from one of his education." This was virtually the impression John Evelyn received of him the next summer. Hatton had written to his brother just the week before: "Dampier's Voyage takes so wonderfully, 2 editions are already sold of, and he tells me he is fitting ye second part for ye press."[2]

Furthermore, Dampier's publisher, James Knapton, knew that he had put forth a popular book. Spurred by the exhaustion of three editions of the *New Voyage* in so short a time, he heralded the second volume, *Voyages and Descriptions*, with a liberal display of advertising, announcing it eight months before it appeared. Three months before, he advertised it to be out in a few days. It was published early in February 1699, graced with an index to both volumes. The index manifested the publisher's conception of them as a set; in fact, the first part of the long title of *Voyages and Descriptions* was "Voyages and Descriptions, Vol. II. In Three Parts." As I have said, this volume was a supplement to the first, completing the story of Dampier's first long voyage. Gaps that he had purposely left, here he filled. Curious experiences in Central America, trading and cutting logwood in Campeachy, preceding the voyage proper, pieced out the hitherto scant autobiographical remarks. A whole section was devoted to a meteorological study of winds and tides of the world. Here was literary fare for all: escapades with the buccaneers, solemn observations of curious natural phenomena, hardships on land and sea, accounts of Indians, South Sea islanders, and the Chinese—a grand total from twelve and one-half years of voyaging.

Knapton kept up his advertising, but the sale of Volume II was much slower. It went to a second edition in June

---

[2] *Hatton Correspondence* (edited by Edward Thompson, 1878) (Camden Society Publications, n.s., XXII–XXIII), II, 224, 225.

1700 and to a third only in February 1705. An early monthly journal with the heavy name of *The History of the Works of the Learned*, which began in 1699, devoted four pages of its February number to the contents of Dampier's new volume. Whereas the editor was impressed by the usefulness of Dampier's information, particularly the "Discourse of Winds," we are pleased to note that he recommended it to the "Sedentary Traveller" because of its "variety of descriptions and Surprizingness of the Incidents."

Voyages and Descriptions carried Dampier to what was probably the highest point in his career. His new friend, the Earl of Orford, to whom he dedicated it, recommended him in turn "to the greatest Encouragers of public-spirited undertakings that the age produced." Soon he was to set forth, a naval captain, heading an official expedition to explore the coasts of New Holland. In a later preface Dampier himself admitted the favorable reception of his first two volumes, so favorable that he dared next time to recount the adventures of an expedition that failed in its purpose and bred dangerous enemies for him. But even his enemies admitted the "good Reception and universal Approbation" which his *Voyages* met. Just how great an effect upon his time this really was, neither Dampier, his publishers, nor the world knew. But we shall see.

On February 25, 1703, Dampier gave to the world his third volume of voyages. This was *A Voyage to New Holland, in the Year 1699* . . . . *Vol. 3, Written by Captain William Dampier, printed for James Knapton at the Crown* . . . . *where may be had Capt. Dampier's first and second Volumes of Travels.* The greatest care was taken to advertise it in the *Daily Courant*, as something of an event. Notices before and after February 25 are more numerous for it than for other books. Only quack medicines held their space so persistently. At least ten notices appeared in February and March. The faithful *History of the Works of the Learned* digested the contents, as before, but proffered no opinion except that it had one advantage over its companion volumes, the inclusion of drafts and five cuts to picture the rareties. The earlier volumes had maps only. The cuts of fish and plants were of no little significance. The voyage to New Holland had been a real scientific expedition and would unquestionably have swept Dampier on to much greater fame, this time as the explorer and true discoverer of Australia, had not the British Admiralty stupidly furnished him with a mutinous, inexperienced crew and a ship so mellow with age that it went down on the return trip off the coast of Africa with the irreparable loss of most of Dampier's papers.

Despite all this Dampier was at the height of his fame. Although demoted in the Navy for cruelty, his books went forth, a neat set of three octavo volumes from the pen of "Captain William Dampier," and he was engaged to go privateering before he could finish his account of New Holland. It was not until February 1709 that he was able to complete Part II, the supplement.

Dampier's vogue was tremendous. Professor Edward Arber, analyzing the bibliographical records from 1668 to 1709 as he found and published them in the *Term Catalogues*, declares that the most popular secular works in the Age of Anne were voyages and travels and geographical works in general, to a taste for which we are indebted for *Robinson Crusoe* and *Gulliver's Travels*. "James Knapton set the fashion in this, with *Dampier's Voyages*. That led the way to the Collections of Voyages by Hacke, Churchill, Harris, and others; even to a monthly Geographical Journal, the Atlas Geographus."[3] If we probe back of this interesting comment we shall see Dampier in a new rôle as the great fountainhead of a swift stream of books that was to cut its way deep into English literature.

[3] Edward Arber, *Term Catalogues, 1668–1709 A.D.* (London, 1903–1906, 3 vols.), III, viii.

DAMPIER'S FAME

It was Dampier's books, we may repeat, and not his exploits that made him famous. Six years of his life following his first circumnavigation were so completely buried that we can only conjecture what he was doing, whereas his "Painted Prince," Jeoly, made something of a sensation. A handbill still exists, announcing the exhibition of this "just wonder of the Age"; and a chapbook of twenty-seven pages by an unknown scribe gives a perfectly fictitious "Account" of him, with a full-length portrait. Neither of these so much as mentions Dampier's name. All London knew of the much-tattooed Jeoly. No one knew Dampier. After 1697 all was different. Dampier, the famous buccaneer, was now much sought; Jeoly, dead of the smallpox, had faded from the picture. This is John Evelyn's impression in August 1698 of the dinner with the Secretary of the Royal Navy:

6th August. I dined with Mr. Pepys, where was Captain Dampier, who had been a famous buccaneer, had brought hither the painted Prince Job, and printed a relation of his very strange adventure, and his observations. He was now going abroad again by the King's encouragement, who furnished a ship of 290 tons. He seemed a more modest man than one would imagine by the relation of the crew he had assorted with. He brought a map of his observations of the course of the winds in the South Sea, and assured us that the maps hitherto extant were all false as to the Pacific Sea, which he makes on the south of the line, that to the north end running by the coast of Peru being extremely tempestuous.

A modest man, Dampier, going around with maps stuffed in his pocket, full of the knowledge of seas and shores and their winds. Next he was presented to Queen Anne. His goings and comings were noted in the newspapers. Narcissus Luttrell made eight different entries in his diary regarding the movements of "the famous Captain Dampier." His word was authority. His portrait was painted at the suggestion of

Sir Hans Sloane, and represents the famous sea captain holding a copy of *Dampier's Voyages* in his hand: to the artist he was author first, not sea captain. This portrait now hangs in the National Portrait Gallery in London. An engraving was made from it and published during Dampier's lifetime.

Certain casual references indicate that Dampier was read widely. He was quoted by the journalist Tutchin to prove points in arguments for British trade. "Whoever read Captain *Hack's* Collection of Voyages, Dampier, Wafer, [Basil Ringrose], and others, will soon conclude how valuable a trade to the Spanish *West-Indies* would be to the English." Defoe read him and possibly knew him personally. Addison quoted from him in the *Tatler* and the *Spectator* and Knapton advertised Dampier in the *Spectator*. Steele relates in the *Englishman* two famous episodes from Dampier's voyage with the Bristol privateers. Swift's "Cousin Sympson" in *Gulliver's Travels* calls him "cousin Dampier."

Other writers of voyages accepted his word as final authority. He was so widely known that upon meeting an English vessel upon the high seas (off the Cape of Good Hope) and going aboard her he was immediately recognized. Evelyn felt that Dampier was the sort of great man to be commemorated by a medal, and so recommends in his *Numismata: A Discourse of Medals* (1699).

In a list of 716 ships to whom letters of marque were granted in the War of the Spanish Succession, published in *Notes and Queries* (December, 1928), Dampier's name appears as commander of the "Saint George," and he is further described there by the registrar of the High Court of Admiralty as "the celebrated author of the *Voyages*." This list was sent to the Queen.

We have seen that Dampier and Wafer were consulted with regard to the plan of the Scottish Colony at Darien. It was the descriptive passages in their books concerning this region that attracted the attention of William Paterson, the promoter of the colony. Archibald Foyer in *A Defence of the Scots Settlement at Darien* (Edinburgh, 1699) depends upon Dampier and Wafer for his descriptions. He proves his point regarding the legality of Scottish occupation at Darien because of Dampier's account of the freedom of the Indians and so exonerates Captain Sharp for trading and buccaneering on that coast. Jeremy Collier refers to Dampier and Wafer regarding Darien, under the heading "Caledonia," in his *Great Historical, Geographical, Genealogical and Poetical Dictionary*. And, finally, Oldmixon's *History of England* (1725) quotes Dampier in its account of the beginning of the trouble at Golden Island.

Other writers of voyages soon after Dampier avoided the subjects treated by him, imitated his manner, digested his chapters, referred to him, or in other ways showed his influence upon them. The editor and reviser of the third edition of Exquemelin's *History of the Bucaniers of America* justifies the inclusion of Basil Ringrose's narrative on the grounds that it was "said by *Mr. Dampier* to be very exact." Wafer seems to avoid much that Dampier carefully described, such as detailed description of the South Sea coast and of logwood cutting. When Wafer was buccaneering with Dampier, Dampier was a man of no prominence at all, merely one of the buccaneers. Wafer, however, a year after Dampier's book had appeared, takes pains to say in his own, "Here I first met with *Mr. Dampier* and was with him in the Expedition in the S. Seas." In Captain Hacke's preface to his collection of voyages similar remarks are made. Captain Cowley is described as one *"who went from* Virginia *in Company with Capt.* Dampier, in *Capt.* Cooks *Ship."* As a matter of fact Dampier was at the time in a position (probably that of common sailor) subordinate to that of Cowley, who was sailing master. Again, in telling of the Mosquito Indian of Juan Fernandez he finds it necessary to say that Dampier was present at the leaving of him.

William Funnell explains that he says little of winds and other things that his hated superior Dampier has given account of, and in the dedication and the preface of his *Voyage Round the World* (1707) he compliments Dampier on the exactness of his descriptions and observations. This is either balm for his conscience or a grudging admission, for the book itself attacks Dampier's judgment and skill. Like Dampier, he includes a table of each day's run in the South Sea.

The accounts of the Bristol privateers also very naturally mention Dampier a good deal because of his presence, but they also depend upon his books for many things. Captain Edward Cooke, whose narrative of the expedition is loaded with the history of the countries near which they sailed (a practice not characteristic of Dampier), retells from Dampier the activities of the buccaneers on the coast of Peru and on the South Sea coast of North America, "having no Design to compile a History of Robberies, but only to mention those Persons who have been remarkable in those Seas, or give some Particulars which others have not done." Dampier qualifies for both of these, and Cooke ends the passage, "as may be seen in Dampier's Travels." He also makes much of Dampier's tremendous reputation among the Spaniards, to their discredit. Captain Woodes Rogers' account, *Cruising Voyage* (1712), which is still sometimes catalogued under the name of Dampier, makes clear the Spaniards' fear of him and necessarily refers often to him as pilot of the expedition. But it also refers familiarly to "his Book."

In several other places Rogers' book shows the hand of Dampier. Dampier had described the humming bird of Yucatan as "a pretty little feather'd Creature, no bigger than a great over-grown Wasp." Twice thereafter he compares it to a bee gathering honey. Rogers declares that the humming bird is "no bigger than a Humble Bee." His description of the sloth, which I quote later in this chapter, is derived from Dampier's more picturesque description.

A rather well-known description in Dampier is that of the South Sea outrigger canoes, which he calls "proes." Poles run out from the side of the canoe, says Dampier, "by the help of which the little Boat is made firm and contiguous to the other." In Rogers the poles are "fasten'd to a large Log shap'd like a Boat, and near half as long, which becomes contiguous to the Boat." Such coincidences of phraseology are more obvious in their respective mention of trade at the Peruvian port of Guayaquil. Says Dampier, "All imported Goods for the City of Quito pass by Guiaquil: By which it may appear that Guiaquil is a place of no mean Trade." Rogers writes, "All sorts of European Goods come hither from Panama . . . . which shows that the Port of Guiaquil is no mean Place of Trade in this Part of the World." The inhabitants of Bouton are "small and well shaped" in Dampier. They are in Rogers "a well-set People, of a middle stature, or rather small."

In the course of his journal, Rogers quotes from many travel-works, enough to make a considerable library. Others he merely mentions, among them Dampier's *Voyages.* He either carried these with him on the expedition or consulted them at home in preparing his account for the press, the former being more likely. He does not, however, mention Dampier's books except in a slighting way. "He tells us he was at them," writes Rogers, recording a discussion among his officers regarding their failure to locate certain South Sea islands where Dampier said they should be: "He tells us he was at them formerly when he was a Buccaneer, and has describ'd 'em in one of his Volumes he calls his Voyages." Captain Rogers, a privateer, had great contempt for buccaneers, yet neither his expedition nor his book was complete without Dampier.

Again, Frezier and Shelvocke, two other notable navigators, make their bow to Dampier. Frezier supplements his description of the cotton-flower from Dampier. Shelvocke's

Voyage Round the World shows perhaps more acquaintance with Frezier than with anyone else among his predecessors in the South Sea. Yet at Juan Fernandez he plants his commission high and dry among the rocks, "remembering how Captain Dampier had been served in these seas." No important voyage of the period escaped the influence of Dampier.

John Harris originally prepared his great collection of voyages without comment on the authors or the exploits. He included most of the *New Voyage* of Dampier verbatim; the others he digested. In this first edition, Dampier's voyages stood well along in the second volume, and yet the unsigned map of the world in Volume I shows the courses "of Sir Francis Drake, William Schouten and Capt. William Dampiers Voyages Round it." In the eyes of his contemporary Harris, then, Dampier ranked with Drake and Schouten. Later editions of this work, I may repeat, pay further tribute to Dampier's importance by digesting and rewriting his voyages least of all, although purging them from errors. Campbell, the editor, makes much of Dampier's discoveries in New Holland and provides a map particularly to show them. He makes the comment that propositions made to great ministers, like those of Dampier to the Earl of Pembroke regarding discoveries that could be made in a voyage to New Holland, are very rarely agreeable, but that the Lord High Admiral did listen to Dampier, encouraged him, and brought about the voyage.

The collection of voyages made by the Churchill brothers is less flattering to Dampier. In the introduction to the *History of Navigation,* Dampier's first voyage round the world and the voyage in the "Roebuck" are mentioned. In the "discourse" on the "character &c. of Books of Travel" the three volumes of Dampier are very briefly described. The only comment is regarding the *Voyage to New Holland,* "which has no great matter of discovery."

Maps and geographical works in general acknowledged the importance of Dampier's *Voyages*. I have already referred to the general impetus lent them by Dampier. Herman Moll, illustrator of Dampier's volumes, quickly incorporated in both text and maps of his geographical works matter from Dampier. In the *Atlas Geographus*, maps of New Guinea show Dampier's Passage. Dampier's bearings for Shark's Bay, where he landed on the coast of New Holland, are given side by side with Moll's own, which are different, as though Moll disagreed with Dampier but did not dare to displace his records. In describing New Holland, New Guinea, New Britain, the west coast of South America, and the Isthmus of Darien, Moll quotes frequently from Dampier as an authority. Dampier is Moll's only authority for New Holland (excepting one paragraph), for the routes of the three Acapulco ships to and from the Philippines, and for California. For the Bay of Campeachy, Dampier is his principal authority. Moll's map of America (1726) in his *Atlas Minor* clearly shows by the lettering of the "Pacific Sea" that he accepts Dampier's definition of it. The maps of trade winds in Dampier are unsigned, but they probably were made by Moll. A Moll map of the world in the first volume of Harris' *Navigantium* clearly shows the use of Dampier's maps of trade winds. The arrows and many notations of both of Dampier's maps have been combined into one. Many of the notations are identical (the shifting trade winds of the Arabian Sea and elsewhere, the term "Shifting Winds" in the Indian Sea, etc.). The legends or footnotes beneath the maps have been telescoped into one and reprinted in the exact phrases.

A Moll map of trade winds appears also in the second volume of Osborne's *Collection of Voyages and Travels* of 1745. This is also based on Dampier's maps, with the addition of east-and-west compass-variations. Moll died in 1732. These maps therefore must have been made at least thirteen years before the Osborne collection, being still standard. And finally, "Dampier's Voyages" were in the catalogue of "newest and best" authorities from which Moll took his descriptions of Asia, Africa, and America, written "wholly new," in the fourth edition of his *Compleat Geographer.*

Thus there is no question that Dampier's *Voyages* commanded respect. They set a standard in writing. Not only were they popular books, but they became the prime authority in many matters and remained so for forty years or more. They were the most influential books of their kind in England in the hundred years following 1631.

Two amusing derogatory comments upon Dampier should be recorded. In referring to other stories of men left alone on Juan Fernandez, the anonymous author of the pamphlet, *Providence Displayed,* in order to win confidence to his own false account, doubts the truth of Dampier's story of the Mosquito Indian left there. "But whatever there is in these stories," he says, "this of Selkirk I know to be true." In Tom Brown's *Amusements Serious and Comical,*[4] a bookseller is met by the traveler about town, who is "a tearing those Calculations of gain in a Fury which he had made, and assur'd himself of before Dampier's last unsuccessful Voyage." Perhaps other booksellers besides James Knapton saw their business rise and fall with the successes of the exquisite buccaneer.

HIS STYLE

"The keeping of a Sea Journal is a Thing reduced to a settled Method, and is as much the Business of the Navigator, as the Care of the Ship; but the turning that Journal into an historical Relation of the Voyage, and the Circumstances attending it, is a thing quite out of his Way, and which very few Seamen can do without Assistance."

[4] For this I am indebted to Professor Katherine Hornbeak.

Thus writes John Campbell, reviser of Harris' *Navigantium*. And this is why many sea-journals are hard to read. A dreary repetition of bearings, soundings, winds, tides, currents, and courses raises such a barrier of dullness for the lay reader that a Captain Fireball or a Captain Gulliver arises to satirize them. It is a style without style. The "settled Method" is deadly.

The thing that first wins the reader to Dampier is the attractiveness, the freshness, of his material. To be sure, there are bearings, soundings, winds, and tides, and all the rest, but they are on the whole so well relegated to subordinate places or special sections in the book that they rarely offend. And it is quite plain that Dampier studies to keep his account fresh and full of variety, even though his purpose is to be useful and not primarily entertaining. What is familiar and has long been known he refuses to include. Honestly, exactly, and simply he sets forth what he believes is strange and unknown and yet withal useful. He thus writes in the rugged style known best in English letters through Defoe and Swift. Hardships, adventures, and disappointments unparalleled in his time he relates with modesty and naïveté sometimes approaching archness. For us who read at a distance of over two hundred years there is also the flavor of quaintness.

Certainly few have objected to Dampier's way of writing. Because he was serious and minimized adventure instead of playing it up, some contemporaries apparently found his "Accounts and Descriptions of Things . . . . dry and jejune." John Campbell himself objected to his harshness and lack of order, but he praised Dampier in unstinted terms in other places. And he left the voyages practically untouched on his pages "that they might remain as entertaining as ever."

Dampier is fresh. More than this, he has a real feeling for words. His descriptions abound in the homely simile that drives an impression home, or the metaphor that easily illumines. That his perceptions were clear is revealed in his sharpness of delineation. That his imagination played over what he saw at the moment of observation seems guaranteed by the perfect fitness of his figures.

A good illustration of the attractiveness he gave to commonplace objects is found in his description of the sloth, which I have said supplied Captain Rogers a foundation for his own.

They are very mischievous to the Trees where they come, and are so slow in Motion, that when they have eaten all the Leaves on one Tree, before they can get down from that and climb another, and settle themselves to a fresh Banquet (which takes them up five or six Days, though the Trees stand near,) they are nothing but Skin and Bones, although they came down plump and fat from the last Tree. *—Dampier's Voyages*, II, 162

They say it feeds on the Leaves of a certain lofty Tree, and when it has clear'd one, before it can get down and walk a little Way to find and climb another, would grow lean and be almost starved. —Rogers, *Cruising Voyage*, p. 246

If the charm of the old travel-writers really lies in their homely yet individually pungent phrases, Dampier's style justifies the encomiums heaped upon it. One might select many examples of his felicity of expression, but a few will suffice. His descriptions of storms and birds are noticeable. In an open boat in an East Indian storm, "The Sea was already roaring in a white Foam about us . . . . Our little Ark in danger to be swallowed by every Wave." Two pages farther on he writes the rhythmic line, "In this wet starveling plight we spent the tedious Night." The stormy petrel "is a Bird not much unlike a Swallow . . . . They fly sweeping like Swallows, and very near the Water. They are not so often seen in fair Weather; being Foul-weather Birds, as our Seamen call them, and presaging a Storm when they come about a Ship. . . . . In a storm they will hover close under the Ship's Stern . . . . And there as they fly (gently then) they pat the Water alternately with their Feet, as if they walk'd upon it; tho' still upon the Wing. And from hence the Seamen give them the Name of Petrels, in Allusion to St. Peter's walking upon the Lake of Gennesareth." The description of the Hottentots dancing in the moonlight is extremely engaging. One can see Dampier, crammed with curiosity, staying up all night and walking solemnly forth occasionally, to learn about this strange dancing. "They seem[ed] all very busie, both Men, Women, and Children, dancing very oddly on the green Grass by their Houses. They traced to and fro promiscuously, often clapping their Hands and singing aloud. Their Faces were sometimes to the East, and sometimes to the West."

This is of the "dry conciseness" of which Professor Lowes speaks.[5] Dampier's similes are splendid because they are at once homely and exact. The Corpus Sanct "resembles a great Glow-Worm." Ambergris is "of a dusky colour, towards black, and about the hardness of mellow Cheese." The enclosed fruit of the plantain is "no harder than Butter in Winter."

It is not my purpose to eulogize the style of Dampier. Scholars and poets, biographers and laymen, have already done it. But I shall remark further upon Dampier's method of composition to indicate that he was by nature, whatever may have been the assistance received by him, aware of certain qualities of good writing, and he strove to compose his manuscripts with care to such ends. He had a strict regard for the reader, traces of which are to be found throughout.

In the "Letter to Cousin Sympson" in *Gulliver's Travels* Swift expresses what was a common idea regarding Dampier: that someone else helped him compose his books from his journals (that perhaps he merely dictated while the other person wrote). A remark of Charles Hatton also indicates

[5] J. L. Lowes, *The Road to Xanadu* (1927), p. 319. I am indebted to Professor Lowes for many suggestions regarding Dampier.

this. "He [Dampier] is a very good navigator, kept his journal exactly, and set down every day what he thought remarkable; but, you must imagine, had assistance in dressing up his history, in wch are many mistakes in naming of places." There is some indication of this but more to the contrary. In answer to this charge, Dampier himself wrote: "As to the latter; I think it is so far from being a Diminution to one of my Education and Employment, to have what I write Revised and Corrected by Friends; that on the contrary, the best and most eminent Authors are not ashamed to own the same Thing, and look upon it as an Advantage." Very clearly here Dampier admits editorial assistance, but he also definitely says that he composed the manuscripts originally, for his friends to help correct. There is no reason to think he is avowedly misstating or understating the case. There was no honester mind than his.

There is no settling the point by referring to manuscripts, because the Sloane manuscript of the *New Voyage* in the British Museum is not the final copy that went to the printer. It is in the hand of a copyist, with marginal notations by Dampier. The text is not like the printed version, lacking observations on natural phenomena and containing some matter on Wafer, Swan, and Harris, his associates. Furthermore, not all the marginal notations are to be found in the book. It seems clear, therefore, that Dampier worked over his material carefully, adding and rejecting, and that this manuscript is but one of many in a process of much revision.

Another statement of Dampier, an artless apology for his shortcomings in the way of style, indicates further that it is his composition that we see in his works. Certain it is that his *Voyages* are remarkably uniform throughout in a style plain, modest, and scrupulous in detail like the man himself. It is easier, and more natural, to think that it is largely his own rather than that he had such good fortune as to engage an anonymous scribe (perhaps a hack) skilful, sympathetic, and consistent enough to maintain such a style through four books composed at intervals through twelve years.

But to return to his method of composition. Dampier's purpose, it should be remembered, never was to write an exciting story of adventures, or to be literary. He was well aware of the incredulity and prejudice generally lent to travelers' wild tales. His own serious turn of mind made it impossible for him to be lively. His seafaring life left him no time to be literary. He could give only an honest and plain account. His zeal was only for the promotion of useful knowledge. Unknown to the world of letters and science, he sought no literary patron. Instead, he wisely dedicated his *New Voyage* to the president of the Royal Society. This dedication and all the others should be read carefully for any complete understanding of the man.

Accordingly, Dampier wrote "a mixt Relation of Places and Actions," choosing rather to be too particular in places and be generally understood than to spice his useful matter with high adventure and be suspect. "I write for my Countrymen," he said. And he wrote with care, extreme care for a seaman. The state of the Sloane manuscript accords with all other proof of this. For one thing, he was not content to write hastily. Despite this, he had to write the *Voyage to New Holland* hurriedly. "I am ashamed, my lord," he wrote to the Earl of Pembroke in the dedication, "to offer You so imperfect a Present, having not time to set down all the Memoirs of my last Voyage." He was ashamed, because he had been able to spend great care on the *New Voyage* and the *Voyages and Descriptions* but could not do so here.

Again, in composing the *New Voyage*, he indefatigably bore the reader's attention in mind. He seems to have experienced the impatience of plowing through the rambling accounts of others to find what he wanted, particularly the parts thrown in "to divert and gratify the Curious Reader." So solicitous is he that he is sometimes awkward in his frequent expression of concern. At the very outset he condenses in a summary the events of his life up to his departure from Captain Sharp in 1681. This is in order to begin in the midst of things. Basil Ringrose and others had given accounts of these adventures with buccaneers. Why should he tire the reader with a repetition of them? He calls this summary an "Introduction . . . . that the Reader may the better perceive where I mean to be Particular," and that the "Tour of the World" may "correspond to the Title." Of his thirteen months in Virginia he says nothing, that country being "so well known to our Nation." He furthermore does "not detain the Reader with the story" of his own "Affairs, and the troubles that befel" him during his stay there, interesting as those details unquestionably would be. Having one object in mind (to present the extraordinary and useful), he unifies his material accordingly. Farther along he omits another large mass of material (the voyage to Tonquin), fearing once more to spoil the effect of a continuous voyage around the world. Observations regarding winds he leaves for a separate essay. He literally cuts out enough matter to make a whole volume. (It forms the volume of 1699, *Voyages and Descriptions*.)

All this but confirms the belief that Dampier wrote his own accounts, that he wrote painstakingly, and that he had a keen appreciation of the fundamental principle of all artistic endeavor, unity of impression. His language betrays in him a certain felicity of expression, particularly in description, and his methods of composition betray in him the hand of a sincere writer. His purpose is practical, but his mind is the mind of an artist. The result is a plain, unassuming book of travel-information with a minimum of narrative but, flashing through it, the delicate piercings of a rare mind. Being of an honest and hearty nature, he writes an honest and hearty tale. Such is the style of Dampier.

IV

THE SILVER AGE OF TRAVEL

The travelling I mean is in books, the only way of travelling
by which any knowledge is to be acquired.

—Parson Adams

THE GREAT FOLIO COLLECTIONS

ARBER said Knapton "set the fashion" for travels in
Anne's age with the publication of Dampier's *Voyages*. The trend of this fashion can be detected in the activity
of the publishers, who presented their public with many great
folio collections of voyages, both foreign and English. The
significance of these will be made more clear if we note first
the popularity of travel literature just before.

It should not be assumed from what I shall say that voyages and travels had not sold well before Dampier. On the
contrary, an examination of any bibliography of voyages[1]
reveals that a constant, though not necessarily large, stream
of publications of this kind flowed from the London presses
from Hakluyt's time to Dampier's. Following 1626, however, a definite lull can be detected. Somewhere between
1626 and 1630 the Elizabethan enthusiasm for books of
travel waned. It followed naturally a lull in daring exploits

---

[1] There is no good bibliography of voyages for the seventeenth and
eighteenth centuries. One may turn to the catalogues of large libraries, to
standard bibliographical manuals, such as Lowndes, or to the amazingly incomplete, inaccurate, and misleading list in Vol. XVII of Pinkerton's
Voyages and Travels, 1816.

like those of Drake, Hawkins, and Raleigh. After the death of Raleigh in 1618, until 1631 when the plans of James and Fox to explore Hudson's Bay were being completed, there was "almost a blank as regards maritime enterprise."[2] And following 1631 almost a generation passed before there was any distinct renewal of it. The names of Drake and other Elizabethans soon passed into legend, which romantically set them forth as the grand heroes of the good old days when England was England. Tutchin and Defoe, somewhat later, in lamenting Britain's weakness on the sea, had only to refer to Raleigh, Hawkins, Drake, or Cavendish to call up visions of the Royal Navy in all its ancient glory.

Accounts of Drake had considerable vogue, it is true, between 1600 and 1653. Books about him continued to appear throughout the century—and still do. But it is commonly overlooked that Hakluyt's *Principall Navigations* never went to a second edition. And legend has it that Purchas died in distressed circumstances, in consequence of losses sustained by the publication of his *Pilgrimes.* The *Purchas his Pilgrimage* went to four editions only between 1613 and 1626, and the *Hakluytus Posthumous* (1625–26) was not reprinted until 1906.

The stormy middle portion of the century left little time or energy for voyages of exploration and discovery. At various times the navy fell into neglect. England was occupied with affairs at home more than abroad. There were published, however, various scattered collections of voyages. Drake's voyages were issued in collected editions in 1652 and 1683. In 1662 Olearius' *Voyages and Travels of the Ambassadors* was translated from the Dutch. Titles appear more frequently toward the end of the century. In 1684–85 came the most notable book immediately preceding Dampier.

---

[2] W. L. Clowes, *Naval History* (London and Boston, 1898), II, 92 and 538.

This was Exquemelin's *History of the Bucaniers of America*, a translation from the Dutch. It became a very popular book, going to a second edition in three months' time. According to Charles Hatton, it suffered after Sir Henry Morgan's successful action against Crooke, the publisher, for defamation of character. Then "his History of yᵉ Buccaneers wase looked upon as fabulous and sold for noe more than wast paper."[3] A third edition, however, did not appear until Dampier's books were well known and had helped revive it. One more notable book appeared just before Dampier—*A Collection of Several Late Voyages to the South and North* (1694), significant for the narratives of Sir John Narborough (who had been sent by Charles II to explore the coasts of Patagonia and Chile) and of Janszoon Tasmen, the greatest of the Dutch navigators. It was not, however, reprinted soon. Another collection that might be mentioned is one by J. Ray in 1693, consisting of "curious" travels from Dutch and English sources.

These are the principal collections of the century—not many for a period of seventy years. They show little more than that voyages were read, when one compares with them the state of things at the very beginning and the end of the century. Such a bibliography as Davies' *Bibliography of British History* notes only two collections of English voyages prior to 1697. A recent student of Defoe, in tracing the tradition of the story of adventure in far-off lands, skips from Raleigh to Dampier.[4] John Hughes says nothing in his essay *Of Style* (1698) of books of travel, although at the end he recommends the essay because it is a varied and delightful type of writing. The complaint of Defoe and Swift

---

[3] *Hatton Correspondence* (edited by Edward Thompson, 1878) (Camden Society Publications, n.s., XXII–XXIII), II, 225–26.

[4] Paul Dottin, *Daniel De Foe et ses romans* (Paris and Oxford, 1924), II, 324.

twenty years later against the tediousness of travelers came because of the abundance of voyages in the interim. Had these been so many in Hughes's time, he too might have mentioned them.

When the outburst following Dampier is set beside this period of relative inactivity, but one conclusion can be drawn: that Dampier had something to do with it. Certainly between 1697 and 1710 voyages and travels were extremely popular. The subjects of William and of Anne might have been just as hungry for geographical knowledge had Dampier never lived. That is a supposition. But Dampier did live and write, and he wrote books of travel more popular than any that had gone before, at a time when interest in exploration and discovery, in buccaneers, in journeys to remote regions with their attendant adventures was being generally revived. That is a fact.

In the seventy years before Dampier, then, there were but three collections of voyages in English worthy of notice. In the fourteen years following Dampier's *New Voyage* no less than eight completely new collections appeared in London. Others were revived after lying in various states of dormancy, and enjoyed one or more reprintings or editions. These were as follows:

1698 C. D'Acugna, M. Acarete, Grillet and Bechamel, *Voyages and Discoveries in South America*. 8vo.

1699 Hacke, Capt. Wm., *A Collection of Original Voyages*. 8vo.

1699. Exquemelin, *The History of the Bucaniers of America*. 8vo.

> Another edition of the second, with additions. The bibliography of Exquemelin presents a knotty problem. I have depended principally upon Sabin, *A Dictionary of Books Relating to America* (1868–81), VI, 314–16.

1703 de Rennevile, R. A. C., *A Collection of Voyages undertaken by the Dutch East Company.* 8vo. Translated from the French, which was from the Dutch.

1704 Churchill, A. and J., *A Collection of Voyages and Travels.* 4 vols., folio.

A great collection; still standard. It appeared on November 15, 1703, but bore the date 1704 on the title-page. It was announced as early as September 5, 1700. In 1732 it was reissued in 8 vols., folio, and again in 1744–47, a third edition, 8 vols., folio.

1704 Exquemelin, as above. A second edition corrected.

1704 Exquemelin, as above. Third edition. A complete revision.

1705 Harris, John, *Navigantium atque Itinerantium Bibliotheca or, A Compleat Collection of Voyages and Travels,* 2 vols., folio.

A great collection; still standard. Proposals were made for it as early as March 20, 1701 (*London Gazette*). It was revised, with large additions, by John Campbell in 1744 and 1764, 2 vols., folio.

1707 Ray, J., *A Collection of Curious Travels and Voyages,* 2 vols., 8vo. A new edition.

1707 *A Collection of Voyages,* 7 vols. 8vo.

1707 *Miscellanies containing a Collection of Travels,* 3 vols., 8vo.

1708–10 *A New Collection of Voyages and Travels, with historical Accounts of Discoveries and Conquests in all parts of the World,* 4to.

Knapton's serial.

1710 Tellez, Balthazar, *A New View of the Universe; or a New Collection of Voyages and Travels into all parts of the World,* 4to.

Perhaps originally, but certainly eventually, a part of Knapton's serial.

1711 [Stevens, Capt. John] *A New Collection of Voyages and Travels*, 2 vols., 4to.
Knapton's serial republished.

1708–17 Moll, H., *Atlas Geographus.*
A serial, not strictly a collection of voyages, but derived principally from voyagers' accounts. Republished in 1717 in 5 vols., 4to.

Another work of Moll might have been inserted above, but is also not strictly a "collection." This is *A System of Geography*, 1701, 2 parts, folio, "The whole abstracted from the best Ancient and Modern Geographers and from the esteem'd Modern Travelers."

William Dampier thus marks the beginning of a second great period of travel-literature, if the bibliographical record above has meaning. The reception of his own books being unquestionably great, he marks the beginning of the second, or silver, age of travel.

DAMPIER AND KNAPTON

James Knapton, Dampier's publisher, was a keen business man and contributed not a little to Dampier's fame then and to the significance of his works now. John Dunton of tireless pen and morality, the lesser Defoe of his time, extolled Knapton in this way: "A very accomplished person, not that sort of animal that flutters from Tavern to play house, and back again, all his life made up with Wig and Cravat, without one dram of thought in his composition; but a person made up with sound worth, brave, and generous; and shews by his purchasing *Dampier's Voyages* he *knows how to value a good copy*."[5]

Knapton's activities did so much for Dampier that we must speak somewhat of him. Reputable, industrious, and shrewd, knowing good copy when he saw it, he undertook,

[5] *Life and Errors* (London, 1705), p. 295.

following his success with Dampier, the publication of voyages on no small scale. A search through the *Term Catalogues* and the advertising pages in his own books (usually at the end) shows this. Dampier was his first book of voyages. The long list of books on the last few pages of the *New Voyage*, for example, contains no title of a travel work. Yet after the success with Dampier, he soon engaged to publish three other books of this kind, Lionel Wafer's *A New Voyage and Description of the Isthmus of America* (1699), Roberts' *Voyages and Cruising* (1699), and Capt. William Hacke's *Collection of Original Voyages* (1699).[6] From then on, he advertised them (and Dampier) prominently at the top of lists of books "also published" appearing inside the back covers (sometimes in both the front and back). The preparation of two of these (Wafer and Hacke) Knapton announced in the *Term Catalogues* along with Dampier's second book (*Voyages and Descriptions*); and they were thenceforth to be closely associated with each other and with Dampier. For example, when Dampier's third book appeared, it was a signal for the second edition of Wafer's book. In 1729 when the Knaptons collected Dampier and his associates into four volumes, Wafer went to a third edition, as is indicated in the table of editions on page 58. Thus Wafer was drawn along in the wake of Dampier, and became to the trade one of *Dampier's Voyages*. This third edition was still being advertised almost two years later. Even the plates used to illustrate it were marked for the printer, "Damp. Voy. Vol. 3." The map in it is identical with one to be found in the early pages of any of the first six editions of Dampier's *New Voyage Round the World*. Wafer, thus, was absorbed by Dampier.

[6] Hacke's *Collection* contained "Cowley's *Voyage round the Globe,* Sharp's *Journey over the Isthmus of Darien* . . . . , Wood's *Voyage thru the Streights of Magellan,* and Roberts' *Adventures among the Corsaires of the Levant.*"

Nor was Wafer alone in this. Captain Hacke's whole collection became the biggest part of volume four of Dampier, although connected only by the association of Dampier's name with the expeditions of Captain Cowley and Captain Sharp related therein. And still further, the account of the last expedition that Dampier himself commanded, written by a mutinous subordinate officer and therefore scarcely favorable to Dampier—even this became a part of the collected edition. This was William Funnell's *A Voyage Round the World*.

Funnell's book always had masqueraded as one of Dampier's, and it seems intentionally so.[7] An announcement of it preceding publication was worded, "Within a few Days will be published, An Account of Captain *William Dampier's* late expedition into the South Sea, in the 'St. George' . . . ." Funnell's name was not mentioned. When the book appeared a month later (March 1707) its title-page still exploited the good name of Dampier. It was, *A Voyage Round the World. Containing an Account of Captain Dampier's Expedition* [etc.] . . . . *With his various Adventures, Engagements, &c.* . . . . *By William Funnell, Mate to Captain Dampier.* The *History of the Works of the Learned* for March 1707 made its usual digest of the contents but treated it exclusively as a voyage of Dampier. "The World can't but be acquainted with the character of Capt. *Dampier* whose three Volumes of Voyages have met with such a favorable Reception from the Publick," wrote the hack reviewer. He [the reviewer] was giving the reader, he said, "the most Material of Capt. Dampier's Adventures, knowing that the world was in great Expectation of the Success of this

[7] Some writers on the subject charge Funnell, others Knapton, with the responsibility for this: Sir Albert Gray, "Introduction" to Dampier's *New Voyage Round the World* (London, 1927), p. xxx; *Early English Voyagers* (London, 1886), p. 451; Joseph Sabin, *A Dictionary of Books Relating to America* (New York, 1868–1881), V, 189.

THE EDITIONS OF DAMPIER'S *VOYAGES* TO 1729*

	EDITION AND DATE						
	[1st]	(2d)	(3d)	(4th)	(5th)	(6th)	(7th)
A New Voyage Round the World	1697	1697	1698	1699	1703		1717
Voyages and Descriptions				[1st] 1699	(2d) 1700	(3d) 1705	
A Voyage to New Holland:							
Part I					[1st] 1703	(2d) 1709	
Part II						[1st] 1709	

A Collection of Voyages:
  Vol. I: *A New Voyage Round the World* .... 7th edition ⎫
  Vol. II: *Voyages and Descriptions* .... [4th edition] ⎬
  Vol. III: ⎪
    A Voyage to New Holland, Part I .... 3d edition ⎪
    A Voyage to New Holland, Part II .... [2d edition] ⎬ 1729
    Wafer, *A New Voyage and Description of the Isthmus of America* (1699) .... 3d edition ⎪
  Vol. IV: ⎪
    Funnell, *A Voyage Round the World* (1701) ...... [2d edition] ⎪
    Voyages of Cowley, Sharp, Wood, Roberts (Hacke's *Collection of Original Voyages*, 1699) .... [2d edition] ⎭

*This table is based on that of N. M. Penzer, Esq, general editor of Dampier's *New Voyage Round the World*, 1927. I have corrected and extended it to show particularly the miscellaneous character of Volumes III and IV in the collected edition.

Expedition; and would be willing to know the Circumstances of his Disappointments."[8] Funnell's *Voyage*, furthermore, appeared in the index of this journal under the name of Dampier, not that of Funnell.

Years later (1744 and 1764) John Campbell, the editor of Harris' great collection of voyages, found it necessary to explain why he had put Funnell's name in the title of Funnell's voyage. "This Voyage has usually passed under the Name of Captain *William Dampier;* but as he proceeded only to the South Seas . . . . I thought that his [Funnell's] Name should stand in the Title than that of *Dampier's,* with whom, in the Voyage, we have much less to do."[9]

Harris' collection has a closer connection with Dampier than this. In the midst of Dampier's popularity, and certainly in some part because of it, the London booksellers engaged in 1702 Dr. John Harris, scientific writer, divine, and topographer, to compile a huge collection of voyages. This was to be abridged from the principal works of the kind from Hakluyt and Purchas to his own time. It appeared in 1705 in two folio volumes, under the impressive title, *Navigantium atque Itinerantium Bibliotheca or, A Compleat Collection of Voyages and Travels,* and contained over four hundred voyages. The list of subscribers' names in the first volume shows that Dampier's publisher signed "for seven books." We have already seen with what respect he treated Dampier.

Nine years after his collected edition, Dampier was apparently still a much read contemporary and was not considered by William Oldys as rare or scarce.[10] By 1776, however, one editor of his "Voyages and Adventures" declared

---

[8] *History of the Works of the Learned,* IX, 179–90.

[9] John Harris, *Navigantium atque Itinerantium* . . . . (ed. 1764), I, 131.

[10] His *British Librarian* (1738) does not mention Dampier.

that editions of Dampier were "extremely scarce" and the language somewhat obsolete.

By 1705 Knapton had on his shelves Dampier, Wafer, Hacke, and Harris, being responsible as publisher for the first three. He himself added many more titles to this interesting list. In 1705 he published Bosman's *New and Accurate Description* . . . . *of Guinea.* In 1707 he published Funnell's *Voyage Round the World* and let it go as one of Dampier's. Herman Moll, the ingenious geographer and cartographer, with whom Knapton had close relations, catered to the now growing demand for geographical knowledge by beginning in June 1708 a monthly magazine of geography. This was called *Atlas Geographus.* It ran until 1717, and was then republished in five volumes. Nothing like it had before been attempted. Its long run proved new possibilities in publishing this kind of matter. In December of 1708 Knapton and four others also published a travel serial, which we may safely assume was done in imitation of Moll. This was *"A New Collection of Voyages and Travels with Historical Accounts of Discoveries and Conquests in all Parts of the World* translated from foreign accounts into English for the first time." So runs the title-page. The translator's name, Captain John Stevens, is not mentioned. This serial appeared somewhat irregularly from December 1708 to some time in 1710 and was republished in 1711 in two volumes. In this form it exists today, as Stevens' *Voyages.*[11] It may have been published also in competition with Awnsham and John Churchill's famous collection of voyages of 1704 and later, which had already made a name for itself and its publishers.

The London booksellers of this time split up into various

---

[11] It may be found catalogued also under *A View of the Universe* in 7 vols., 1708–1710. These are the seven parts of the serial. Stevens was well known in his day as a Spanish scholar and translator. Swift satirizes his style in the introduction to *Polite Conversation.*

groups or syndicates, one group publishing law books and another books of science and so on. James Knapton appears to have belonged to such a syndicate, composed of himself (named first), A. Bell, D. Midwinter, W. Taylor, A. Collins, and J. Baker. These men took over Knapton's serial, apparently, for they were responsible not only for its republication in 1711 but for an earlier digest of voyages translated by one Balthazar Tellez (1710) and forming a considerable part of the present Volume II. A separate title-page for Part IV in the series (it stands first in Volume II), *The Travels of the Jesuits in Ethiopa* by Balthazar Tellez, bears the date 1710 and the names of the Knapton-Bell-Midwinter syndicate. Title-pages are lacking for the numbers following this in the copy that I examined,[12] but it is safe to say that Knapton and four others began a travel serial in 1708, which passed by 1710 at least into the hands of a publishing syndicate of which Knapton was a prominent member. It forms an interesting and significant addition of books of travel to the list of James Knapton.

Many other books of this character bear the imprint of this enterprising bookseller. By 1729 he was advertising, besides those already mentioned, the following:

A Relation of Two Several Voyages made into the East Indies . . . . Done out of the Dutch by S. L., by Fryke and Schewitzer, 1699.

Atlas Maritimus & Commercialis; Or a General View of the World, so far as relates to Trade and Navigation . . . . The Construction of Maps and Globes . . . . in which the present State of Geography is considered, 1717.

Moll's *The Compleat Geographer, or the Chorography and Topography Of all the known Parts of the Earth,* fourth edition, 1723. A folio with elaborate title-page in black and red.

---

[12] In the Astor Library, New York City.

*An Historical Geography of the Old and New Testaments
. . . .* by Edward Wells. (*New Testament,* 1708, 1712,
1718; *Old Testament,* 1711, 1712; *Old and New Testaments, ca.* 1712.)
*A Treatise of the Situation of Paradise To which is prefix'd
a Map of the adjacent Countries,* by P. D. Huet, Bishop
of Soissons, *ca.* 1729. Translated from the French.

One would not presume to prove the flourishing state of
voyages and travels in Queen Anne's time and thereafter by
the record of one publishing house, albeit a good one. The
two titles given last in the list above may be examined with
profit, however. It is all very well to print bona fide voyages. It argues for an interest in them to do so. But when
bishops and others proceed to do over Biblical works in
popular guise and in doing so choose to appeal to the reader's
fondness for geography, it is for us to mark it well. One of
the most amusing but none the less significant titles to be
found advertised at this time runs as follows:
"*The Travels of the Holy Patriarchs, Prophets, Judges,
Kings, our Saviour Christ, and his Apostles, as they are related in the Old and New Testaments: with a Description of
the Towns and Places to which they Travelled, and how
many English Miles they stood from Jerusalem,* by Henry
Beunting, fourth edition, 1704, with additions." In other
words, the Bible done over into a book of travels, with all
the rights and privileges, the signs and symbols, appertaining
thereunto.

Did the interest in travel spread to others? Was it general? Much that I have just said with regard to the activity
of James Knapton and the general reception of Dampier
shows that it did. It can be shown more definitely, however,
that a widespread interest in travels followed a line of development similar to that of the books of the house of
Knapton.

The ultimate limits of its penetration into English life I do not presume to tell, but enough can be demonstrated to show that it went far. The serial publication of atlases and voyages has already been pointed out. It is not improbable that a greater impetus to serializing than at first appears was lent by Moll's initial enterprise. Daniel Defoe imitated Moll and Knapton in this by issuing his *General History of Trade* (1713) and his *History of the Principal Discoveries and Improvements, in the Several Arts and Sciences: Particularly . . . . Commerce, Navigation, and Plantation* (1726–1727) in monthly numbers.[13]

In the back of the fourth edition of *Robinson Crusoe* is advertised *A Treatise of both Globes. To which is added, a Geographical Description of our Earth.* Defoe cast satire into the form of voyages in *Atalantis Major* (1711) and *The Comical Pilgrim, or, Travels of a Cynick Philosopher* (1722). Steele recommended in *The Ladies' Library* that reading the best authors on the subject of *"Histories* of other *Nations,* Accounts of *Voyages* and *Travels,* the Lives of *Heroes* and *Philosophers"* not only would be "pleasant and instructive Entertainment" for the fair but would "enlarge and elevate their Souls, and give them a Contempt for the common Amusements of the Sex." Michael de la Roche in *Memoirs of Literature* (1712)[14] and John Cockburn in *A Journey over Land from the Gulf of Honduras to the Great South-Sea* (1735)[15] assured their readers that a voyage round the world, or anywhere, was always acceptable—so popular as to need no apology. Robinson Crusoe, on his way to China from Bengal, refers the reader for a description of the voyage "to those journeys and travels of Englishmen,

---

[13] The title-page of the former and the Preface (pp. iii to viii) and Conclusion (p. 303) of the latter indicate this.

[14] Michael de la Roche, *Memoirs of Literature,* V, 42.

[15] John Cockburn, *op. cit.,* Preface, pp. [iii]–iv.

many of which I find, are published, and more promised every day." A bishop complained in the *London Journal* that "books of Voyages and Travels, filled with monstrous and incredible Stories" had become popular because they satisfied a "morbid taste" for extravagant fiction. And Defoe's Colonel Jacque did not dream that his memoirs would be so popular as he finds "custom and the humour of the times has caused" such autobiographies to be. Lemuel Gulliver, upon being asked by his rescuer why he did not write and publish his adventures in Brobdingnag, complains that England is "overstocked with books of travels" so that "nothing could now pass that was not extraordinary." William King, humorous writer, wit, and friend of Swift, Pope, and Gay, wrote in the preface[16] of his satirical *Voyage to Cajamai:*

> After a diligent Search of what probably might Please, he [the Author] consider'd that the Liking of the Town generally runs in the same Vein for some time together. At one Season nothing Pleases but Novels, then Translations from the French, then Tragedies . . . . then all again is swallow'd up in Bickerstaff's Astrological Predictions and Tatling: *but that which seems most generally to have prevail'd, is the Pleasure taken from the Perusal of Accounts given by Travellers.* The Success at Darien gave no inconsiderable Amusements, *nor were Dampier's Relations less acceptable to the Ladies* than the Men of Business.[17]

Paradise and the Holy Land were laid out for geographical demonstration, and the Bible was converted for the mildly pious into a book of travels. Cuts and drafts and maps and indexes made unimportant books seem important. Announcements in the *Term Catalogues,* and daily papers and

---

[16] Pp. [2] and [3] in *Useful Transactions,* for May–September, 1709. Italics are mine.

[17] Psalmanaazaar's *Island of Formosa* and the *New Atalantis* are also mentioned by King.

the title-pages of books took care to say, when possible, "adorned with cuts and maps," "with a map of the country," or the like. One is struck by the number of maps advertised for sale, usually in sets. Through the activities of Herman Moll and William Dampier, particularly, new interest was aroused in charting the unknown, especially the shores of New Holland. Moll became the greatest hydrographer of his time. His geographical works already noted were plentifully supplied with maps. James Knapton engaged him to draw maps for his best travel books: Dampier, Wafer, Funnell, and others. Some unsigned maps in these works bear every sign of the pen of Moll, too. The map of the world in the fourth edition of *Robinson Crusoe* looks much like Moll's map of the world in Dampier's *New Voyage*. "Maps by H. Moll" was worth displaying on a title-page. A glance at some of his more important sets[18] for sale indicates something of the popularity and appeal of maps alone. Atlases were so common that Swift conveniently described the size of the little book carried by Gulliver's Brobdingnagian nurse as "not much larger than a Sanson's atlas," a folio book.

Despite the strong suspicion of mariners' tales entertained throughout this period, they yet found an eager audience if they bore a semblance of truth. One thinks immediately of the accounts of Alexander Selkirk, both true and false. Steele devoted one whole number of the *Englishman* to an account

---

[18] *The World Described; or a New and Correct Sett of Maps . . . . each map . . . . printed on two Sheets of Elephant-Paper* (1708–36, folio); *Atlas Manuale: A New Sett of Maps of all Parts of the Earth . . . . Wherein Geography is Rectify'd by Reforming the Old Maps according to modern Observations* (1711); *A View of the Coasts, Countries, and Islands within the limits of the South Sea Co.* (1711); *The English Gentleman's Guide* (1717), a "new and complete Book of Maps of all England and Wales"; *Atlas Minor*, n.d. (*ca.* 1732), sixty-two small maps dated around 1725, advertised in D'Anvers' *Craftsman* in November 1729, but map No. 41 dated 1732.

of him, and himself confessed elsewhere that he delighted in no books more than in travels into remote parts. Addison, furthermore, writes a book of voyages himself. At least, he refers to his *Remarks on Several Parts of Italy* as "my voyage" and takes pains to explain that his book is an improvement over Misson's *Voyage d'Italie*. It is typical, although in a literary manner, of the kind of work known as a "voyage" in its descriptions of cities, rivers, mountains, soil, etc. Steele and Addison think of the *Iliad* and the *Odyssey* as "voyages," and Steele in *Tatler* No. 6 does over a small part of the *Iliad* in the manner of a traveler's journal. Anthony Henley writes to Swift on the subject of "the use which may be made of modern travels."

Providence Displayed was a broadside devoted to the story of Selkirk, and the chapbooks of the time show an interesting number concerned with travel.

The story of the Bristol privateers told by Captain Rogers became so popular that the book lay open at Elford's Coffee-house to be "seen and read Gratis"—an inducement to enter Elford's. So great became the vogue for voyages that Defoe in 1725 protested against the commonness of voyages around the world, and then proceeded to write a fictitious one. The fictitious voyage, by no means a new thing, enjoyed a prosperous revival at the hands of many. A voyage to somewhere became almost a stock device for satire.[19] George Psalmanaazaar, that strange impostor and pillar of piety, could never have fooled the public with his fraudulent account of Formosa had not the readers of 1704 been travel-crazy. The index to Gay's *Trivia* and the alphabetical catalogue of "Names, Plants, Flowers, Birds, Beasts, and other Material

[19] William King, *A Journey to London in the year 1698* (London, 1699); *A Voyage to Cajamai* (1709); *Crapulia;* cf. *Remains* (1732).

Ned Ward, *The Merry Travellers; or, a Trip upon Ten-Toes, from Moorfields to Bromely* (1721–1722).

Tom Brown, *Amusements* (1708).

Things, mentioned in these Pastorals" appended to his *Shepherd's Week* seem done in the very manner of the voyagers and natural philosophers. Certainly the second part of *Polly* with the scene in the West Indies where Macheath is a pirate exploits the general interest in voyages, pirates, and the West Indies. Stage sailors like Farquhar's Captain Fireball[20] and Congreve's Ben begin to appear.

One must be careful not to assign too much to the influence of Dampier alone. The excitement over the South Sea Bubble in and about 1720, and the actual activities of pirates (Kyd, Avery, and Gow) contributed much indeed. Captain Fireball says to Colonel Standard: "The whole house [the Chocolate House] was clearly taken up with the two important questions, whether the Colonel [Standard] was a Cuckold? or Kid a Pyrate?" Charles Johnson's play, *The Successful Pyrate*, was produced at Drury Lane in November 1712 and was published the next year. His *General History of the Robberies and Murders of the Most Notorious Pyrates* (1724) went through four editions in two years. I shall speak later of Defoe's interest in Captain Avery and Captain Gow. It would be scarcely pertinent here to go into the details of the stir created by the South Sea Bubble. It is sufficient to note that these things all fed a stream of interest in voyages revived at this time by William Dampier and his shrewd publisher, James Knapton.

[20] *Sir Harry Wildair.* In Act III the dullness of seamen's journals is satirized by Clincher, who reads Captain Fireball's daily log of winds, courses, bearings, sailing terms, whales sighted, etc., and then exclaims, "Odso! Great News Faith."

V

THE STRANGE SURPRISING ADVENTURES
OF A YORK MARINER

And what does else want credit, come to me,
And I'll be sworn 't is true: travellers ne'er did lie,
Though fools at home condemn them.
—Antonio in *The Tempest*

ALL the world knows Robinson Crusoe. At least, all the world knows about his shipwreck and his piously resourceful life on an uninhabited island vaguely located in southern seas. Most of the world forgets, however, that that is not half the story, that Crusoe comes home, returns to his island, sails to the East Indies, where he is marooned, takes care of himself as admirably in the East Indies as he did in the West Indies, is for years a trader to the Spice Islands, the Philippines, and China, and finally, as an old man, accomplishes a long trek overland back across Siberia down into Germany and so home. In other words, if we go back to our boyhood classic, we find it to be not simply a tale of a plain sailor alone on an island for twenty-eight years, but a two-volume prose romance of a hero who wanders three-quarters the way round the globe, suffering many vicissitudes at the hands of fortune and seeing many wonderful sights and distant lands. His tale is a fictitious voyage much like the actual accounts of real voyages current in Defoe's day.

We have seen that Dampier's *Voyages* made a stir in the world, fanning into flame the eagerness of a curious reading public for strange tales of far-away places. It is this appetite for travel, caught at its height just before the disillusionment and panic of the South Sea Bubble, that Defoe deliberately satisfies. Being a journalist, and not a sailor, he drew his remarkable fund of nautical information from books, among them the very same popular travel works noted in our last chapter.

Old-fashioned scholars and students of Defoe thought him either a grand liar or a magician. His amazing knowledge of all places and things—the courses of rivers in unexplored middle Africa, the private lives of Madagascar pirates, the natural life of tropic seas, the fortunes of slaves in America, trade in the Philippines, and the lives and customs of the Chinese—all this was hard to explain except by the fertile imagination or the divining rod. For years England's first great journalist was thought to have manufactured wholesale all necessary details for his romances. He lied like the truth; he had a genius for verisimilitude. Remarks like these became almost canonical. But the steadier hand of modern scholarship has turned upon him the white ray of patient research. Defoe's reading has been examined with great profit. Possessing a tenacious memory and an insatiable capacity for rapid reading, Defoe read and read and read. The marvel of it is that he read so much while engaged in a dozen political and journalistic enterprises at once. Thirty-odd years ago a list of the books in his library was published. Since then the secret of Defoe's genius for nautical detail has awaited only the patient soul who would read the books. That has been done for his important works, and we now look at him in a new light. No longer magician or liar, he now stands before us as the journalist par excellence. Every possible experience was grist for his mill, in life and in books. He had, among many things, a genius for parquetry, piecing together bits from everywhere in new designs.

The best authority on Defoe's narrative method summarizes his transmutation of reading in *Robinson Crusoe* thus:

"Robinson Crusoe" is not a creation entirely from Defoe's imagination. He has his hero do a series of things well known in the literature of travel; suffer storm and shipwreck, endure slavery in Barbary at Turkish (or Moorish) hands, duplicate the experiences of desert island life, and participate in both commerce and travel. But in the large aspect, Defoe's genius has play in unifying in the experiences of one man these diverse elements of adventure undergone by several men. As he says in the preface to part one [of *Robinson Crusoe*], "The wonders of this man's life exceed all that (he thinks) is to be found extant; the life of one man being scarce capable of greater variety." Crusoe's character colors the whole so well that we are not aware (except for the distinct loss of interest when the island story ends) of the diversity of his sources. Especially is this true of Crusoe's life on his island; here the author has blended and unified his materials from Rogers, Knox, Dampier, and the rest, until they are scarcely distinguishable—an artistic method that has made the search for these originals so difficult. But even the later story has this unity of tone. We are totally unaware of the point at which Defoe ceases to depend upon Dampier and turns to Le Comte and later to Ides.[1]

The names just mentioned (Knox, Dampier, Rogers, Le Comte, and Ides) are those of authors of travel books current in Defoe's day having to do with long voyages, shipwrecks, marooned men, and the wonders and hardships of overland travels in Asia told by Jesuit missionaries. Robert Knox recounts in *An Historical Relation of Ceylon* (1681) his adventures for twenty-eight years on that island, a kind of captivity and desert-isle experience combined. Woodes Rogers, as we have seen, was captain of a successful privateering expedition famous not only for riches but for the rescue of Alexander Selkirk. His *Cruising Voyage* (1712) tells of

[1] A. W. Secord, *The Narrative Method of Defoe* (1924), *University of Illinois Studies in Language and Literature*, Vol. IX, No. 1, pp. 109–10.

fighting the Spaniards, describes Juan Fernandez, and in general supplies us with reliable information on Dampier's activities for three years. Father Louis Le Comte, a French Jesuit missionary, wrote a description of China, one of the standard works in the seventeenth century for things Chinese. This was translated in 1697 as *Memoirs and Observations Made in a Late Journey through the Empire of China*. The details of Robinson Crusoe's adventures in China depend heavily on this book. E. Ysbrants Ides's *Three Years Travels from Moscow Overland to China*, translated from the Dutch in 1706, is an account of Siberia written by an Ambassador to China from the court of the Czar of Muscovy. If we reverse Ides's journey from Archangel to Pekin we have Robinson Crusoe's journey from Pekin to Archangel, towns, rivers, comments, and all.

Other titles should be added to these: Hakluyt's *Principall Navigations and Discoveries,* and Purchas' *Hakluytus Posthumous, or Purchas his Pilgrimes,* the classic collections in our tongue of voyages and travels, compiled in the years from 1589 to 1600 and in 1625, respectively; collections like Adam Olearius' *Voyages and Travels of the Ambassadors* (translated from the Dutch in 1662) and Exquemelin's *Bucaniers of America* (1684); accounts of pirates like Captain Charles Johnson's *General History of the Pyrates* (1724); and numbers of accounts of shipwrecks and desert-isle adventures, especially that of Alexander Selkirk. Other accounts of this the most famous marooned man were available in Defoe's day in Captain Edward Cooke's two volumes, *A Voyage to the South-Sea and Round the World* (1712), in Steele's *Englishman,* No. 26, and in an anonymous pamphlet, *Providence Displayed,* thought by some to have been written by Defoe himself.

Such were the materials at Defoe's command. Those convincing details in *Robinson Crusoe* that have made Defoe a great realist have come from books like these. With few exceptions, everything from Robinson Crusoe's earliest desire to run away to sea to his long inland journey home across Siberia when he had become an old man can be traced or identified thus.[2] Study of *Captain Singleton* and the *New Voyage Round the World* reveals the same thing.

"ROBINSON CRUSOE," PART I

This, then, is how Defoe worked. Our eye, however, should rather be upon William Dampier, whom we now have left from the list above. Fortified with knowledge of Defoe's method of composition, we turn to the greatest contemporary English travel works, celebrating England's greatest buccaneer, fully expecting a contribution to this mélange of matter. And we are not disappointed. Many things point to the fact that Defoe used Dampier more than he used any other as a storehouse of information and a mine of adventure and suggestions of adventure.

It is impossible to think that the greatest journalist of Queen Anne's day should be unfamiliar with the works of the greatest buccaneer and explorer. Idle speculation has it that Defoe met and talked with Dampier. Evidence is not lacking, however, that he knew Dampier's volumes, apart

---

[2] The reader cannot do better than turn to Mr. Secord's book for complete illumination. He proves his points by using three principal prose romances of Defoe: *Robinson Crusoe, Captain Singleton*, and the *Memoirs of Captain Carleton*. In the course of his discussion, however, he touches provocatively other narratives, notably the *King of Pirates*, the *Memoirs of a Cavalier, Colonel Jacque*, and *A New Voyage Round the World*. Being concerned with William Dampier primarily, I have retraced Mr. Secord's steps in two of these narratives. Our findings coincide except where I have corrected, added new, or made a different application of the old. Inasmuch as my purpose is to determine how far the influence of Dampier penetrated, I have had to take for my province all of Defoe's work pertaining to adventures at sea or in lands described by Dampier. It is following such an investigation that I declare Defoe dependent on Dampier more than on any other single travel work.

from the unmistakable imprint they made on his prose romances.

"He [the English gentleman] may go round the globe with Dampier and Rogers and kno' a thousand times more in doing it than all those illiterate sailors," he writes familiarly in the *Compleat English Gentleman*.[3] Before *Robinson Crusoe* appeared, all of Dampier's books had been published and had risen to fame. The *New Voyage* had gone to the sixth edition in 1717 and the others were in their third, second, and first editions, respectively. Defoe's wide and accurate knowledge of geography would alone have led him to Dampier.

Forty-nine titles of books of voyages, travels, descriptions of foreign countries and treatises upon geography and navigation were in his library.[4] In his works he mentions others. He thought himself a master of geography[5] and thus styled himself in a list of his intellectual accomplishments in which no one of the others is thus emphatically described. If he were master of geography, he became so from a perusal of "maps, attlasses, and measurements of our mathematicians," which are the terms of his recommendations for such proficiency in the *Compleat English Gentleman*. No "Master of Geography" in his time would dare call himself such without having known the maps of Herman Moll and the books of William Dampier.[6]

[3] Ed. by Bülbrig, p. 225.

[4] *Athenaeum*, June 1, 1895.

[5] *Review of the Affairs of France*, VII, 455.

[6] The attacks of Gildon and others emphasize this (Gildon, *Life of . . . . Mr. D— DeF——, of London, Hosier . . . . With Remarks . . . . upon the Life of Crusoe*, 1719). Lee quotes a communication in *Read's Journal* two days after the publication of the second volume of *Robinson Crusoe* professing to discover a geographical mistake in the foreign news of *Mist's Journal* (for which Defoe was writing) and ending with the sneer, "Certainly the infallible *Robinson Crusoe*, that great Trav-

Defoe was, furthermore, especially familiar with the coast of South America in the region of the mouth of the Orinoco River. In 1719, besides publishing *Robinson Crusoe*, he published also *An Historical Account of the Voyages and Adventures of Sir Walter Raleigh*, at the end of which he made a proposal to the South Sea Company of founding an English colony in Guiana. Should they listen to it, he said, he was "ready to lay before them a Plan or Chart of the Rivers and Shores, the Depths of Water, and all necessary Instructions for . . . . Navigation."[7] His knowledge of Raleigh was from Hakluyt, but his practical information for such a plan could only have been modern. His was a changing world, especially in geography. In *Robinson Crusoe* he made use of Dampier's routes of travel, some of his phraseology, and groups of small (but telling) details. Take the first part of the story, the island experience. Recall the outstanding details: Robinson Crusoe's overwhelming desire to run away to sea, the shipwreck and the salvaging of goods, the building of his abode, the tedious construction of a canoe, the discovery of the footprints in the sand and the subsequent faithful service of his man, Friday, many details of his resourceful solitary existence, and his final rescue.

Fresh from the pages of Dampier, we note first the large amount of matter that would surely have struck Defoe's eye: early longing for the sea, voyages to remote places, storms at

---

eller and Geographer, could not be guilty of so Monstrous a Blunder" (*Life of Defoe*, I, 306).

A contributor to the *Gentleman's Magazine* in 1785, who had read in Defoe only *Robinson Crusoe*, asks, "Whence came so able a geographer?" (Vol. LV, p. 882).

A definite connection between Defoe and Moll is to be found in the second and third volumes (1724, 1727) of Defoe's *Tour*, which contained maps by Moll.

[7] Defoe, *An Historical Account of the Voyages and Adventures of Sir Walter Raleigh*, p. 55. For specific mention of the Orinoco, cf. pp. 40 f.

sea, shipwrecks, marooned men, South Sea islands, especially Juan Fernandez, a description of the country of Brazil and the reef-infested islands off the coast of Brazil, and nautical details galore for the West Indies and coasts of Central and South America such as winds, tides, and currents, not to say anything of rafts, ladders, umbrellas, tame goats, parrots, penguins, and the like. But similar matter often existed, usually in less degree, in other works. We are therefore led to give most credence to those matters that are found only in Dampier. I shall select a few of these latter, leaving the former to be drawn in the wake of positive identifications and an accumulation of things.

Going back to Robinson Crusoe on his island, we find Defoe following rather closely Dampier's directions for making a canoe by hollowing out a cedar log. This is how Robinson Crusoe does it. Finding the ship's boat, beached high and dry, too heavy to move, he wonders "whether it was not possible to make myself a *canoe, or periagua,* such as the natives of those climates make, even without tools, or as I might say, without hands, viz., of the trunk of a great tree . . . . and to work I went. I felled a cedar tree; I question whether Solomon ever had such a one for the building of the Temple at Jerusalem. It was five feet ten inches diameter at the lower part next the stump, and four feet eleven inches diameter at the end of twenty-two feet, after which it lessened for a while, and then parted into branches."[8] The stupendous labor of hollowing was finally accomplished with no other tools but mallet and chisel. This "canoe or periagua" never saw the water, it being too heavy to move. It was not until years later that Crusoe made another attempt, less ambitious, and successful only after he had dug a canal to bring the water to the craft.

Dampier says, "We reckon *Periagoes* and *Canoes* that

[8] *Robinson Crusoe* (Oxford ed., 1840), I, 149–50. References to *Robinson Crusoe* are to this edition unless otherwise stated. Italics are mine.

are made of Cedar to be the best of any; they are nothing but the Tree itself made hollow Boatwise, with a flat bottom, and Canoa generally sharp at both ends, the Periago at one only, with the other end flat." Finding that the lack of boats was a serious impediment to their buccaneering designs Dampier and his friends went to a small island off the coast of Darien, St. Andreas, still marked on modern maps, where "we might build Canoas, it being plentifully stored with Cedars of its own . . . . the largest that ever I knew or heard of; the Bodies alone being ordinarily 40 or 50 Foot long, many 60 or 70 and upwards, and of a proportionable Bigness."[9] Dampier elsewhere pauses in his narratives to tell how natives in various parts of the world build and operate small boats.[10]

In another part of his first volume, Dampier describes Mindanayan [Philippine] craftsmen.

> Every Man almost is a Carpenter, for they can work with the Ax and Adds. Their Ax is but small, and so made that they can take it out of the Helve, and by turning it make an Adds. They have no Saws; but when they make Plank, they split the Tree in two, and make a Plank of each Part, plaining it with the Ax and Adds. This requires much pains, and takes up a great deal of time; but they work cheap, and the goodness of the Plank thus hewed, which hath its Grain preserv'd entire; makes amends for their cost and pains.[11]

Dampier here provides the idea of great West Indian cedars for canoes and of heavy, tedious work done with small hand tools. Defoe's frequent use of *periagua* gives a particular flavor of Dampier, for it is a favorite word with him, too, in this connection. More than once we find Defoe susceptible to the great buccaneer's language.

---

[9] *Dampier's Voyages*, I, 60.

[10] Particularly at Guam. See Dampier, *op. cit.*, I, 308–309.

[11] *Dampier's Voyages*, I, 339–40.

Dampier's description of hewing out planks from solid logs at great labor also seems reflected in that of Defoe's canoes. Says Robinson Crusoe,

However, I made abundance of things even without tools, and some with no more tools than an adze and a hatchet, which, perhaps, were never made that way before, and that with infinite labour. For example, if I wanted a board, I had no other way but to cut down a tree, set it on edge before me, and hew it flat on either side with my axe, till I had brought it to be thin as a plank, and then dub it smooth with my adze. It is true, by this method I could make but one board out of a whole tree; but this I had no remedy for but patience, any more than I had for the prodigious deal of time and labour which it took me up to make a plank or board. But my time or labour was little worth, and so it was employed in one way as another.[12]

The only difference between Crusoe's method and that of Dampier's Mindanayan carpenters is that Crusoe made but one plank from a single tree, whereas the others made two.[13] Otherwise the similarity is too striking to pass by.

[12] *Robinson Crusoe*, I, 79–80.

[13] Readers are again referred to Mr. Secord's *Narrative Method of Defoe*, pp. 46 and 59. Robert Knox, hero of an adventure on the island of Ceylon, wrote, in addition to his published book, a manuscript of supplementary data which was in existence at the time of the composition of *Robinson Crusoe*. In this manuscript, it appears, are some apparent sources for details in Defoe's narrative, among them notably Defoe's method of making plank. The situation is perplexing because it cannot be proved that Defoe knew Knox (who was alive and in London) or had seen this manuscript. It is certain that he was familiar with Dampier. It may easily be that he saw both accounts. As it stands, the connection with Dampier is surer, the similarity with Knox more striking. It is, furthermore, more like the observed practice of Defoe to change some single external feature rather than to follow meticulously each particular in his source. This also would suggest Dampier rather than Knox.

Since I first wrote this, Mr. Secord has called my attention to Defoe's reference in *The Plan of English Commerce* (Oxford ed., 1928, p. 27) to the Muscovites' practice of making a single plank from a tree.

As for the cedar canoe, in another place, building another canoe, Crusoe does not know the kind of wood used. His own remark concerning it further ties Defoe to Dampier: "nor can I tell to this day what wood to call the tree we cut down, except it was very like the tree we call fustic, or between that and the Nicaragua wood, for it was much of the same colour and smell."[14] In the course of Dampier's famous descriptions of the logwood industry he treats the subject of dye-woods. Other dye-woods have the same reddish color as logwood, he says, particularly blood-wood and stockfish-wood; and blood-wood, so far as his experience goes, grows in the North Sea *only in the Gulf of Nicaragua.*[15] This appears to be the same as Defoe's "Nicaragua wood." In another place,[16] but also on the subject of dye-woods, Dampier mentions definitely fustic, a yellowish wood.

In the *Mercator* (a journal of trade, successor to his *Review*) for July 1, 1714, Defoe shows that logwood and Nicaragua wood are associated in his mind as the timber cut by the buccaneers, Dampier's logwood cutters, for the Jamaica trade. Thus, Crusoe has cut down a logwood tree, but Defoe cannot call it logwood because Crusoe's island is not located where logwood grows. He therefore cleverly explains his ignorance of this wood by comparing it with others even as Dampier compared logwood.

A suggestion for Crusoe's difficulty in getting his canoes to the sea is also given in Dampier.[17] In remarking about the hardship of cutting logwood at Cape Catoch, he explains that the cutters abandoned the region and went to the Bay of Campeachy where the timber stood nearer to the shore. At Catoch it had to be carried 1,500 paces, whereas at Campeachy it had to be carried only 300. To get these large

---

[14] *Robinson Crusoe*, I, 272.
[15] *Dampier's Voyages*, II, 159.
[16] *Ibid.*, II, 394.   [17] *Ibid.*, II, 115–16.

trees to water, a very large path was cleared through the woods for 300 yards.[18] Crusoe could not get his first canoe to the shore at all. The second he launched not only by clearing a path, but, being alone, by cutting a canal and bringing the water "almost half a mile" to it.

So much for cedar trees and canoes. Dampier's pages lead us on. One of the best-known incidents in *Robinson Crusoe* is the history of Friday. The footprint in the sand is memorable. Here is the passage:

> It happened one day, about noon, going towards my boat, I was exceedingly surprised with the print of a man's naked foot on the shore, which was very plain to be seen on the sand . . . . How it came thither I knew not, nor could in the least imagine. But after innumerable fluttering thoughts, like a man perfectly confused and out of myself, I came home to my fortification . . . . terrified to the last degree, looking behind me at every two or three steps, mistaking every bush and tree, and fancying every stump at a distance to be a man.[19]

Several sources in the literature of travel have been suggested for this vivid scene, but none is so close as a passage in Dampier where "much footing of men and boys" on the sandy shore of a West Indian island "troubled us a little" for fear of Spaniards.[20] No other source has the combination of the print in the sand and the fear induced in the spectator.

Friday himself is probably the only other interesting character in the tale, with his ecstasies, his piety, his fidelity, and his impossible English. He belongs to that sociological phenomenon raised on high in the eighteenth century and now called the "noble savage." Much has been written about Alexander Selkirk as the original of Robinson Crusoe. No one, however, has done more than suggest an original Friday.

[18] *Ibid.*, II, 181.   [19] *Robinson Crusoe*, I, 182–83.
[20] Secord, *op. cit.*, p. 61; *Dampier's Voyages*, II, 137.

The search for Alexander Selkirk takes us to a famous episode in Dampier, that of a Mosquito Indian marooned for over three years on Alexander Selkirk's island, Juan Fernandez, from which he was rescued by Dampier and made one of the world's famous solitaries. He has long been rather vaguely considered one of the originals of Robinson Crusoe. Dampier's account of this Indian in chapter four of his *New Voyage Round the World* goes in part as follows:

March the 22nd, 1684, we came in sight of the Island, and the next day got in and anchored in a Bay at the South end of the Island, in 25 fathom Water, not two Cables lengths from the shore. We presently got out our Canoa, and went ashore to see for a Moskito Indian, whom we left here when we were chased hence by 3 Spanish Ships in the year 1681. . . . .

This Indian lived here alone above three years, and altho' he was several times sought by the Spaniards, who knew he was left on the Island, yet they could never find him. He was in the Woods, hunting for Goats, when Capt. Watlin drew off his Men, and the Ship was under sail before he came back to shore. He had with him his Gun and a Knife, with a small Horn of Powder, and a few Shot; which being spent, he contrived a way by notching his Knife, to saw the Barrel of his Gun into small Pieces, wherewith he made Harpoons, Lances, Hooks and a long Knife; heating the pieces first in the fire, which he struck with his Gun-flint, and a piece of the Barrel of his Gun, which he had hardened; having learnt to do that among the English. The hot pieces of Iron he would hammer out and bend as he pleased with Stones, and saw them with his jagged Knife, or grind them to an edge by long labour, and harden them to a good temper as there was occasion.[21]

---

[21] A long descriptive essay, entitled "The Mosquito Indian and his Golden River; Being a Familiar Description of the Mosquito Kingdom in America," said to be written in 1699 by "M. W.," reposes in Churchill's *Collection of Voyages and Travels* (1732), Vol. VI. This unsympathetic account, viewing the Mosquito as barbarous and debauched, has little in common with Dampier and Defoe. Furthermore, it apparently was not in print before 1732, as it does not appear in the Churchills' first col-

Here are numerous suggestions for Robinson Crusoe. And they are followed by still more: how savages hollow out logs for rough canoes with sharp instruments and fire, how Will supplied himself with fish and the flesh of goats by home-made tools, how he had a little hut a half-mile from the sea, lined with goatskins, how his bed was a barbecue of sticks also covered with goatskins, and how he wore only a goat-skin when found.

Will, it seems, saw the rescuing ship the day before it anchored, his sharp eyes telling him that it was English. Then in accordance with the solemnity of the occasion he prepared a royal feast of welcome—excellent goat from his mountains and sweet cabbage from his trees. Says Dampier:

He came then to the Sea side to congratulate our safe Arrival. And when we landed, a Moskito Indian, named Robin, first leap'd ashore, and running to his Brother Moskito Man, threw himself flat on his face at his feet, who helping him up, and embracing him, fell flat with his face on the Ground at Robin's feet, and was by him taken up also. We stood with pleasure to behold the surprize, and tenderness, and solemnity of this interview, which was exceedingly affectionate on both sides; and when their Ceremonies of Civility were over, we also that stood gazing at them drew near, each of us embracing him we had found here . . . . He was named Will, as the other Robin. These were names given them by the English, for they had no Names among themselves; and they take it as a great favour to be named by any of us; and will complain for the want of it . . . . saying of themselves they are poor Men, and have no Name.

All who remember their Defoe see here accumulating

lection (1704) or anywhere else. There is the barest suggestion of the identification of Friday with Dampier's Mosquito Indian in Thomas Wright's *Life of Defoe* (1894, p. 231), and in a footnote in Paul Ver-beek's *William Dampier's Leben und Werke, Deutsche Geographische Blätter*, Vols. XXII–XXIII (1899–1900). The recent edition of Wright's *Life* also fails to follow up the clue.

suggestions for the desert-island episode in *Robinson Crusoe*. Set the extravagant ecstasies of Friday and his father beside the "exceedingly affectionate" demonstration of Robin and Will, and one knows for certain that the roving eye of Daniel Defoe paused here. Friday, one recalls, went back to England with Crusoe, leaving his father behind on the island. When he returned with Crusoe's shipload of tools and other supplies, it was one of Friday's great moments. Offshore it was he who first sighted human beings on the island. Writes Defoe:

> The fellow, it seems, had better eyes than I, and he points to the hill above my old house; and tho' we lay half a league off, he cries out, we see! we see! yes, we see much men there, and there, and there. I look'd, but I could see no body, no not with a perspective glass.

Then when they land, Friday is first ashore.

> I order'd no body to go on shore at first but my self, but there was no keeping Friday in the boat; for the affectionate creature had spy'd his father at a distance, a good way off of the Spaniards . . . . and if they had not let him go on shore, he would have jumped into the sea. He was no sooner on shore than he flew away to his father like an arrow out of a bow. It would have made any man have shed tears in spight of the firmest resolution, to have seen the first transports of this poor fellow's joy when he came to his father; how he embrac'd him, kiss'd him, strok'd his face, took him up in his arms, set him down upon a tree, and lay down by him; then stood and look'd at him . . . . then lay down upon the ground, and strok'd his legs . . . . and then got up again, and star'd at him.

This went on all the next day. The Spaniards, too, welcomed them lavishly, embracing Robinson Crusoe. "It would be endless," says Defoe, tasting Dampier's words, "to take notice of all the ceremonies and civilities."

Clearly here is an interesting parallel, as striking as that of Selkirk and Crusoe. Robin and Will, the Mosquito Indians in Dampier, have become Friday and his father in Defoe. The affectionate greeting has merely been enlarged upon by Defoe, and the effect of it upon hardened spectators emphasized, as in Dampier.

Friday has many of the general characteristics of the "Moskito Man," such as extraordinary eyesight, great valor, expertness with a rifle, and absolute fidelity to Englishmen. In fact, no other contemporary account of the Mosquito Indians is so detailed in these matters as Dampier's. Neither is there any so sympathetic. There Defoe learned that the Mosquitos were a small native Central American tribe inhabiting the eastern coast where Honduras and Nicaragua now come together, and that they had in common a hatred for the Spanish. They often sailed with Englishmen, especially the buccaneers, who naturally found use for them in their enterprises. They were such good hunters and fishermen that it was "very rare to find Privateers destitute of one or more of them." They were "tall, well-made, rawbon'd, lusty, strong, and nimble of Foot, long visaged, lank black Hair, look stern, hard favour'd, and of Copper-colour Complexion." They were extremely skilful in throwing a lance or harpoon and thwarting arrows shot at them. They had "extraordinary good Eyes, and discry a Sail at Sea farther, and see any Thing better than we." Among the privateers they learned to use firearms and proved "very good Marks-Men." They were "very bold in fight, and never seem to flinch or hang back; for they think that the White Men with whom they are know better than they do when it is best to fight, and let the advantage of their Party be never so great, they will never yield or give back any while any of their Party stand."[22]

Such is Dampier's glowing tribute. If we turn back again to *Robinson Crusoe*, we cannot but be struck with the char-

[22] *Dampier's Voyages*, I, 39–40.

acter of Friday. We have already seen that his eyesight was phenomenal. So also was his marksmanship. When savages appear off the island and Crusoe and Friday prepare to fight, Friday obeys to the letter Crusoe's orders, sends each bullet home, and declares, "Me die, when you bid die, master." He does die later, fighting bravely the savage enemies of his master, all as Dampier describes the valor and fidelity of Mosquitomen at such times:

> I order'd all my men to keep close, lest they should shoot any more arrows, and made all our guns ready; but being so near as to be within hearing, I made *Friday* go out upon the deck, and call out loud to them in his language to know what they meant, which accordingly he did . . . . but immediately *Friday* cry'd out they were going to shoot, and unhappily for him poor fellow; they let fly about 300 of their arrows, and, to my inexpressible grief kill'd poor *Friday*, no other man being in their sight. . . . . We buried him with all the decency and solemnity possible, by putting him into a coffin, and throwing him into the sea: and I caus'd 'em to fire eleven guns for him; and so ended the life of the most grateful, faithful, honest, and most affectionate servant that ever man had.[23]

So, along with Alexander Selkirk we must place Robin and Will, the Mosquito Indians, who served also as models for Defoe. Dampier, whom Defoe sought as friend and guide, brought them all together. Dampier rescued both Selkirk and Will, and Dampier's *New Voyage* made Will so famous a solitary that a later account of Selkirk significantly reminded its readers that Dampier's Mosquito Indian was marooned on the selfsame island, too. As Crusoe had his Selkirk, so Friday had his Will and Robin.

In the light of this knowledge of Dampier and Defoe, we can turn with renewed interest to an old subject: the origin of the name, Robinson Crusoe. Of little importance in itself, it has, nevertheless, drawn enough speculation and

---

[23] *Robinson Crusoe*, II, 189–93.

comment from time to time to show that readers of Defoe still enjoy puzzling over it. Some explanations already made are as follows:

1. A simple coinage based on the common English name "Robin," variant for "Robert."

2. "Cruso," an English family name. A Timothy Cruso was a school-fellow of Defoe and later became a prominent dissenting minister.

3. "Kreutznaer," the German name from which Defoe himself declares "Crusoe" was derived by corruption. This is phonetically akin to the German *kreuzen*, to cross, to clash, to cruise, and *das Kreuz*, a cross. An English Cruso family wrote *"sub cruce"* for its motto. Also, a German imitation of *Robinson Crusoe* in 1722 called its hero "Bernhard Creutz."

4. "Robert" Knox, the name of the famous castaway who lived nineteen years on the island of Ceylon, and whose adventures (*An Historical Relation of Ceylon*, 1681) bore some resemblance to those of Robinson Crusoe.

5. The name, "Robinson Crusoe," seen on a tombstone thirty-five years before by Defoe as he escaped from some skirmish in the battle of Sedgemoor.

There may be some others. If, however, we discard them all temporarily and begin afresh with what Defoe himself tells us and what we know was in his mind at the time of composition, we arrive at something different. It may be just another item to add to the list above, but it at least has the virtue of being arrived at through the natural association of fresh ideas.

"Robinson" clearly comes from the familiar "Robin"; for Crusoe taught his famous parrot to call him nothing but "Robin Crusoe." Thus when he fell into sleep of exhaustion after the almost disastrous exploration of the coast of his island in his canoe, he was awakened by Poll, who kept repeating, "Robin, Robin, Robin Crusoe, Poor Robin Crusoe."

Now Robin was not only a common English name, but in the well-known passage just cited from Dampier appeared appropriately associated with the life of a marooned man. Here Robin, the rescuing Mosquito, was second in importance only to his marooned friend Will. The whole atmosphere of buccaneers at Juan Fernandez was the most suitable imaginable, as we shall see. But what is more, if we recall the last sentence of the passage in Dampier, we perceive that, while all this was being stamped upon the tenacious mind of Defoe, it was attended by Dampier's remark that the names Will and Robin were given the Indians at their request by the English. "They take it as a great favour to be named by any of us." Here was certainly a strong suggestion for naming a person Robin(son).

As for the name, "Crusoe," the way is not so clear; and what I have to offer is brought forth as reasonable speculation. We should always remember that Defoe's head was full of travelers' accounts, tales of buccaneers like Dampier, and narratives of Jesuit missionaries when he wrote these strange adventures. His next novel, *Captain Singleton*, was to have a pirate for its hero; and other accounts of pirates were soon to come from his pen. The bold sea-adventurer Raleigh was his lifelong hero. Anyone who cruised against the Spanish, particularly if he had plans of establishing an English colony, pleased him mightily. And there is, I think, a connection between this business of cruising and the name "Crusoe."

"Kreutznaer," the origin according to Defoe, we have seen has been connected with *kreuzen* and *Kreuzer*, the underlying idea being that of the Latin *crux*. Now *das Kreuzer* means, as well, a cruiser, a privateer. An older form and spelling, I am told, might easily have been "Kreutzenaere," which is close indeed to Defoe's "Kreutznaer." It would be like Defoe to change it in just a letter or two. If he knew the first meaning (cross), in all probability he would know the second (cruise). And he would know that *Kreuzer* meant a cruiser or privateer. The thing passes beyond the realm of mere probability when we learn from etymological dictionaries that the word came into the German, French, and English languages from the Dutch in the seventeenth century. The only mention of *kreuzen*, and the second meaning of *Kreuzer*, in Friedrich Kluge's *Etymologisches Wörterbuch* (ed. 1921) are in this nautical sense and are thus explained. This can mean but one thing. Through the Dutch classic of buccaneering (Exquemelin's *De Americaensche Zee Rovers* [Amsterdam, 1678], translated into English in 1684–85), the sea rovers of the Spanish Main contributed this word (and incidentally also the word, "buccaneer") to at least four European languages. With the knowledge of buccaneers came the language of buccaneering and the English language acquired "buccaneer" and "cruiser." The established English idiom in Defoe's day had become, as we know, "cruising," as in "cruising against the Spaniard," or *A Cruising Voyage Round the World*, title of Woodes Rogers' narrative. Thus the fictitious name "Kreutznaer" and the idea of buccaneering would be mutually suggestive, and it becomes reasonable to attach some significance to the phonetic similarity between "cruise" and "Crusoe." This Indian, Robin, was cruising against the Spaniard with England's greatest buccaneer when he rescued his friend Will. In Dampier we have Robin, cruising, and a famous solitary; in Defoe, Robinson Crusoe.

Permit us to carry nautical genealogy one step farther. It has been shown that in naming Friday Defoe followed a common practice of mariners who named newly discovered places. St. Matthias Island was named thus by Dampier, who found it on St. Matthias' Day.[24]

Our association of Alexander Selkirk with Dampier's

---

[24] For the naming of Friday, see Secord, *op. cit.*, p. 57.

Mosquito Indian has one other implication worth recording. William Dampier is inextricably caught in the affairs
and accounts of Selkirk. Few scholars care to exclude Selkirk from his rightful place as prototype of Crusoe and perhaps as the germ of the whole desert-isle tale. It should be
noted again in passing that Dampier was the most famous
person with the expedition that rescued Selkirk and came
back with his story. Not only is this to be seen in the
account by Woodes Rogers, but in the separate accounts of
Selkirk. *Providence Displayed,* a twelve-page pamphlet
which appeared contemporaneously, was an account fabricated from Rogers' *Cruising Voyage* but advertised as, "Written by his own Hand." In this, Dampier's name appears
three times: (1) because he recommended Selkirk to Captain
Rogers, (2) because he sowed "good turneps" on Juan Fernandez formerly, and (3) because he had rescued the famous
Mosquito Indian also.[25]

To say, therefore, that Defoe took the various accounts of
Selkirk as the basis upon which to build the character of
Robinson Crusoe is to bring him into the very presence of
Dampier and Will, the Mosquito Indian. It is, furthermore,
very striking to re-read, apart from the account of Selkirk
but still only as a tale of a marooned man, Dampier's account
of the Mosquito Indian.

The details of Dampier's story we have seen include the
following: Will, the Mosquito Indian, was in the woods
hunting goats at the time his captain took away his men.
Left alone, he made his living by means of a gun, a knife, a
small horn of powder, and a few shot. Having spent his
shot, he notched his knife to saw the barrel of his gun into
small pieces. With these he made other small instruments
for procuring food. He killed and ate seal, fish, and goats.
He ate seal at first, but afterwards killed them only to make

[25] *Harleian Miscellany* (ed. 1810), V, 430–32.

thongs of the skins. He made a hut and lined it with goat skins. His couch was of sticks two feet from the ground in barbecue fashion and spread with goat skins. And he wore skins when he was found. He ate also cabbage and herbs. Dampier, furthermore, comments on the agricultural possibilities of the island. Its valleys were well suited for excellent pasturage and for growing corn, wheat, peas, yams, and potatoes.

These facts fit into the life of Crusoe as easily as do the experiences of Selkirk, who was provided with a sea chest, bedding, a firelock, one pound of gunpowder, a large quantity of bullets, a flint and steel, a few pounds of tobacco, a hatchet, a knife, a Bible and other books of devotion and navigation, mathematical instruments, and provisions for two meals. He ate turtles, goats, sea-lions; and he dressed in goat skins. He domesticated cats and goats and built a hut and a bower. He observed regular devotions and suffered at first from Melancholy.[26]

Defoe unquestionably was influenced by both Selkirk and Dampier's Mosquito Indian.

"ROBINSON CRUSOE," PART II

The *Farther Adventures of Robinson Crusoe,* we should remember, carries Crusoe back to his island, where he establishes an orderly living community, an island-commonwealth. Then he sails for Brazil to send back stores before departing for the Cape of Good Hope and the East Indies. Stopping at Madagascar, he witnesses dreadful slaughter of the natives by the ship's crew. He differs sharply with his nephew, the captain, over the affair and makes himself so disagreeable that he is marooned somewhere in the road to Bengal, the ship having coasted in the meanwhile along the Arabian shore and the Gulf of Persia. From Bengal he goes on a trading voyage to Achin on the island of Sumatra and

[26] Steele's account in the *Englishman,* No. 26.

to Siam with an English merchant. Returning to Bengal, he makes a second voyage, this time to the Spice Islands. A third trading voyage takes him in his own ship through the Straits of Malacca to China. He is forced ashore at Cambodia and is frightened by being taken for a pirate. Ashore again south of the Bay of Tonquin, he is attacked by natives. Next he stretches over to the Philippines and up to Formosa and finally to China at a point farther north than European ships go. Disposing of his ship, he returns to England across China, Tartary, and Muscovy, with a caravan to Archangel. Trading up to the last, he sails down the Baltic to Hamburg and The Hague and comes home rich, a circumnavigator at seventy-two, ready to retire, having been away on this voyage ten years and nine months.

I have given generous detail from this second part of *Robinson Crusoe* because it is the less-known part of the story and because it furnishes the clearest example of borrowing from Dampier. Until Crusoe starts home overland, the events take place in regions where Dampier spent many years and which he describes with great detail. Defoe bases the entire history of his hero in the East Indies upon Dampier's accounts.

Let us start at Bengal. Crusoe is abandoned by his nephew and his ruffian crew here. Dampier, long watchful for opportunity to escape from an uncongenial ship, is allowed to go ashore at the Nicobar Islands in the Bay of Bengal. Crusoe had so harangued the ship's crew because of cruelty to Madagascar natives that they would not sail with him. Dampier was glad to get away from the remnants of a buccaneering expedition. Crusoe, it should be noted, accepts the situation cheerfully enough and like Dampier expects to make the best of things and so get home in English ships from Achin. They both contemplate the possibility of returning home by way of Persia, the caravan routes to Aleppo and Scanderoon, but both decide otherwise.

Crusoe next undertakes eight years of trading out and back from Bengal: to Achin, Siam, and Surkan; to Borneo, the Spice Islands, and Manila; and finally to Tonquin and China. Dampier, using Achin (Sumatra) as his base, trades for three years to various places, notably Tonquin, which he describes fully in his second volume. His route from Achin to Tonquin Crusoe follows closely, touching the same spots. Where Dampier says pirates lurk, Crusoe is taken for a pirate. Where Dampier finds the natives treacherous (a notable thing in his pages) and likely to seize shipwrecked sailors as lawful slaves, Crusoe finds the same thing. Crusoe's phrases even betray the page of Dampier. "We coasted northeast to the point of land which opens the great bay of Tonquin," says Crusoe. In Dampier we find, "We coasted along to the eastward . . . . to the Point of Land that bounds the S.W. part of the Bay of Tonquin." Where the hostile natives threaten, Crusoe remarks, "If they had found us there [they would have] carried us away for slaves to their king, or whatever they call him." In Dampier's explanation of this custom, seamen who escape shipwreck "become Slaves to the King."[27]

Crusoe's uneasiness from learning that his ship had been purchased from renegade pirates apparently springs from the anecdote of Captain Johnson in Dampier, in which the owner and captain of a ship are killed by Malayans and the crew wonder what to do with a ship not their own.[28]

To close this part of the comparison, we might note that both Dampier and Crusoe express here their uncontrolled desires to wander in order to see the world. Also, Defoe makes an indirect reference to Dampier's journals and his detailed method of writing. Dampier closes his first volume by deliberately leaving out descriptions of his trading voy-

[27] *Robinson Crusoe*, II, 245, 246; *Dampier's Voyages*, I, 561, 562.
[28] Secord, *op. cit.*, pp. 51–52; *Dampier's Voyages*, II, 40–47.

ages. Having carried his reader to Sumatra on his way around the world he will not take him back upon his course, but all such descriptions and observations "I shall refer to another place, where I may give a particular Relation of them. In short, it may suffice, that I set out to *Tonqueen* with Captain Welden about *July* 1688, and returned to *Achin* in the *April* following."[29] It is only in his next book that he gives details. Crusoe, having found a companion in Bengal, plans a short trading voyage. "There are so many travellers who have described the places upon this proposed voyage," he declares, that he will not attempt it.

Those things I leave to others, and refer the reader to those journals and travels of Englishmen, of which many I find are published, and more promised every day. 'T is enough to me to tell you that I made this voyage to Acheen, in the island of Sumatra [one of Dampier's notable adventures], and from thence to Siam . . . . a great voyage . . . . eight months out . . . . and returned to Bengal.[30]

Whereas single details here and there might point suggestively, though not conclusively, to similar details in Dampier, a chain of events involving similarity in fact, in sequence, in language, and incidental comment like Crusoe's adventures between Bengal and China is unmistakable evidence that Defoe used Dampier freely. It gives some weight of credence to a hundred other details. For example, authority for all of Defoe's meteorological observations in *Robinson Crusoe* in seas known to the great buccaneer can be found in the pages of Dampier. Like most great geniuses, Defoe creates by appropriating what he needs wherever he finds it and then he vitalizes it in its new situation. To this creative process William Dampier's *Voyages* were a principal contribution.

[29] *Dampier's Voyages*, I, 489.

[30] *Robinson Crusoe* (Oxford ed., 1840), II, 227–28.

VI

PIRATES

When I wrote these things down, I did not foresee that the
writings of our own stories would be so much the fashion in
England, or so agreeable to others to read, as I find custom, and
the humour of the times has caused it to be.

—COLONEL JACQUE

THE KING OF PIRATES

ROBINSON CRUSOE was a good man. His greatest sin was
filial disobedience. Following the course of Defoe's
narratives, we now notice a series having to do with persons
lower in the social scale. "With few exceptions, the men of
whom he wrote were, like Moll Flanders and Roxana, people
more or less outside the pale of respectable society. Thieves,
pirates, adventurers, charlatans, these were the men whose
lives he places before us."[1] That he had a keen interest in
pirates and buccaneers is only too obvious. He not only pored
over his copies of Esquemeling, Wafer, and Dampier but
he wrote pamphlets on Captain Avery and Captain Gow,
famous contemporary pirates. He mentions Captain Kidd
in *Robinson Crusoe*. Being close to King William, he probably knew of Dampier's advices regarding the Madagascar
outlaws. The nautical parts of his narratives bristle with
them. He may even have had a hand in composing *A General History of the Most Notorious Pyrates* (1724).

[1] George Aitken in "General Introduction" to his edition of *Robinson Crusoe*, I, xlii.

93

The fifty years preceding the publication of *Robinson Crusoe* was a time of great activity among thoroughly piratical adventurers as well as among the more protected buccaneers, the favored sons of piracy. Defoe's interest in these adventurers was lifelong.[2] Either because of the success of *Robinson Crusoe* or because of some stir created by actual pirates at the time,[3] Defoe turned his pen in late 1719 and 1720 to the business of recording fact and fiction about them. His next long narrative had for its hero not only a wandering sailor but a confessed pirate. This was *Captain Singleton* (1720). Just before he published this tale, however, he wrote *The King of Pirates*, a pamphlet on the famous Captain Avery, purporting to give the only true relation of him. Defoe's interest in Avery was also one of long standing.[4]

This pamphlet not only preceded *Captain Singleton* by a few months, but it was one of the sources of the longer narrative.[5] To phrase it differently, Defoe reworked the life of Avery when he came to write *Singleton*. This is of double

[2] Three years before his death he put forth a project for stamping out the pirates of the Mediterranean (*Plan of the English Commerce* [1728], pp. 321–23).

[3] Such as Anne Bonny and Mary Read, famous women pirates, and Captain Rackam, who were convicted of piracy in 1720 (Gosse, *The Pirate's Who's Who*, pp. 57, 256). Capt. Woodes Rogers came to public notice again when he went out in 1718 to be governor of the Bahamas and to stamp out piracy.

[4] In his *True Account of . . . . the South-Sea Trade* (1711), he argues that one of the advantages of a South Sea company would be the trade with the Madagascar pirates (p. 21). He then subjoins an account of these pirates made in 1703 by five "captains" apprehended but pardoned. According to this, Avery had 700 of his own men. All told, there were 1,500 men with 5,000 pounds a man, each willing to give a quarter of it for a general pardon: "Six millions sterling to the Government" (pp. 21–23).

[5] Secord, *Narrative Method of Defoe*, pp. 115–16, 140–45, 160–61.

significance to us because it is clear that Defoe depended on Dampier for material in both tales.

Pirate John Avery flourished in 1695 and became famous in legend for taking a ship belonging to the Great Mogul having on board it the Great Mogul's granddaughter (or daughter), and also for establishing a kingdom of pirates on the Island of Madagascar. Little is actually known about this romantic figure, so that any lengthy account of him is of necessity a mixture of much fiction with little fact. Professor J. K. Laughton in the *Dictionary of National Biography* provides a short sketch only. According to this, he was a West Indian pirate who furnished himself there with a ship, who cruised in the Red Sea and took the Great Mogul's ship, who returned to the West Indies, dispersed his crew, and disappeared. Large rewards offered failed to produce him. There is no mention of Madagascar.

Now the great legendary exploits of Avery were: capturing the fabulous wealth of the Mogul's ship, ravishing the beautiful Oriental princess and her female retinue, and creating the glorious pirate kingdom at Madagascar. This legend may be read in the following places:

1. An octavo pamphlet of sixteen pages entitled, *The Life and Adventures of Captain John Avery, the Famous English Pirate (rais'd from a Cabbin-Boy, to a King) now in Possession of Madagascar . . . .* , and claimed to be the true deliverances of a Dutch merchant, Adrian Van Broeck, who was captured by Avery, but who escaped. It bears no date, but is thought to belong to the year 1709.[6]

2. An octavo pamphlet attributed to Defoe, entitled, *The King of Pirates: being an account of the Famous Enterprizes of Captain Avery, The Mock King of Madagascar with His Rambles and Piracies; where in all the Sham Accounts for-*

_____

[6] The Yale copy is so considered. See also the *Dictionary of National Biography* and the British Museum catalogue.

merly publish'd of him, are deleted. In Two Letters from himself: one during his Stay at Madagascar and one since his Escape from thence. London . . . . 1720.

Mr. George Aitken declares that it was first published on December 10, 1719, between the appearance of the first and second parts of *Robinson Crusoe*, but carried the date 1720 on the title-page.[7] It was first included in an edition of Defoe's works by Mr. Aitken.[8] This account is divided into two parts, one letter from Madagascar and one from Constantinople.

3. An account of twenty pages, placed prominently at the very beginning of Captain Charles Johnson's *A General History of the . . . . Most Notorious Pyrates*, third edition, 1725. This is a confused account, introducing the Bristol privateers and Captain Woodes Rogers, who flourished in 1708–1711.

All three of these insist, in the journalistic argot of the time, that they are giving the true account and not following the wild romantic tales of Avery previously told. Defoe's pamphlet is branded by the *Dictionary of National Biography*, along with the pamphlet of 1709, as "fiction, with scarcely a substratum of fact." In it, Defoe makes a number of references to the extravagances of the 1709 account and himself declares Avery never to have ravished or even married decorously the Mogul's granddaughter. He let her go with the loss only of her wealth. He further declares that Avery's gang on Madagascar was much smaller than reported and that Avery himself had already left it.

There is no question that it is mostly fiction. The interesting things to observe here, as always in Defoe, are the particulars that Defoe added and where he got them. It is

---

[7] Aitken's edition of Defoe, *Robinson Crusoe* (1895), XVII, ix–x.

[8] Professor Trent includes it in his bibliography of Defoe, *Cambridge History of English Literature*, IX, 477.

among these additional details, found in none of the other accounts, that material appears that could have come only from Dampier. The pamphlet has already been said to be founded on Dampier.[9]

The first letter opens with an attack by Avery on "a most ridiculous book entitled, 'My Life and Adventures'." Like Dampier he was a wanderer with an early lust for the sea. He was, he writes, "bred to the sea from a youth," being somewhat envious of the buccaneers.

I had been some years in the Bay of Campeachy, and though with patience I endured the fatigue of that laborious life, yet it was as visible to others as to myself that I was not formed by nature for a logwood-cutter any more than I was for a foremastman . . . .

He aimed at being master of a good ship.

It was many years after this before I could bring my purposes to pass; and I served first in some of the adventures of Captain Sharp, Captain Hawkins, and others in their bold adventures in the South Seas, where I got a very good booty; was at the taking of Puna, where we were obliged to leave infinite wealth behind us . . . . was among that party who fought their way, sword in hand, through all the detachments of the Spaniards, in the journey overland, across the isthmus of Darien to the North Seas; and when other of our men got away, some one way, some another, I with twelve more of our men, by help of a periagua, got into the Bay of Campeachy, where we fell very honestly to cutting of logwood, not for want, but to employ ourselves till we could make off.[10]

Here is a mixture of material from Esquemeling and Dampier, with unquestionably more from Dampier. The story of the adventures of the bold buccaneers across the Isthmus of Darien with Sawkins and Sharp is told by both;

[9] Sir Albert Gray, "Introduction" to Dampier's *New Voyage Round the World* (1927), p. xiii; Secord, *op. cit.*, p. 141.

[10] *Captain Singleton* (ed. Aitken), XVI, 8–9.

but Dampier is the only possible source of information regarding the life of logwood-cutters themselves.

When Dampier returned from the South Sea across the Isthmus of Darien he and his companions joined with a large group of privateers but later went off in a vessel of their own to cruise along the shore and among the islands. They planned to attack a Spanish town at one time in canoes and "periagoes."

As I have already remarked, Esquemeling, though he often mentions Campeachy, deals very little with the logwood trade. But Dampier worked for three years with the logwood-cutters, although not by choice. From his account it is clear that he endured the life merely in order to see the world. It is he who tells us that the labor was hard, the climate very inclement, the returns but little. Also, as planter in Jamaica, Dampier was "clearly out of [his] Element," and so returned to the sea. Accordingly, it is to Dampier that we must turn for the suggestion of the following phrases, already quoted: "though with patience I endured the fatigue of that laborious life." "I was not formed by nature for a logwood-cutter." "It was many years after this before I could bring any of my purposes to pass." "We [thirteen men] fell very honestly to cutting logwood."

The mention of the taking of Puná is another possible detail from Dampier. Puná was a small Indian town belonging to the Spaniards on the island of Puná lying at the mouth of the Guayaquil River, for a century prey to English rovers. Here all ships bound into the river of Guayaquil anchor, says Dampier, and must wait for a pilot, the entrance being very dangerous for strangers. Once again, Dampier seems to be Defoe's source. Ringrose, who sailed with the buccaneers along this coast, and whose journal is printed as Part IV of the *Buccaneers of America*, makes no mention of Puná at all. Coxon, Sharp, and Sawkins were aiming for Arica, farther north. Dampier, on the other hand, being there again a few years later, describes the island and the town fully. His party takes the town. Whereas they fail to take Guayaquil, they capture 1,000 negroes on three barks, a great prize according to Dampier. "There was never greater opportunity put into the Hands of Men to enrich themselves than we had, to have gone with these Negroes, and settled ourselves at Santa Maria . . . . and employed them in getting Gold out of the Mines there." However, all but a few were turned ashore and left behind. This was a serious loss to Dampier, and he half apologizes by writing, "But these may seem to the Reader but Golden Dreams."[11]

Dampier was twice again at Puná, once in the "Saint George" in 1704 and once in 1709 when he attended another by no means completely successful attempt upon Guayaquil, this time under Woodes Rogers of the Bristol privateers.

Another account of Puná available to Defoe was in Funnell's *Voyage Round the World*. This story of Dampier's expedition in the "Saint George" boasted more particular descriptions of the coasts of Peru and Chile than had ever before been made public, yet the passage on Puná is brief and contains no mention of plunder.[12] Woodes Rogers displays Puná and Guayaquil on the title-page of his *Cruising Voyage*, and much was made in England of the ransom paid (in part) to him here. It is in Dampier, however, that Defoe read about a golden dream of wealth like Avery's that had to be left behind.

When Captain Avery arrives at Madagascar with his men,

[11] *Dampier's Voyages*, I, 172–81, *passim*. Admiral Benbow's men some years later proved Dampier's plan to be a good one. At Santa de Cana near Santa Maria, they took the town evacuated by the Spaniards and put seventy negroes to work for twenty-one days in the gold mines and got eighty pounds weight of gold dust from it (Defoe, *True Account of . . . . the South-Sea Trade*, pp. 16–17).

[12] Funnell, *A Voyage Round the World. Containing an Account of Captain Dampier's Expedition into the South-seas in the Ship St. George* (1707), Preface, pp. [3]–[4]; also pp. 54–55, 171–7[3].

they do "not care to make the south part of the island [their] retreat." Accordingly they coast north but run into a tornado and are forced ashore under a great headland (near 14 degrees north latitude). Their sloop comes to anchor but their ship is lost. Because of this, they build huts ashore and dwell there eight months. This is an episode that owes something to Dampier, and that Defoe reworks with greater elaboration in *Captain Singleton*.

Other details in the *King of Pirates* that Dampier's *Voyages* may easily have suggested are: the plundering "of some towns on the shore near Guayaquil"; the killing and salting of beef in Cuba; the loading of fish and hogs at the Bay of All Saints; the whole business of sending Avery into the South Seas and especially to Juan Fernandez; and Avery's route to Constantinople.

"CAPTAIN SINGLETON"

The Life, Adventures, and Pyracies of the Famous Captain Singleton was Defoe's second long story of adventure. It appeared, hastily composed and lacking a preface, in the busy year 1720, during which, besides other activities, Defoe wrote five volumes.

Apparently the vein struck by *Robinson Crusoe* a little less than a year before warranted further working. This time the wandering adventurer is thoroughly bad until the very end—a buccaneer and pirate. Stolen as an infant and sold to gypsies, he is corrupted at an early age. At twelve he makes a voyage to Newfoundland. Returning, he is captured by a Turkish rover, then by the Portuguese. Carried to Lisbon, he becomes cabin-boy in a Portuguese vessel bound for the East Indies. His shipmates complete his schooling in the profligate life of the sea. Returning from this voyage, the vessel is driven back from the Cape of Good Hope and puts in at the island of Madagascar. Here Singleton is one of twenty-seven men set ashore as a result of mutiny. Like

Crusoe, this group eventually get off in a boat of their own making. Going over to the mainland of Africa, they disembark and make a remarkable tour across the heart of the continent. From the West African coast, Singleton returns to England to spend his fortune.

Having done this, he goes to sea again and joins a desperate crew as lieutenant and engages in a series of piratical escapades begun with a vessel seized from its owners by the crew. He cruises in the West Indies, along the coast of South America, off the Arabian shores, in the East Indies, the Spice Islands, the Philippines, and Formosa. Having risen to the command of a thirty-eight-gun frigate loaded with stolen wealth, he returns to England by way of Persia and Venice, disguised as an Armenian merchant, having ended his seafaring with an added flourish of exploring the then unknown southern coast of Australia. Repenting his evil days, he marries the sister of his Quaker companion and lives virtuously thereafter.

There are thus two parts to the narrative. And it is the first principally that has attracted the attention of scholars and geographers — Singleton's adventures in the heart of Africa, a continent as dark geographically then as it has been thought to be spiritually. Defoe has received unanimous praise for making these experiences vivid and accurate. He has even been credited with a kind of sixth sense for African geography, particularly in the location of lakes and the courses of rivers. "The two matters of greatest interest in the book," says Mr. George Aitken in the introduction to his edition of *Captain Singleton*, are "the journey across Africa and the character of Quaker William." Recent scholarship, however, once again shows Defoe to be after all a perfectly reasonable, though skilful, user of accessible materials: maps and travel books.[13]

[13] Secord's *Narrative Method of Defoe*, pp. 127–39, should be read in this connection also.

Our pursuit of Dampier finds us more interested in the second part of Singleton's story than the first. Dampier had nothing to do with Madagascar or the interior of Africa, but he was very familiar with the regions in which Singleton did most of his buccaneering. And the expectancy with which one turns from an examination of *Robinson Crusoe* to this story of a pirate-hero is well rewarded. Defoe leaned more heavily on Dampier here than in his more famous tale.

It is obvious, as the commentators prove, that books of travel and the gossip of Defoe's seafaring friends are the sources of *Captain Singleton*.

Three streams of influence contributed to Defoe's story: (1) the general literature of travel, (2) the more or less authentic narratives of privateers, buccaneers, and pirates of the half-century preceding 1720, and (3) the reports of the half-mythical pirate, Captain John Avery. More specifically, Defoe made use of four writers of travel and foreign adventure, namely, J. Albert de Mandelslo ("Voyages and Travels," a part of Olearius' *Voyages and Travels of the Ambassadors*, 1662), Robert Knox (*An Historical Relation of Ceylon*, 1681), Dampier (*Voyages*, 1697–1709), and Maximilien Misson (*The Voyage of François Leguat*, 1707, itself a compilation from previous works).

Already aware of Defoe's practices, we may assume a skilful weaving together of strands from these four authors and turn to a particular examination of the part played by William Dampier. Immediately certain details of Singleton's early life sound familiar. Singleton's first voyage, at the age of twelve after a few years in various parish schools, was to Newfoundland with "a master of a ship, who took a fancy" to him and had employed him in building the ship at "Bussleton."

Dampier, upon the death of his parents, was removed from a "Latin school to learn Writing and Arithmetick" and was soon after placed with "a Master of a Ship at Weymouth." With this shipmaster Dampier made his first voyage of any length, to Newfoundland. He was then eighteen. It was a chilly voyage and made him decide to go on his next voyage toward the south—to Java, in fact.

Singleton's next voyage, after some preliminary adventure with Algerine rovers, was to Goa on the Malay Peninsula in a Portuguese ship from Lisbon. He was too young to keep a journal, he reminds the reader, but recalls with some vividness the insolence, cruelty, perfidy, and debauchery of the Portuguese at Goa. They were "a nation the most perfidious and the most debauched, the most insolent and cruel, of any that pretend to call themselves Christians, in the world." He lays much of the responsibility for his own education in wickedness upon his idle months among them at Goa. "Abominable lewdness," "cowardice," "barbarous and tyrannical" are words attached to their conduct in a description immediately following.

Dampier, too, is particularly severe in describing the Portuguese at Goa. It was the only East Indian place left in the hands of the Portuguese, he writes, "than whom there are not a more despicable People now in all the Eastern Nations." They were "the first Discoverers by Sea of the East Indies and had thereby the Advantage of Trade" but "presuming on the Strength of their Forts . . . . they fell into all Manner of Looseness and Debauchery; the usual Concomitant of Wealth, and as commonly the Fore-runner of Ruin. The Portuguese, at this Place [Malacca], by Report, made use of the Native Women at their Pleasure, whether Virgins or married Women . . . . and it is probable, they as little restrained their Lust in other Places."

Furthermore, Singleton, because he "understood some Latin," picked up enough of the Portuguese language to make use of the captain's "charts and books" and began "to get a little superficial knowledge of navigation." So also with Dampier. "In this Voyage," he writes, "I gained more

Experience in Navigation, but kept no Journal." He had learned enough at Latin school to be able to carry on a conversation in Latin.

It may not be without point to notice here that on the same page where he speaks of these early voyages Dampier describes taking precautions in shipping as a seaman to Jamaica that he would not "be trepann'd and sold as a Servant" after his arrival. The boy Singleton finds that his captain considers him his slave.

One more parallel might be noticed. Singleton sails both times to the Cape of Good Hope and the East Indies by Dampier's route: first to the coast of Brazil, then across to Africa. In fact, Defoe's heroes who travel in these regions always do this. It is rendered more significant in the case of Singleton by a remark added to explain the route: "not that it is in the course of sailing the way thither."

Thus at the very outset of the narrative, Defoe keeps close to Dampier in a good many major and minor details. Because of obvious dependence on Dampier in parts that follow, it is quite clear that he is consciously doing so.[14]

---

[14] The reader should consult the first few pages of *Captain Singleton*, and *Dampier's Voyages*, II, 84–85, 108, 109. Dampier not only chose a more westerly route south than was common, but he discussed in at least two places the calms and troublesome land winds to be avoided off the African coast (coming north as well) by crossing the equator in mid-Atlantic or even near the South American shore (*New Voyage Round the World*, chap. xx, and the "Discourse of Winds"). The longer way round is sometimes the shorter, he told those who would be enlightened on the point. As a result it became the English route south. Dampier's international reputation in the eighteenth century contributed to common knowledge what had been the annoying experience of separate individuals before his time. A century later when the French naturalist Peron, who had been sent by his government to explore southern lands, read his paper before the Imperial Institute (June 9, 1806), he complained of a stubborn captain who lost time for him by hugging the coast of Africa, whereas good mariners since the time of the precise and dependable Dampier had known that the best time to the Cape of Good Hope could be made the long way

THE MADAGASCAR EPISODE

The next escapade takes place on the island of Madagascar. The general knowledge of this region Defoe got from de Mandelslo and Misson. Some details, however, seem to be fitted in from Dampier. There is a seven months' cruise of the party in open canoes up the west coast of the island and around the northern end to the east coast. This journey was dangerous and fatiguing and bears many marks of similarity to a very vivid part of Dampier's first narrative: his trip in an open boat from one of the Nicobar Islands to Achin.

Singleton's coasting trip around Madagascar included the following events. Lacking tools and nails to make a larger vessel, the abandoned party make three very good "periaguas" or canoes. (The use of the word *periagua* by both Dampier and Defoe has already been commented upon.) Two of these are fitted up with masts and sails. They proceed north and meet and barter with friendly natives who have small canoes with mats for sails. At Point Desperation they encounter gales, "violent rains, with thunder and lightning, most unusually terrible to us." They turn their "frigates" toward the shore, therefore, "being exceeding wet, and fatigued with the heat, the thunder, lightning and rain." Here they build four huts and live four months, after which they put out again. Singleton, it may be noted, liked the country and would have been content to stay. Their canoes proving poor sailers, they give up attempts to cross against the wind to the African main, and put about again for the shore. They could sail only with the wind, or monsoon, which blows six months from the southeast and six months from the northwest. For two days they are without water and provisions. It is "a terrible adventure." Again they pitch

down. Dampier was his accepted authority. (Peron, "Voyage for the Discovery of Southern Lands," in Pinkerton, *A General Collection of Voyages and Travels*, XI, 751–52).

camp and find friendly natives who assist them in building huts under the direction of "one of their captains or kings."

Dampier's canoe trip was of the same general kind and proceeded from a similar circumstance. Disagreeing with Captain Read and desiring to be set ashore, he is placed on one of the Nicobar Islands with four Malays and a Portuguese, a party large enough to defend itself, as was true of Singleton's. Dampier plans to coast to the south end of Nicobar Island in a canoe purchased for an axe, and there wait for the monsoon to carry him over to Sumatra. The Malays make a mast for the canoe and rig thereon a sail of mats. He calls it "our new Frigot." The natives he finds friendly unless mistreated. Indeed, he devotes two pages to a disquisition on what he feels to be the myth of cannibalism. He even plans to stay and develop a trade in ambergris. At Sumatra, "one of the Oramkai's or Noblemen . . . . came in the Night to see" them. They are brought food and are provided with a hut, "a large House." On the way over from Nicobar, with the western monsoon, the party suffers scorching heat at first, then bad gales, thunder, lightning, and cold rain. It is "the most doleful Night" that Dampier ever experienced.

The circumstance of being set ashore, furthermore, is the same in general in both accounts. It was a common enough thing among the buccaneers to abandon men thus, and some even preferred to be left rather than to go on with a riotous crew. Such were Alexander Selkirk and Dampier. Both Singleton and Dampier wished to leave their captains. Both were joined by others from the ship a bit later. Dampier and one of Singleton's men both managed to carry from the ship a pocket compass.

Thus the Madagascar episode also points to the use of Dampier.[15]

[15] *Captain Singleton* (Oxford ed., 1840), pp. 42, 46, 47; *Dampier's Voyages*, I, 468–84.

CRUISING IN THE EAST INDIES

In the second part of *Captain Singleton*, says a recent writer, Defoe uses no more descriptive, geographical, or ethnographical elements than he had already used in *Robinson Crusoe*.[16] This is probably true. But it is in the second volume of *Robinson Crusoe* that Defoe most clearly depends on Dampier. Similarly, in *Captain Singleton* the second part borrows routes and fills in details freely from the same source.

When Singleton reaches the region of the Spice Islands, the Philippines, and Formosa, he is in water described with such care by the great English buccaneer that men of Defoe's time got much of their knowledge of the adjacent countries and peoples from him.[17] Many other accounts existed, but Dampier's was the most popular and, with regard to the Philippines, the most detailed. The matter that Defoe uses from Dampier, moreover, is not to be found in any of the other narratives. Not only the facts upon which Defoe fabricated the adventures of Singleton but also certainly some of the adventures come from Dampier.

For example, in sailing the waters of the Spice Islands and the Philippines both men encounter dreadful storms. In Dampier it is one of his worst, and provides a vivid description of the Corpus Sanct or St. Elmo's fire. It is one of those descriptions that fired the mind of Coleridge and supplied an image for the *Ancient Mariner*.[18] Defoe could not have missed it, not only having read the account but having also a keen eye for the unusual and exciting. So into Singleton's narrative at this point he brings a bad storm.

---

[16] Dottin, *De Foe et ses romans* (1924), III, 633.

[17] E. Heawood, *A History of Geographical Discovery in the Seventeenth and Eighteenth Centuries* (1912), pp. 188–89.

[18] J. L. Lowes, *The Road to Xanadu* (1927), p. 85.

There was a "gale of wind S. W. by W. . . . . from a
dark cloud which hovered over our heads, came a flash, or
rather blast, of lightning, which was so terrible and quiv-
ered so long among us, that not only I, but all our men,
thought the ship was on fire." Men's faces were scorched.
Then followed the "terriblest clap of thunder that was ever
heard by mortals." Singleton felt it to be the vengeance of
God upon him, although he was "afflicted at the punishment
but not at the crime." After it was over, the boatswain
"found that part of the head [of the ship] was gone."

Dampier's storm came also from the southwest. "It was
now the time of the Year for the S. W. Monsoon." The
wind, however, did a good deal of "whiffling about" in this
case, coming first from the northeast and then from the
southwest. It blew exceeding hard. "It thundered and
lightened prodigiously, and the Sea seemed all of a Fire
about us; for every Sea that broke sparkled like lightning."
Then follows a description of the Corpus Sanct in which
Dampier expresses the opinion that it is a kind of creeping
jelly. "I was never in such a violent Storm in all my Life;
so said all the Company." Afterwards, they found that the
rails of the ship's head had been washed away and further
damage threatened to the bows by the loosening of an
anchor.

Here again is a parallel that could scarcely have been
written without an eye on the text, or at least from a clear
memory. In both accounts the narrator not only himself emphasizes the dire nature of the storm but brings to his support the opinions of the others present. Striking use is made
of lightning playing about like fire, quivering. The direction
from which the storm comes is the same, the same destruc-
tion is done in the same part of the vessel, and in describing
it Defoe carelessly falls into Dampier's language again. The
ships are sailing at the time in the same general region, i.e.,
the Spice Islands and the Philippines. Defoe has not only

found random suggestions in Dampier for all that he needs but he has adapted a whole episode.[19]

Singleton's storm is felt to be an act of God in punishment of a wicked life. This might well be nothing more than the uneasy thoughts of any person in imminent danger. Sailors proverbially pray, if ever, during violent storms and just before shipwrecks. As one perceives that the outlines and much detail for Singleton's activities in the East Indies are out of Dampier, one cannot but suspect that here, too, Defoe has in mind Dampier's Nicobar-Achin journey.[20] Here he suffers the buffets of a tropical storm with a few companions in an open boat, and, watching the ominous thing creeping upon them out of the sky, repents his freebooting life. This is a part of Dampier that certain writers have insisted is the one unmistakable general influence on Defoe.[21] Certainly Defoe was inclined to wring all the morality and Divine Providence possible out of every situation, especially catastrophes. His *Storm* is such a sermon, and *Robinson Crusoe* is in great part upon the same theme. But in this particular instance, the connection with Dampier is forced upon us. Defoe was familiar with the famous storm-passage and had used it previously in the story. It was therefore fresh upon him. Singleton, unusual among Defoe's heroes because of lightness of heart and freedom from misgivings, has his first thoughts of God and fit retribution for his life of crime in circumstances like those of Dampier.

Defoe with his usual care describes the winds again as if with particular regard for the maps and text of Dampier, particularly the blowing of the monsoons, six months of the year in one direction and six months in the opposite. Cruis-

[19] *Captain Singleton* (Oxford ed.), pp. 241–43; *Dampier's Voyages*, I, 408–409, 411.

[20] *Dampier's Voyages*, I, 479–83.

[21] Clennel Wilkinson, *Dampier* (1929), p. 244.

ing north between the island of Madagascar and the coast of Africa, Singleton is careful to mention the blowing of the monsoon half the year in one direction and half the year in the opposite. It is in this very place that Dampier's map of trade winds shows by arrows the blowing of the monsoon.

Singleton's proposal to go to the Bay of Campeachy to recruit more hands for the business of cruising suggests Dampier and his rough companions, the logwood-cutters. Singleton remarks that he did not doubt he should ship as many men there as he pleased; "and so we did." Soon they "had taken two or three sloops from New England and New York . . . . going for Jamaica and Barbadoes." Defoe's pamphlet on the life of a famous pirate, John Gow, written five years later, repeats this idea and almost the very phrases. In fact, the idea of buccaneers in the Bay of Campeachy was a favorite with Defoe.

"COLONEL JACQUE"

On the twentieth of December, 1722, Defoe published *The History and Remarkable Life of the Truly Honorable Colonel Jacque,* which William Lee has called the "male counterpart to *Moll Flanders.*"[22] Colonel Jacque is a London rogue, pickpocket, and thief, but instilled in him is the belief that he is a gentleman. He is therefore something short of the lowest kind of thief. He early abhors the worst part of his trade. As a boy he sleeps in the ashes of the glass house and roams the streets, graduating from small crimes to larger. After twenty-six years of this life he is kidnapped through the devices of his uncle and transported to Virginia. Here by honest effort he becomes a trusted overseer, is tutored by a felon, acquires property, and returns to England, where he marries several times but always unfortunately in one way or another.

---

[22] *Daniel Defoe: His Life and Recently discovered Writings* (1869), I, 365.

En route to England his ship is taken by a French pirate. He goes to France in 1700 and enlists in an Irish regiment in the French army, fighting in Italy for over a year. Returning to Virginia, he tends his estate, recovers a former wife, and begins trading to the West Indies. He is taken by the Spaniards. Under the Spanish flag he trades by stealth from Havana, particularly with merchants at Vera Cruz. He makes several voyages in sloops to Virginia and New England and back to Cuba and Mexico. Eventually, he is driven by the Spaniards into the Gulf of Mexico. He lands at Vera Cruz, but his men, attempting to dodge the Spanish frigates, have to run their vessel ashore at the mouth of the Mississippi. Thirty miles from Vera Cruz he has time to repent and write his memoirs, living among the friendly Spanish merchants. With their help he finally is able to return to England by way of Cadiz.

This story is a moral one intended for the wicked. There are some nautical parts, but it is not a tale of the sea, primarily. There is a very interesting passage in the early part, however, which, if taken to be autobiographical, as Mr. Aitken suggests,[23] adds considerable weight to the belief that Defoe personally knew William Dampier. Says Colonel Jacque:

Particularly, I loved to talk with seamen and soldiers about the war, and about the great sea-fights, or battles on shore, that any of them had been in; and, as I never forgot anything they told me, I could soon, that is to say in a few years, give almost as good an account of the Dutch war, and of the fights at sea . . . . as any of those that had been there; and this made those old sailors and tars love to talk with me too, and to tell me all the stories they could think of . . . .

By this means, as young as I was, I was a kind of historian; and though I had read no books, and never had any books to read, yet I could give a tolerable account of what had been done, and what was then adoing in the world, especially in those things that our own

[23] Introduction to his edition of *Colonel Jacque*, p. xii.

people were concerned in. I knew the names of every ship in the navy, and who commanded them too, and all this before I was fourteen years old, or but very soon after.[24]

If such an interest in the sea were truly Defoe's he could not have missed talking with so attractive and famous a mariner as William Dampier.

In the latter part of the story Colonel Jacque assumes a character more like Defoe's better-known wandering heroes, indulging in a variety of escapades that suggest to Defoe's latest biographer mere padding to fill up the book. His adventures in trading and smuggling bring us back into the kind of life very evidently dear to Defoe's heart. It is as though he could not write of a pickpocket without eventually making him a pirate or smuggler. At any rate, he carries Colonel Jacque through a short series of typical adventures he had long been familiar with in his favorite travel works. We shall not drudge through a list of these but pause only on two episodes that seem rather surely to have sprung from Dampier.

Colonel Jacque is frequently beset by pirates and suffers the usual vicissitudes of the sea. The five-day storm that drove him off his course from Virginia to Bermuda involves the master and the mate of the ship in a quarrel like one described by Dampier in the same region. Colonel Jacque originally set sail from the capes of Virginia for England. The storm injured their stout ship so much that it was decided to run for the Bermudas, but the captain (or master) and the mate engaged in a hot dispute as to their direction. They differed "to an extremity . . . . The master being a positive man, insulted the mate about it, and threatened to expose him for it when he came to England." The mate, who was "an excellent sea artist, and an experienced sailor, but withal a modest man," was right, but "made no inde-

---

[24] *Colonel Jacque* (Oxford ed., 1840), pp. 9–10.

cent use" of his victory. They then sail away for the Canary Islands, these being the nearest land.

Dampier, sailing from Virginia, with the buccaneers under Captain Cook, runs into one of the worst storms he ever saw when his ship is a few days out from the capes. It "lasted above a week." The details of it he put in chapter six of his *Discourse of Winds:*

> The Ship by the mistake of him that con'd, broched too, and lay in the Trough of the Sea. . . . . The Master, whose Fault this was, rav'd like a mad Man, and call'd for an Axe to cut the Mizen Shrouds, and turn the Mizen Mast over Board . . . . Captain Davis was then Quarter-master, and a more experienced seaman than the master. He bid him hold his Hand a little, in hopes to bring her some other way to her Course . . . .

It was Dampier and another who finally saved the day by going in the shrouds forward and spreading the flaps of their coats. This made enough of a sail to turn the ship so that her sails functioned again. They then sailed for the Cape Verde Islands, only a little south of the Canaries.[25]

The two situations are not precisely the same, but much is common to both. There is a master of the vessel responsible for its plight in a storm off the Virginia coast. There is a younger officer, more experienced, who opposes him. In one the master insults the mate. In the other he raves like a madman, and there is clearly an argument. Defoe's description of the mate, furthermore, admirably suits Dampier, particularly, "withal a modest man."

Colonel Jacque is but one more wandering hero like Robinson Crusoe, Captain Singleton, Lemuel Gulliver, and William Dampier. Wanderlust consumes him. "Knowledge of things begat a desire of increasing it."[26]

---

[25] Compare *Colonel Jacque* (Oxford ed.), pp. 189–90; *Dampier's Voyages*, I, 189–90, and II, 283.

[26] *Colonel Jacque* (Oxford ed.), p. 253.

A kind of left-handed compliment is paid by Defoe to his own previous narratives and to mariners' tales like Dampier's. Of his memoirs, Colonel Jacque remarks, "When I wrote these things down, I did not foresee that the writings of our own stories would be so much the fashion in England, or so agreeable to others to read, as I find custom, and the humour of the times has caused it to be."[27] So whatever Defoe's purpose may have been when he began to write *Colonel Jacque*, it is very certain that near the end he thinks of his tale as a travel-memoir.

[27] *Colonel Jacque* (Oxford ed.), p. 334.

VII

A JOURNALIST DREAMS

I would to God I were once in a place where I might cause
your burning zeale to bee knowen to those that have authority,
power, and abilitie to recompense your travelling mind and
pen, wherewith you cease not day nor night to labour and
travell to bring your good and godly desires to some passe,
though not possibly to that happy ende that you most thirst
for.—ANTHONIE PARKHURST, Gentleman, in a letter to Richard
Hakluyt, 1578

W E COME now to 1724 and Defoe's last long narrative,
A New Voyage Round the World by a Course Never
Sailed Before.[1] It appeared on November 9, but was post-
dated 1725. This is not one of Defoe's best books—in fact
it is rather pedestrian—but it is especially interesting to us.
It marks a kind of cycle in Defoe's long narratives. Beginning with Robinson Crusoe, he was primarily interested in a
wandering hero who was left alone for many years on an
uninhabited island but who also wandered for many more,
trading in various ships. Beyond our rather narrow interest

[1] It was an octavo volume. There is, however, an interesting and exceedingly rare folio copy in the Harvard Library. It bears the name of a
different printer (G. Read) but no date. The year 1725 is written in
ink on the linen title-page. The pages measure thirteen and one-half
inches by eight and one-half inches. It is divided into two parts, Part II
beginning in the middle of the voyage where the expedition heads south
for Valdivia in Chile. The Harvard Catalogue describes it as the first
issue of the first edition. It may have been a presentation copy.

in Defoe and Dampier, it reveals its creator's intense interest
in trade, in planting colonies, in morality, and in pure geography. Soon after, his interest was drawn rather closely to
rogues and criminals and their life histories. Not only do
the titles of narratives immediately succeeding indicate this
but also his interest in Applebee, the publisher of lives and
confessions of dying criminals. Thus there flowed from his
pen *Captain Singleton, Captain Avery, Moll Flanders,
Colonel Jacque, The Fortunate Mistress,* and the *History of
John Sheppard.* This sort of thing continued, it is true, in
1725, 1726, and 1727, but only in shorter pieces. In his
New Voyage he comes back to the long story of the sea,
directly imitating that typical travel work of his day, the
voyage around the world. He returns to a current of interest perhaps the longest and strongest of his life. Whereas it
takes the careful student to remind us of the dominance of
travel in *Robinson Crusoe,* it stands out at every point in
The New Voyage. Just because this narrative has not been
worked into shape and its materials sublimated in a fiction
like *Robinson Crusoe* or *Captain Singleton,* it is all the more
valuable as a laboratory specimen. Here is the somewhat
undigested raw material of travel paraded with little dis-
guise. We see Defoe at work with mariners' journals spread
out before him. To the initiate his *New Voyage* smacks
strongly of the voyages of Sir John Narborough and Captain
William Dampier.[2]

The story, told in the first person, is supposed to be related by a nameless owner's agent who takes a nameless merchant vessel around the world on a most prosperous voyage
by a route never sailed before.[3] The purpose of the voyage
is threefold: trade, buccaneering, and discovery. In Spanish

---

[2] John Masefield, *Masters of Literature: Defoe* (1909), p. xix; Secord,
Narrative Method of Defoe, p. 153.

[3] Lee says that a map of this new route around the world was published
afterwards separately (I, 397–98), but I have seen no trace of it.

territory these nameless heroes pose as Frenchmen, there being a French captain and thirty-two Flemish seamen on board. On the high sea, meeting with Spaniards, they are English cruisers with letters of "mart" [marque] and, not having heard of the recent peace, are "fitted for the attack." In the East Indies they are to spread "imperial colours" and transact business as they "found occasion." They are, further, to make what discoveries they can toward the South Pole. The owners are British merchants designing to set up an East India trade in Flanders.

With this engaging prospect the narrative begins under double responsibility for a lively tale because Defoe devotes the first few paragraphs to a loud complaint against the usual manner of writing sea journals. Such books leave out the most interesting parts, he says. Then he proposes to write a "voyage" full of variety. The book is disappointing, however, there being in it nothing so diverting as Robinson Crusoe on his Indian island. It is filled, on the other hand, with a good deal of matter obviously intended merely to promote trade, discovery, and colonizing in South America and the Pacific.

The nameless ship sails from the Thames in 1713. After stopping at Dunkirk to pick up its complement of Frenchmen it is provisioned in Ireland and drops down to the Canaries. A council of officers here decides against the plan of the owner's agent (narrator of the story) to sail first to the East Indies by way of the Cape of Good Hope. Accordingly, they sail to the Brazilian coast. They fail to round the Horn, however, and have to submit to the contrary winds, which blow them safely across to the Cape of Good Hope as originally planned. The men, however, become mutinous, being on so long and uncertain a voyage. Defoe (as I shall call the narrator) is able to quell this only with the aid of a Dutch captain at the Cape of Good Hope and by threatening to put the ringleaders ashore on the island of Madagascar. With a brigantine bought from a Dutchman at the Cape they sail into a storm that drives them to the island of Madagascar. Learning that only a few pirates and miserable derelicts still live in the northern part of the island, they coast north and recruit more men from among them, all willing and anxious to get away. From here they go to Ceylon and the East Indies, trading by stealth to great advantage, particularly at the Philippines. They cross the Pacific by sailing far to the south and discovering much new land. Reaching the South Sea coast, they cruise for Spanish prizes for a short time, but finally, being rich, they divide their company: one half to go over the mountains from Chile to Patagonia; the other to sail the vessel around the Horn and join the land party. This is done, with lengthy descriptions of the land in Chile and Patagonia suited for colonization and trade. Defoe ends with a definite recommendation of this region for an English colony. He speedily brings the ship to England and the voyage to an end.

DEFOE AND LE MAIRE

So much for a review of the narrative. It is surprising that it has not suffered close scrutiny before now, for the first thing that strikes us in this professed "journal of a voyage" is the author's confession that it follows the journals of William Cornelius van Schouten and Jacques Le Maire, the navigators of Hoorn who in 1616 first passed around the famous South American cape. They passed "in part, the same way I have given account of," Defoe writes, "as by their journals which I have by me at this time." Like them, he combines in his voyage trading and discoveries toward the South Pole, by a new route. Strange lands like those that the Dutchman sighted or touched upon without fully describing Defoe makes much of, supplying from elsewhere the details he felt they did not know or failed to mention. Approximately one-fourth of the book is given to these South Sea discoveries. Much of the latter part of it is concerned with travel over the Andes and across Patagonia, an idea which he got probably from Narborough and others who described these regions.

Further similarity between the *New Voyage* and these journals is to be observed in the illegal manner of trading and the presence of a second person of importance (Le Maire) who sailed as supercargo, or owner's agent. But it is only in a general way that Defoe follows Schouten and Le Maire. Defoe's route around the world is "by a course never sailed before." This is to the east by way of the Cape of Good Hope, the East Indies, the Philippine Islands, the South Pacific, the coasts of Peru and Chile, and across Patagonia. Le Maire and Schouten and all their kind had always gone the other way. Defoe spends much time on the subject of mutiny, of pirates at Madagascar, on trading in the Philippines, on cruising and trading in South America, on the possibilities of settling Patagonia. Much of this lies outside the routes of the Dutchmen and the scope of their journals. Many sources are without question involved in the composition of this tale of "the richest ship and cargo that ever came out of those seas." Defoe mentions definitely the accounts of Sir Francis Drake, Sir Martin Frobisher, Sir John Narborough, and Captain John Wood, besides those of Schouten and Le Maire. He had already used Dampier. Inasmuch as our business is not with all the sources of the book, but with Dampier, we shall deal with him first and treat the others only as it is necessary to validate our remarks. Suffice it to say here that Dampier's *Voyages* stand out prominently among several sources for Defoe's *New Voyage Round the World*.

ROUTES

The route that Defoe sails is a new one, and to all actual appearances a bad one. All the voyages around the world, before his time, had been by the usual way east to west across the Pacific, where equal and constant trade winds are met. Where Defoe got this idea is completely hidden, except that we already know he has taken a given route of an actual traveler and in his fiction simply reversed it. Dampier specifically recommends trading to the Philippines by way of the Horn, and furthermore specifically prefers it to the route past the Cape of Good Hope because of counter-winds surely to be met with in the Straits of Malacca or thereabouts. Defoe apparently winks at the difficulties in order to tell his unusual tale, and to boost English trade.

Certain details of the narrative, however, rather clearly reflect Dampier. First of all, in the journey from England to the east of the Cape of Good Hope Defoe has many experiences like those of Dampier on his voyage to New Holland. Defoe's route is elaborate (he makes Newport Pitts, Dunkirk, and Galway, Ireland, after leaving the Thames), but he makes one rendezvous of the customary two, the Canary Islands. (Dampier stopped at the Cape Verde Islands, just south.) Defoe sails from the Canaries on February 11 for the coast of Brazil. Dampier sailed from the Cape Verde Islands for Brazil on February 22. This leg of the journey occupies Defoe twenty-six days. It occupied Dampier twenty-seven days. Defoe strikes the coast of Brazil at Cape St. Augustine, north of the Bay of All Saints (Bahia). Dampier, changing his original plan of going to Pernambuco on Cape St. Augustine, struck the Brazilian coast twenty leagues north of Bahia and coasted down to it. Both were at Bahia the last of March. Having used a description of this port from Dampier in *Robinson Crusoe,* Defoe does not repeat it here. But it may be significant that he brings his heroes to the same ports often, ports given especial prominence in the accounts of Dampier.

Dropping down to Buenos Aires Defoe makes desperate attempts to round the Horn, but he succeeds only in being blown so far to the east that he finds it expedient to go on to the Cape of Good Hope. Dampier, knowing all about such things, sailed with intention directly south from Bahia in order to strike westerly winds in southern latitudes that would carry him to New Holland by way of the Cape of Good Hope. The reader should be reminded that Dampier's route to New Holland by way of Brazil was unusual, and that Defoe's adherence to it more than once is therefore striking. Beyond the Cape of Good Hope Defoe temporarily leaves Dampier's route,[4] going by way of Madagascar and Ceylon to the Spice Islands.

When Dampier was at the Cape Verde Islands he "meditated on the Process of his Voyage," having a green crew and desiring to refresh them for the long run ahead. He sailed for Pernambuco as the best place for this, but his men became so discontented that he was forced to stand for Bahia, a place more likely to furnish protection in case of mutiny. Sailing from the Canaries, Defoe calls a council to determine which way they should go. He was for the Cape of Good Hope, but, the other officers being against it, he was forced like Dampier to change his plans.

Furthermore, when Dampier arrived at Bahia, he found a busy harbor in which was the Portuguese Brazil fleet of

---

[4] Mr. Secord states in his *Narrative Method of Defoe* (p. 153) that Defoe follows Dampier through the Gilolo passage. But this is not so. Dampier sailed from Timor to Banda and then struck the coast of Guinea on the *western side*. Following this, he rounded the *northwestern* end (the Gilolo passage) and coasted down the other shore towards the southeast (II, 507–20). This end of New Guinea lies under the equator. Defoe not only approached New Guinea from the Ladrones, far to the east, at 17 degrees south latitude, but his route through the Spice Islands lay much farther north than the Gilolo passage. It was through the Straits of Malacca and up in a northeasterly direction along the north shore of Borneo (Oxford ed., pp. 90–91, 93).

Page references to Defoe's *New Voyage* are to the Oxford edition, 1840, unless otherwise stated.

thirty vessels, making ready to sail for Europe with two men-of-war for convoys. He further explained here, in a manner characteristic of him, that the two other great Brazilian ports (Pernambuco and Rio Janeiro) also have "2 Men of War to each Place for their Convoys."

So also when Defoe arrives at Bahia he learns of three Spanish merchant ships at Buenos Aires ready to sail for Europe and "they expected two Spanish men of war to be their convoy because of the Portuguese men of war which were in Brazil, to convoy the Brazil fleet."[5]

MUTINY

Mutiny plays a large part in the story of Defoe's *New Voyage*. Lying in the Plate River in an uncomfortable climate, his "men began to be very uneasy, being crowded together so close all in one ship; so we made the best of our way south." But it seems they had other reasons for being discontented. Somewhat later on Defoe tells us that ever since the council among the officers at the Canary Islands when opinion had been unanimous against him the crew, who had heard of the argument among their superiors, had looked upon him "with an evil eye, as one that was against their interest." Finally, after the failure to pass the Horn and the decision to go for the Cape of Good Hope, as Defoe originally outlined it, the crew, led by the second mate, a surly boatswain, and a gunner, broke out in actual mutiny. Defoe enlarges upon the ignorance of a crew who have only vague ideas of where the expedition is headed and are swayed by petty officers, and gives advice to captains warning them not to let an argument among the officers be known among the crew. He puts in at the Cape of Good Hope and there secures the valuable aid and protection of the Dutch officials ashore and of a Dutch captain lying in the road. Now this is very much like the situation that threatened Dampier. His

[5] *New Voyage*, pp. 8–10; *Dampier's Voyages*, II, 373–400, *passim*.

green crew gave him trouble before he reached the coast of America. As has just been remarked, they were the cause of changing his course against his better judgment. But that his men did much more than this is clear. His lieutenant, one George Fisher, began making trouble at the Cape Verde Islands, and by the time the "Roebuck" was well over to the American coast Dampier put him in irons and kept him there until he turned him over to the Portuguese governor at Bahia. "I was obliged partly to alter my Measures, and met with many difficulties," wrote Dampier of this trouble. "I mention this much of it in general for my own necessary Vindication, in my taking such Measures sometimes for prosecuting the Voyage as the State of my Ships Crew, rather than my own Judgment and Experience, determin'd me to." And so he slept, armed, with his officers upon the quarter deck, and prevented a final outbreak by turning the ringleader over to officials at Bahia. Substitute the Cape of Good Hope for Bahia and Dutch officials for Portuguese, and the general outline of Defoe's mutiny and Dampier's is the same. Returning from his first voyage round the world, Dampier and his companions were materially assisted by a Dutch captain at the Cape who sent ashore for one hundred men to help trim Dampier's ship and bring it to anchor.

Add to this the comment of both writers upon the ignorance and superstition of the plain seamen. Defoe's crew, not understanding the project, and aware that even the officers differed in opinion among themselves, suspected their commander and grew panicky over imagined hardships and attempts at the impossible. Dampier had already written:

. . . . And anyone who is sensible, how backward and refractory the Seamen are apt to be in long Voyages when they know not whither they are going, how ignorant they are of the Nature of the Winds [etc.] . . . . Anyone, I say, who is sensible of these Difficulties will be much more pleased at the Discoveries and Observations I have been able to make, than displeased with me that I did not make more.

Again he wrote:

. . . . the Ignorance and Obstinacy withal, of some under me, occasion'd me a great deal of Trouble: Tho' they found all along, and were forc'd to acknowledge it, that I was seldom out in my Conjectures, when I told them usually beforehand what Winds &c. we should meet with at such or such particular Places we should come at.

Privateers, he wrote in another place, trying to double Point Pedro on the south shore of Jamaica, fired a gun sometimes "to kill the old Daemon that they say inhabits there to disturb poor Seamen. I have related these odd Passages to show how ignorant Men are that cannot see the Reason of it."

So, too, Defoe's crew, not seeing the reason of it, were led by a ringleader into mutiny, but, being checked in the mutiny and having the project clearly explained to them, repented their rashness and served faithfully.

The last point regarding the business of mutiny is Dampier's reluctance to discuss it. He apologized for mentioning it. He obviously considered it apart from the serious business of keeping a journal. Speaking of the impending trouble with the crew, he remarked, "This, with some other unforeseen Accidents, *not necessary to be mention'd in this place*, meeting with an Aversion of my Men to a long, unknown Voyage, made me justly apprehensive of their Revolting, and was a great Trouble and Hindrance to me. So that I was obliged partly to alter my Measures, and met with many difficulties, the Particulars *of which I shall not trouble the Reader with*." Dampier was vindicating his action against his lieutenant and the general failure of the voyage in the way of new discoveries.

But Defoe, knowing well how interesting those details

would be, complains of the manner of seamen in their journals. A voyage around the world no longer is in itself worth reading because it is so common a thing.

The way is now a common road . . . . we no more look upon it as a mighty thing . . . . It is to be observed, of the several navigators whose Voyages round the World have been published [this must include Dampier] that few, if any of them, have diverted us with that variety which a circle of that length must needs offer. We have very little account of their landings, their diversions, the accidents which happened to them, or to others by their means; . . . . the storms and difficulties at sea or on shore, and have nowhere a full relation; and all the rest of their accounts are generally filled up with directions for sailors coming that way, the bearings of the land, the depth of the channels, entrances, and bars at the several ports, anchorage . . . . and the like things, useful indeed for seamen . . . . but not at all to the purpose when we come to find the history of the voyage.

Another sort of these writers have just given us their long journals, tedious accounts of their logwork, how many leagues they sailed every day; where they had winds, when it blew hard, and when softly; what latitude in every observation, what meridian distance, and what variation of the compass.

Defoe then cites specifically the voyages of Narborough, John Wood, and Martin Frobisher, "all which, are indeed full of their own journals, and the incidents of sailing, but have little or nothing of story in them, for the use of such readers who never intend to go to sea, and yet such readers may desire to hear how it has fared with those that have, and how affairs stand in those remote parts of the world." It is not therefore for the rarity of going around the world or for nautical information but supposedly for the interest of a good story that Defoe publishes his *New Voyage*. "Such a variety of incidents" happened in the voyage, says Defoe, that he resolved to put them all in and make it not only useful but diverting and wholly new in the way of voyages.

Dampier's *Voyages* plead guilty to many of the charges cited by Defoe (soundings, charts, winds, compass-variations, etc.), although Narborough is the writer Defoe has particularly in mind. But Dampier's *Voyage to New Holland* definitely suggests what has been omitted, definitely implies escapades of mutiny more exciting than the simple facts stated. Defoe, reading Dampier and objecting to a certain dryness of style, could not have failed to see the excellent lead offered by Dampier. He then supplied those missing details of human interest. It is like Defoe to do so. It is only one of many connections between the two books.[6]

WINDS

Then there is the matter of winds. Dampier was unquestionably the best-informed man in England regarding the winds of the seven seas. I have already shown that scientists, mariners, and map-makers turned to him in the matter. It would have been as natural for Defoe to turn to Dampier for knowledge regarding winds as to go to Moll for the latest and best maps, as he did in his *Tour thro' the Whole Island of Great Britain,* and as he seems to have done in *Robinson Crusoe.* Examination of the maps of the early eighteenth century shows that Dampier's maps of the winds of the world, drawn by Moll, became the standard for such things.

If the winds of Defoe's *New Voyage* be checked against various statements in Dampier regarding winds, it will be found that Defoe agrees with Dampier except where he wishes to change them to suit his story. Defoe is not troubled by winds sufficiently for comment until he sails south toward the Horn along the coast of South America from Rio de la Plata. Then he remarks: "We met with some stormy

[6] *New Voyage,* pp. 3, 13, 24–54; *Dampier's Voyages,* II, 256, 333–34, 343, 376–77. Italics are mine.

weather in these seas and particularly a north-west blast, which carried us for eleven days a great way off to sea." They beat their way back and try again. This time winds from the southwest and southwest by west drive them back to Port Saint Julian. After a rest they try once more and would have got into the South Seas, "but a strong gale of wind took us at west-north-west, and though we could, lying near to it, stretch away to the southward, yet, as it over-blowed, we could make no westward way . . . . we went away to leeward in spite of all we could do, and lost ground apace." Councils are called to consider what is best to do, "for we did but drive to leeward the longer we strove with it; the gale still held on . . . . blowing like a kind of monsoon, or trade-wind, though in those latitudes [64° South] I know there is no such thing, properly called, as a trade-wind."

The wind abating, they return to Port Saint Julian. Setting forth yet again, they are driven so fiercely by a storm from the southwest that they turn before it and sail for the Cape of Good Hope.

It is noticeable in this attempt to pass around the Horn that the strong westerly winds are encountered *before* the Straits of Le Maire are entered. Most navigators before Defoe's time, it is true, met stormy weather in these regions. They describe the currents upon entering the Straits of Magellan or Le Maire, but it is in the Pacific that they meet the most violent winds. It was not uncommon to be driven back, as Cavendish was, into the Straits for shelter or even back to the Rio de la Plata to winter. There are some records of storms on the Atlantic side of this famous passage, but all (excepting Magellan, who found the Pacific quiet) especially testify in the unadorned language of record to the severe buffeting of the Pacific. But all these pass into the great South Sea eventually, whatever their fate once there. Drake, whose journals Defoe had before him, found good sailing through the Straits, with the tides normal and winds of no particular note.

It is to be noted that Dampier, aiming, in the *Voyage Round the World*, at the Straits of Magellan, could not enter at all. "But the Winds hanging in the Wester-board, and blowing hard, oft put us by our Topsails, so that we could not fetch it." Accordingly, he made for the Straits of Le Maire, farther south. Here, too, westerly gales, dead calms, and strong, choppy currents prevented an entrance. He sailed for the east end of Staten Island hoping to round that: "The Winds hung in the Western quarter betwixt the N. W. and the West so that we could not get much to the Westward and we never saw Terra del Fuego after that Evening that we made the Straight Le Maire."

A month before this he had argued long with the buccaneer commanders to anchor at the Sibbel de Ward (Falkland) Islands in order "to hinder their designs of going through the Straights of Magellan, which I knew would prove very dangerous to us; the rather because our Men being Privateers . . . ." and not well under command for the dangers of a passage so little known.

Dampier, too, finally got through and suffered the customary storm, this time for seventeen days. His descriptions of winds, however, in these several attempts to make the passage are furnished in unusual detail. In the *Voyage to New Holland*, from which the novelist appropriated so much else, lay the special knowledge he displayed regarding the true trade winds (easterly) and the westerly winds in the lower latitudes:

We had the Wind Easterly, and we ran with it to the Southward [from Bahia]. . . . . We were now in *the true Trade*, and therefore made good way to the Southward, to get without the Verge of the *General Trade-Wind into a Westerly Wind's way*, that might carry us toward the Cape of Good Hope. By the 12th of May, being in the Lat. 31 deg. 10 min. we began to meet with Westerly

Winds, which freshned on us, and did not leave us till a little before we made the Cape. Sometimes it blew so hard that it put us under a Fore-course; especially in the Night . . . .

Routes, ports, mutiny, winds—such a combination of circumstances and things is not to be found in the voyages of any other navigator besides Dampier.[7]

Once past the Cape of Good Hope, Defoe departs from Dampier's route to New Holland, in order to reach Madagascar and India. He also puts in at the Cape for a total period of two months and three days, whereas Dampier sails by it. Yet Defoe conducts his voyage according to the information provided on Dampier's maps.

And, finally, Defoe crosses the Pacific from the Philippines to South America by keeping well to the south, out of the easterly trade winds. It was common knowledge in Defoe's time that in order to sail east across the great South Sea one should go either to the north or to the south of the trade wind. The famous Acapulco ships were known to sail to the north. But here again we meet Dampier. It was he who made popular in English the routes and schedules of the Spanish ships. Defoe may have had this knowledge from the street or the coffee house, but it is safe to say that it came in part from Dampier. Also, Dampier's maps of the winds of the Pacific were marked *"Variable Winds"* to the northward and southward of the easterly trade. Defoe's officers, opposing him, argued in favor of going west with the trade wind and getting no fame for it, rather than trusting to "the variable" in the southern regions in the hope of making discoveries and establishing a name for being the first navigators to sail round the world from west to east. The matter of true trade winds and variable winds was a favorite with Dampier.

[7] *New Voyage*, pp. 13, 17; *Dampier's Voyages*, I, 108, 109, 110; II, 407. Italics are mine.

IN THE PACIFIC

When Defoe travels to Madagascar and toward the South Pole he enters regions unfrequented by Dampier. (Dampier mentions Madagascar but twice.) We accordingly expect to find there little in common between them. But when he trades at the Philippines and cruises for Spaniards off the coast of Peru we keep alert, for these are places that contributed greatly to Dampier's fame.

To proceed in the order of Defoe's route, I shall mention the Philippines first. Of these islands Defoe has much to say. Trade there is worth cultivating. He had already told his officers this in explaining his reasons for adopting his strange new route. European goods brought there by the Acapulco ships, he had said, were very expensive because of much landing and reshipping en route, entailing commissions, transportation charges, and fees. Goods shipped directly in English bottoms could be sold 100 per cent cheaper than those shipped by the Acapulco ships, and yet at a profit. Such is Defoe's argument. Accordingly, when his little fleet arrives at Manila, he pictures a thriving, though illegal, trade, the suggestions for which lay in Dampier.

Regarding the Philippine trade, Dampier wrote, "Beside the benefit which might accrue from this Trade with Meangis, and the other Spice Islands, the Philippine Islands themselves, by a little care and industry, might have afforded us a very beneficial Trade, and all these Trades might have been managed from Mindanao, by settling there first."

Of Manila, he wrote:

It is a place of great Strength and Trade; The two great Acapulco Ships before mentioned fetching from hence all sorts of East-India Commodities; which are brought hither by Foreigners, especially by the Chinese, and the Portuguese.

Sometimes the English Merchants of Fort St. George send their ships hither as it were by stealth under the charge of Portuguese Pilots and Mariners: for as yet we cannot get the Spaniards there to a commerce with us or the Dutch, although they have but few Ships of their own.

The Spanish Inhabitants of the smaller Islands especially, would willingly trade with us if the Government was not so severe against it: for they have no Goods but what are brought from Manila at an extraordinary dear rate. I am of the Opinion, That if any of our Nations will seek a Trade with them, they would not lose their labour; for the Spaniards can and will Smuggle (as our seamen call Trading by stealth) as well as any Nation that I know; and our Jamaicans are to their profit sensible enough of it. And I have been informed that Captain Goodlud of London, in a Voyage which he made from Mindanao to China, touch'd at some of these Islands, and was civily treated by the Spaniards, who bought some of his Commodities, giving him a very good Price for the same.

Later, proceeding toward Manila:

Now if we had really designed to have traded there, this was as fair an opportunity as Men could have desired: For these Men [four natives] could have brought us to the Fryar that they were going to, and a *small Present* to him would have engaged him to do any kindness for us in the way of Trade; For the Spanish Governors do not allow of it, and we must Trade by stealth.

These passages stressed the following things: undeveloped trade, trade by stealth, the dear price of Spanish goods, the eagerness of the inhabitants of the smaller islands to trade.

When Defoe arrives at Manila, under French colors, he is refused permission to trade openly, but, by an exchange with the governor of lavish gifts, a brisk trade in reality is begun. Crimson or scarlet cloth from Defoe figures among these gifts each time. The Spanish governor and merchants come aboard and buy the ship's goods, the goods being sent ashore as if presents. Soon the vessel becomes simply "an open fair." Orientals and others come and depart by night. "This trade held a good while [six weeks], and we found that our customers came from other islands than from the island where the governor resided." Everything is sold at immense profit. Whatever is bought is bought cheap. Here Defoe has again filled in the details of an outline laid down by Dampier, even to the giving of gifts and the commerce with the Chinese and the remoter islands. Captain Swan, Dampier writes, hoped to gain the favor of the Mindanayan officials by gifts, one to the Sultan, one to the Raja. In each present there were three yards of scarlet cloth and three yards of lace. Other contemporary accounts of these islands reveal no such descriptions. Dampier's is outstanding for its concern with the possibilities of trade. Other celebrated authors, like Gamelli Careri,[8] Pedro Teixeira,[9] and Argensola,[10] are either concerned only with the customs of the people or with brief mention of the trade then being carried on by the Spanish. Thus it is evident that Dampier's account is the source of Defoe's information.[11]

[8] *Giro del Mondo* (Napoli, 1699–1700).

[9] *Travels of Pedro Teixera*, edited by Sinclair and Ferguson for the Hakluyt Society (Series II, Vol. IX, London, 1902). Defoe mentions Teixeira's account in his *History of the Principal Discoveries and Improvements* (1727), p. 281.

[10] Stevens, *New Collection of Voyages*, pp. 1–260. Cf. the running-title, *The Discovery and Conquest of the Spice Islands*.

[11] This gains weight further from the fact that Dampier is still considered by authorities on Philippine history to be one of the three greatest Englishmen to visit the Islands during England's long hostility with Spain. (W. Cameron Forbes, *The Philippine Islands* [1928], I, 42; E. Heawood, *History of Geographical Discovery in the Seventeenth and Eighteenth Centuries* [1912], pp. 188–89.) The other two are Cavendish, who came too early, and Anson, who came too late for Defoe's purposes. Dampier is to this day quoted in histories of the Philippines because of his "interesting and valuable" account (Blair and Robertson, *The Philippine Islands* [1906], XXXVIII, 13; Forbes, I, 42). Blair depends heavily on Dampier, quoting literally six chapters from the *New Voyage*. Pinkerton's volume (XI) devoted to the Asiatic Islands begins the account of the Philippines with Dampier.

CRUISINGS

Defoe, it has been seen, restrained his expedition from turning privateer at the Philippines. When he arrives at Juan Fernandez, however, near the happy hunting grounds of the buccaneers, he allows his Madagascar ship to go cruising for the Spaniard and refits all the little fleet for the double service of privateer and merchant as the circumstances might provide, at which we are not at all surprised. Whether or not he employed Dampier for this considerable part of the story rests upon similarities in minor details not common to the great body of information and legend about such widely known and romantic figures as the buccaneers of the South Sea. He knew of buccaneering or trading along the coast of Peru and Panama from a dozen sources.

But even here, Defoe sticks mainly to trade. He makes a circular tour from his headquarters on the island of Juan Fernandez, making the Spanish towns on the coast of Chile and Peru from Valdivia north to Lima, then back to the island.

Only one buccaneering escapade is entered upon. As soon as the men are refreshed after their arrival at Juan Fernandez and the ships scrubbed and refitted, Defoe sends out his "Madagascar ship" to cruise. On the ninth day she takes a large Spanish prize containing 16,000 pieces of eight, 200 jars of wheat flour, oil, and some casks of sweetmeats—a most welcome prize. The prize is towed in and a bargain is struck with the captain to keep him quietly stowed away at Juan Fernandez while Defoe's fleet should engage the coast in trade.

This is Defoe's only attempt at cruising in these waters, but it is just here, in the small details of taking this prize, that we are drawn once again to Dampier. Dampier was with Captain John Cook, who had met with Captain Eaton. These two, after having refreshed at Juan Fernandez, sail north to the Lobos Islands, planning an expedition against Truxillo. But from here they spy three Spanish sails, which they chase, capture, and eventually bring in. They prove to be loaded with flour. "In the biggest Ship," besides a letter from the Viceroy of Lima, were also "7 or 8 Tuns of Marmalate of Quinces." Eight hundred thousand pieces of eight had just been removed from her at Guanchaco for fear of the English privateers.

Other items were noted by Dampier, but the flour, marmalade, and money suggest Defoe's flour, sweetmeats, and money.

Furthermore, the presence of two English privateers in Defoe's story is significant. In Dampier they were Captain Cook and Captain Eaton. Are these the prototypes of Defoe's privateers? We have seen that they made rendezvous at Juan Fernandez, that their prizes contained similar cargoes, that they feared a general alarm along the coast. Two other similarities may be added: a case of mistaken identity and the story of the sudden abandonment of men on the island.

In Dampier's account, Captain Cook, fresh from buccaneering in the West Indies and Virginia and not long out of the Straits of Magellan, sights Captain Eaton to the southward of him, giving chase. Not knowing who he was, Captain Cook "lay muzled" to attack her, taking her for a Spanish ship. "They had the same opinion of us," wrote Dampier, "and therefore made sure to take us, but coming nearer we both found our mistakes." Captain Eaton proved to be another privateer, hailing from London. This is a brevity of style characteristic of Dampier in describing action, and already lamented by Defoe.

Defoe accomplishes his meeting with the two English privateers in much the same way but with less economy of words. Lying in the road at Juan Fernandez, they discover that they are watched. Taking the reconnoitering vessel for a Spaniard (she carried Spanish colors), they go out and give chase but lose her. Returning they find two vessels in the road, who upon discovery bestir themselves to escape or give battle. "They were ships of pretty good force and full of men." Then Defoe, with a foresight a little too keen, even for fiction, spreads his true colors to avoid harming fellow-Englishmen if perchance his opponents proved so to be. They do prove so to be. A skirmish is thus narrowly avoided and the ships turn out to be "mere privateers, fitted out from London . . . . but coming last from Jamaica. . . . . They went afterward boldly up the coast and made several good prizes." This description very well fits that of the buccaneers in Dampier.

The last similarity to be noted is the abandonment of men at Juan Fernandez. The part played by it is slight in Defoe's account, merely adding a realistic detail to the scene of the hasty departure of the surprised privateers. "They fired guns twice, which we found was a signal for their boats, which were on shore, to come on board; and soon after we saw three boats go off to them, though, as we understood afterwards, they were obliged to leave sixteen or seventeen of their men behind them, who, being among the rocks catching of goats, either did not hear the signals, or could not come to their boats time enough."

In Dampier's account, the circumstance of being at Juan Fernandez calls for the story of the Mosquito Indian abandoned there in exactly the same circumstances, over three years before, and discussed previously in these pages. The Indian, too, was in the woods hunting for goats, when his captain hastily drew off his men. It is one item more from William Dampier.[12]

---

[12] Compare *New Voyage*, pp. 187–89, 197, 213–19; *Dampier's Voyages*, I, 111, 120–26. This picturesque Mosquitoman was probably far more famous than we now dare assert. In another century he was, with Dampier, a schoolbook classic.

PIRATES AND DISCOVERIES

Routes, winds, smuggling in the Philippines, and privateering: these are the principal points of contact between *Dampier's Voyages* and Defoe's *New Voyage*. From the South Sea Defoe's party returns in two groups, details being given for the group that toiled over the mountains through the interior of Patagonia, down swollen streams to the Atlantic. It is plain that Defoe aims to awaken his readers to the advantages and possibilities of an English colony in Patagonia. This can have no specific connection with Dampier, for he refers to the country only in the most general manner and was never in the interior.[13]

There are, however, some other less important and somewhat more isolated details that we cannot let escape. These are some remarks regarding (1) pirates and (2) new discoveries.

One who reads about Dampier observes from a number of the author's comments and from the character of things that draw his attention that he was not a buccaneer at heart, not a pirate, although for many years he sailed with buccaneers and pirates. In the midst of their carousals and mutinies, their greed and their ignorance, Dampier remains throughout a sober and intelligent observer of natural phenomena. With Captain Swan's men in the Philippines he grows weary of the miserable life, and longs to leave it.

[13] He who reads the early accounts of Chile and Patagonia will find more of Defoe's sources. Defoe himself mentions Sir John Narborough in this connection (p. 304). Certain recommendations of Wafer and Ringrose regarding colonizing and trading may be significant. Defoe owned Frezier's *Voyage to the South Sea and along the Coast of Chili* (1717) and he had access, in the Churchills' *Collection*, to Brawern and Herckemann's *Voyage to Chili in America*, Alonso de Ovalle's *Kingdom of Chili*, and Nicholas de Techo's *History of Paraguay*. There is occasional mention of trade routes up the Plate River to Peru in Hakluyt.

He writes:

While we stay'd here [Pulo Condore] Herman Coppinger our Surgeon went ashore, intending to live here; but Captain Read sent some Men to fetch him again. I had the same Thoughts, and would have gone ashore too, but waited for a more convenient place. For neither he nor I, when we were last on board at Mindanao had any knowledge of the Plot that was laid to leave Capt. Swan, and run away with the Ship; and being sufficiently weary of this mad Crew, we were willing to give them the slip at any place from whence we might hope to get a passage to an English Factory.

Captain Swan himself had already admitted to Dampier that he was sick of the whole business. Dampier wrote:

But I am well assured that he did never intend to cruize about Manila, as his Crew designed; for I did once ask him, and he told me, That what he had already done of this kind he was forc'd to; but now being at Liberty, he would never more engage in any such Design: For, said he, there is no Prince on Earth is able to wipe off the Stain of such Actions.

This discontent he noted in others, too. A buccaneering fray in Central America he described as follows:

We had about 50 Men killed, and among the rest my Ingenious Friend Mr. Ringrose was one, who wrote that Part of the "History of the Buccaneers," which relates to Captain Sharp. He was at this time Cape-Merchant, or Super-Cargo of Captain Swan's Ship. He had no mind to this Voyage; but was necessitated to engage in it or starve.

But Ringrose was, like Dampier, a man of superior intelligence. The others, too, were forever disgruntled, choosing new captains or going off in a seized ship upon the least disagreement with the main party. But when times were hard, when the food was low and the purchase but little, they too easily grew weary of the life of the buccaneer.

A certain Captain Teat easily persuades Captain Swan's men to turn against him.

As for the Sea-men they were easily perswaded to any thing; for they were quite tired with this long and tedious Voyage, and most of them despaired of ever getting home, and therefore did not care what they did, or whether they went.[14]

Histories of the buccaneers abound in dissensions and mutinies of this kind, but it is only in Dampier that one catches a strong spirit of abhorrence of the life. There is a sincere feeling, several times expressed and more often felt in the work, of moral revolt against it. In Dampier there is conflict of the mind, pricking of the conscience, and soreness of heart. Of an impending tropical storm he wrote, very beautifully:

Other Dangers came not upon me with such a leisurely and dreadful Solemnity. A sudden Skirmish or Engagement, or so, was nothing when ones Blood was up, and push'd forwards with eager Expectations. But here I had a lingring view of approaching Death, and little or no hopes of escaping it; and I must confess that my Courage, which I had hitherto kept up, failed me here; and I made very sad Reflections on my former Life, and look'd back with Horror and Detestation, on Actions which before I disliked, but now I trembled at the remembrance of. I had long before this repented me of that roving course of Life, but never with such concern as now.[15]

Now Defoe, as we have seen in *Captain Singleton*, is not the person to pass by such a character and such comments. Next to his versatility in writing is his moral seriousness, sincere or otherwise. When he comes to his Madagascar pirates, he cannot let a good opportunity go, and so like Dampier he shows the dissatisfactions of the life. His earlier pirates, those of *Captain Singleton* and *Colonel Jacque*, do not have quite this spirit. They are restless, mutinying, and perhaps re-embarking under new captains. Invariably the

[14] *Dampier's Voyages*, I, 285–86, 367, 375, 399.
[15] *Ibid.*, I, 481–82. See also above, p. 109.

hero reforms in the end, fulfilling in general a moral purpose. But here in the *New Voyage* for the first time he creates a group of pirates—Madagascar pirates, too—who not
only in a body are at odds one with another but who hate the
life and would leave it if they could.

Defoe has seized Dampier's moral point of view, his dis-
satisfaction and discontent, and given it to pirates whom he
described elsewhere[16] as being so flourishing and rich. They
are disorganized and poor, pursuing their occupation only by
force of circumstances, to save their lives. They have "nobody to command, and therefore nobody to obey." The
pirates' gunner who is won over easily to Defoe says, "If
our people should agree to lend you a boat to go back to your
ship, they would fall together by the ears about who should
go with you, for not a man of them that went with you would
ever come back again hither . . . . though the terms were,
to be hanged when they came to England."

Again: "I can pick out a set of very brave fellows, good
seamen, and most of them such as, having been forced into
the pirates' ships, were dragged into that wicked life they
had lived, not only against their consciences, but by a mere
necessity to save their lives, and that they would be glad at
any price to go off." This gunner admits that he too was
drawn into piracy "against his will" but had long resolved to
leave them.

The second minor point is the matter of discoveries to the
north and south. Part of Defoe's plan was to make discoveries toward the South Pole as far as was possible on a
trading voyage, and this was satisfactorily accomplished on
the voyage from the Philippines to the coast of South America. It was common information of the time that the great
unknown regions of the world lay to the north and to the
south of the familiar trade routes. Terra Australis Incog-

[16] *New Voyage*, pp. 67–68, 70. It is in his *True Account of the South
Sea Trade* that Defoe declares Avery's pirates to be rich.

nita was almost a legend. The Northwest Passage was a legend. Dampier, with more than usual authority, was as ready to suggest regions where discoveries might be made as any other voyager. The habit was so common that Swift later satirized it. Yet part of Dampier's fame was that of an explorer. His geographical knowledge was not to be disputed. Defoe knew well that he could depend upon him.

Outlining the ideal course around the world, Dampier writes:

> Returning you may probably touch somewhere on New Holland, and so make some profitable discovery in these Places without going out of your way. And to speak my Thoughts freely, I believe 't is owing to the neglect of this easie way that all the vast tract of Terra Australis which bounds the South Sea is yet undiscovered: those that cross that Sea seeming to design some Business on the Peruvian or Mexican Coast, and so leaving that at a distance. To confirm which I shall add what Captain Davis told me lately, That after his Departure from us at the Haven of Rea Lejo . . . . he went after several Traverses, to the Gallapagoes, and that standing thence Southward for Wind, to bring him about Terra del Fuego, in the Lat. of 27 South, about 500 leagues from Copayapo, on the Coast of Chili, he saw a small sandy Island just by him; and that they saw to the Westward of it is a long Tract of pretty high Land, tending away toward the North West out of sight. This might probably be the Coast of Terra Australis Incognita.[17]

Similar high land had been seen by others, like Van Schouten and Le Maire.

Defoe, sailing home east from the Ladrones, remarks, "And now, if ever, I expected to do something by way of discovery." Then, having aroused the expectation of new discovery, he supplies it promptly. Sixteen days out from the Ladrones, he sights to the southeast a vast tract of land which extends he believes from the side of New Guinea, "the land lying away from the west-north-west to the south-

[17] *Dampier's Voyages*, I, 357.

east-by-south, still southerly." This land they follow for 120 leagues, when it is suddenly lost. From then on he furnishes new islands and new mainlands aplenty, going as far south as sixty-seven degrees, where he is stopped by cold weather and a mountain of ice. Here Defoe is filling in a scant outline furnished by Le Maire and backed by the authority of William Dampier.

Having discovered new lands, Defoe must people them. His new mainland is clearly an extension of New Guinea with a chain of islands lying off to the southeast, and so the inhabitants take on many characteristics of New Guineans to be found in Dampier's *Voyage to New Holland*, perhaps the most extended account in English. Defoe finds two kinds, friendly natives in the north, treacherous and hostile natives in the south. The New Guineans were well known for their ferocity. Dampier vouches for it, also for their general unattractiveness. They were very black, decidedly negroid, with short frizzly hair. Defoe's northern tribes, however, are quite different, being "a tawny dark brown" in color with long hair falling in ringlets. We suspect Defoe in such cases either to be correct in accordance with the best information available or to be deliberately different for the sake of novelty and variety. We note in Dampier, on one of the first islands visited on the New Guinea coast (Pulo Sabuda), the natives were unlike the "shock curl-pated New Guinea Negroes," being "a Sort of very *tawny* Indians, with *long black* Hair." Their unusual character (doubtless Polynesian) is just what he particularly noted. Furthermore, *tawny* is the precise word used for describing their color in both passages, Defoe using the word at least four other times in the same connection as though fond of it.[18]

Another outstanding feature of Dampier's description of New Guinea is the very large shellfish, or "cockles," in large

[18] *New Voyage*, pp. 121, 132, 135, 141, 142; *Dampier's Voyages*, II, 515.

numbers in shoal water near an island. Because of them he named it "Cockle Island." He filled a boat with them in an hour, one empty shell weighing two hundred and fifty-eight pounds. One cockle furnished wholesome meat for seven or eight men. So Defoe, well down in southern latitudes, finds large oysters, which he conveniently supplies with pearls, allowing his men to spend extra time "shoring" for them. Shoal water, be it known, is the exception rather than the rule in both Dampier and Defoe in these respective regions. Both have shellfish in the shoals but otherwise make frequent reference to deep water close to land. Furthermore, an offshore squall of terrific force in Defoe matches with more than casual similarity the offshore squalls that put Dampier to severe shifts and moved him to name an uncharted island "Squally Island." Native names for gold and extraordinary fondness for hatchets are other converging points in both narratives.[19]

So much for new discoveries in the south. Before Defoe turned southward he discussed with his officers the possibility of discoveries in both the North and the South Pacific. Having to choose one, he decides to go south because of the greater likelihood of meeting islands in the way where provisions could be obtained. He comments, however, considerably on the possibilities in the north, and in doing so leans again definitely on Dampier. At the risk of being tedious, I shall give two long passages which the overladen reader may skip if he choose. Says Defoe, "I had some thoughts of steering away north, to try what land we might meet with to the north-east of the Philippines." He would have made a circle to the north coming down

between the *island of California* and the mainland of America; in which course I did *not question meeting with extraordinary new discoveries*, and, perhaps, such as the age might not expect to hear of,

---

[19] *New Voyage*, pp. 111, 125, 126, 128, 130, 137, 140, 147, 164, 168–72; *Dampier's Voyages*, II, 439, 516–19, 523–24, 528, 530, 536, 537, 549–51.

relating to the northern world, and the possibility of *a passage out of those seas*, either east or west, both which, *I doubt not, would be found*, if they were searched after this way; and which, *for aught I know*, remain undiscovered for want only of an attempt being made by those seas, where it would be easy to find whether the *Tartarian seas are navigable or not;* and whether Nova Zembla be an island or joined to the main; whether the inlets *of Hudson's Bay have any opening into the West Sea;* and whether the vast lakes, from whence the great river of Canada is said to flow, have any communication this way or not.

But the impracticability of following through such a scheme with a trading vessel (and cargo) deterred him. Dampier's recommendations run thus:

This Lake of California (for so the Sea, Channel or Streight, between that and the Continent, is called) is but little known to the Spaniards. [He then recites the rumors about the geography of Lower California] . . . . In my opinion, here might be very advantageous Discoveries made by any who would attempt it: for the Spaniards have more than they can well manage . . . . But the Voyage thither being so far, I take that to be one reason that hath hindered the Discoveries . . . . yet it is possible, that a Man may find a nearer way thither than we came; I mean by the North West.

I know there have been divers attempts made about a North West Passage, and all unsuccessful: yet *I am of opinion,* that *such a Passage may be found.* All our Countrymen that have gone to discover the N. W. Passage, have endeavoured to pass to the Westward, beginning their search along *Davis's or Hudson's Bay.* But if I was to go on this Discovery, I would go first into the South Seas, bend my course from thence along by California, and that way seek a passage back into *the West Seas.* For as others have spent the Summer, in first searching on this more known side nearer home, and so before they got through, the time of year obliged them to give over their search and provide for a long Course back again, for fear of being left in the Winter; on the contrary, I would search first on the less known Coast of the South Sea-side, and then as the Year past away, I should need no retreat, for I should come farther into my knowledge, if I succeeded in my attempt, and should be without that dread and fear which the others must have in passing from the known to the unknown: who, *for aught I know*, gave over their search just as they were on the point of accomplishing their desires. I would take the same method if I was to go to discover the North East Passage. I would winter about Japan, Corea, or the North East part of China; and taking the Spring and Summer before me, I would make my first trial on the *Coast of Tartary*, wherein, if I succeeded, I should come into some unknown Parts, and have a great deal of time before me to reach Archangel or some other Port. Captain Wood, indeed, says, this N. East Passage is not to be found for Ice: but how often do we see that sometimes designs have been given over as impossible, and at another time, have been accomplished. But enough of this.[20]

The precise and constructive suggestions here take the passages out of the classification of the usual blanket recommendation of voyagers. The regions mentioned (Tartary, California, Hudson's Bay, and both the northern passages), the assurance of discoveries to be made there, the new way of sailing for the Northwest Passage—the grouping of these together by both writers could scarcely be coincidence. Defoe adds only the possibility of the western end of the Great Lakes–St. Lawrence system, and names specifically Nova Zembla along the northeast route. Dampier had mentioned Archangel. But especially significant are: the new approach to the Northwest Passage, the use of the term "West Sea," and other similarities in phraseology, such as "for aught I know." The northern voyages of Frobisher and Wood, open before Defoe at the time, contain nothing like this.

DEFOE'S DREAM

There remains something to be said of the relation of Defoe's *New Voyage* to his many schemes and plans for ex-

[20] *New Voyage*, pp. 104 ff.; *Dampier's Voyages*, I, 286–88. Italics are mine.

tending English trade and planting English colonies. The advancement of trade was a lifelong passion with him. In 1697 he wrote against the pressing of seamen (*An Essay on Projects*). One of the major topics of his *Review* was trade. He was very active in the interests of commerce from 1711 to 1714, writing prolifically on trade with France in support of the South Sea project. He engaged in trading ventures himself and was involved in several lawsuits as a result. In 1713 he was urging less of discovery and more trade with known parts of the world.[21]

Walter Raleigh was his greatest hero. In a list of voyagers he declared him the greatest of all because on "the Foot of his genius almost all the English Discoveries were made, and all the Colonies and Plantations . . . . in America were settled and established."[22] In 1719, as we have seen, he prepared *An Historical Account of the Voyages and Adventures of Sir Walter Raleigh,* . . . . in which he recommended the taking over of Guiana by the British. There is, however, a relative lapse in his publications on trade during the period of his novels, 1719–1725. But in 1725 the subject engages his pen again, this time in writing more ambitious pieces, and it is his major concern in the years before his death (1731).[23]

[21] *General History of Trade*, I, 42. Letter to Harley submitting a plan of trade, 1711; *A True Account of the Design and Advantages of the South-Sea Trade* (1712); *The Trade with France, Italy, Spain and Portugal* (1713); *A Brief Account of the . . . . African Trade* (1713); *Considerations of the Eighth and Ninth Articles of the Treaty of Commerce and Navigation* (1713); *An Essay on the Treaty of Commerce with France* (1713); *Some Thoughts upon the Subject of Commerce with France* (1713); *A General History of Trade* (1713); *Mercator: Or, Commerce Retrieved* (May 26, 1713, to July 20, 1714).

[22] *A Plan of the English Commerce* (1728), p. xiii.

[23] *The Complete English Tradesman* (1726); *The History of the Principal Discoveries and Improvements in the Several Arts and Sciences: Particularly the Great Branches of Commerce, Navigation, and Plantation*

In "trade" he distinctly included "navigation and foreign discoveries; because they are, generally speaking, all promoted and carried on by trade."[24] Thus his interest in the sea, in voyages of discovery, and in plantations and trade is all one. It is but natural that books like *Robinson Crusoe, Colonel Jacque, Captain Singleton,* and the *New Voyage* should be written by a man whose greatest interest in life was the development of trade. Defoe's fondest dream was to take a voyage of trade and discovery round the world and establish an English colony.[25] This is what he causes Robinson Crusoe to do in the *Farther Adventures.* . . . . In *Colonel Jacque* he is full of practical advice on how to manage slaves on a Virginia plantation (worth the attention of any modern sociologist). And in the *New Voyage Round the World* he realizes, in imagination, what he has longed to do for years in actuality.

His fondest scheme for colonization was a plan for a settlement in South America below the dominion of the Spanish. When the South Sea project was laid before Parliament in 1711 by the Earl of Oxford, Defoe claimed the idea as his own. In the *Review,* he declared that before King William's death he had laid a plan of colonization on the western shore of South America before him at his Majesty's request and had won his favor. The King, however, died before any action was taken in the matter. He then repeated his idea that there was still room enough left to establish an English colony there. This was in May. On the twenty-third of July he directed to the Earl of Oxford, at the Earl's request, a series of letters laying down his plan in greater

---

in All Parts of the Known World (1727); *A Plan of the English Commerce* (1728).

[24] *Complete English Tradesman* (Oxford ed., 1840), p. 243.

[25] Cf. Masefield, *Masters of Literature: Defoe,* pp. ix–xx; Dottin, *Defoe,* III, 751–52.

detail. This plan was for two settlements, one on the west coast near Valdivia, the other on the east coast somewhere between Rio de la Plata and the Straits of Magellan.[26] The *New Voyage Round the World,* then, was not only Defoe's dream-voyage. It was one of a series of elaborate plans set forth in various ways to promote colonization in South America. John Narborough seems to be his original source of information, but his own previous plans are his source for the last part, which constitutes the most detailed and most imaginative of his schemes, covered only by the thinnest of narratives. A year or so later he repeated the outline of the whole plan in chapter xxii of his *History of the Principal Discoveries and Improvements* (1726–27), "A Proposal for a New Settlement in America."

This whole interest in trade, navigation, and colonization, displayed in plan after plan, running through his narratives as well, but puts the seal of authority upon the frequent traces of Dampier to be found in his narratives. Defoe's enthusiasm for British commerce and his debt to Dampier become sharply and unmistakably focused in the *New Voyage Round the World,* "a fitting close to five years of phenomenal production."[27] It provides a fitting close to this discussion of Dampier's part in the principal narratives of Defoe. Some find the *New Voyage* prosy and dull, but dull is he who has an interest in Defoe and yet cannot see in this book Defoe's imagination "darting forth over the globe . . . . with a sweep and a fervor . . . . which suggest . . . . the spirit of those great Elizabethan adventurers"[28]—and, as I have shown, of William Dampier.

---

[26] *Review of the Affairs of France,* VIII, 165–274. Letters to the Earl of Oxford may be seen in the *British Manuscripts Commission Reports, Report on the Portland MSS,* V, 58–61.

[27] W. P. Trent, *Defoe, How to Know Him* (1916), p. 219.

[28] *Ibid.*

VIII

DAMPIER AND DEFOE

I am not ignorant of Ptolomies assertion, that Perigrinationis historia, and not those wearie volumes bearing the titles of universall Cosmographie which some men that I could name have published as their own, beyng in deed most truly and unprofitablie ramassed and hurled together, is that which must bring us to the certayne and full discoverie of the world.

—RICHARD HAKLUYT, Preface to the
Principall Navigations

MORE PIRATES AND A JOURNEY TO THE MOON

WE HAVE dealt thus far with the better-known narratives of Defoe simply as a natural and easy way of approach. Dampier's influence, however, proves not only to have been strong in this period of Defoe's life but also to have been rather long-lived, appearing once in writings before *Robinson Crusoe* and more than once after the *New Voyage*. To save dragging our weary lengths along any farther in a list of passages and parts, we shall briefly indicate these other places and sum up the grand total for Dampier and Defoe.

In 1705, when Defoe was still known as "the author of the True-Born Englishman," Dampier had published his first three books and was very popular. Defoe had not long been out of prison. He was deep in politics in the employ of Harley, had begun the most influential periodical of the day, the *Review*, but still had time to toss off pamphlets and things like *The Storm* and a dictionary of religions.

In March of this year he put forth a long prose satire called *The Consolidator; or Memoirs of Sundry Transactions from the World in the Moon.* In this work, said to be a forerunner of *Gulliver's Travels,* poets, politicians, wits, and philosophers are satirized by the simple device of a journey to the moon in a machine called a consolidator, from which elevation affairs on earth are viewed with a cosmic and jaundiced eye. The moon-journey begins in Tonquin in Indo-China, a country famous for learning and invention in the mathematical sciences. Certain uncommon points in his description of the Tonquinese, such as their use of firearms and their safety vaults in case of fire and flood, came from Dampier's extended description of these people in *Voyages and Descriptions.* At least no counterparts can be found in other popular works on China and Tonquin.[1]

Advice from the moon amused Defoe for some time later. At least two other papers in this vein appeared before the year was out, *A Second and More Strange Journey to the World in the Moon* and *A Letter from the Man in the Moon, to the Author of the True-born Englishman;* and he was still playing with the idea in the *Review* in April and May, 1710.

On June 11, 1725, occurred a spectacular hanging. A notorious cut-throat and pirate, John Gow, paid the penalty after daringly selling his stolen goods among the Orkney Islands. He was meat for the yellow journalists of the time —a sensation. Defoe, as was his custom, published a pamphlet of his life on the very day of the hanging, advertised as from the very lips of the pirate crew. A paragraph in this yellow sensation betrays Dampier in its mention of Hon-

---

[1] Jean Baptiste Tavernier, "A New and Particular Relation of the Kingdom of Tunquin" in his *Six Voyages of John Baptista Tavernier* (London, 1678); John Nieuhoff, *An Embassy from the East India Company . . . . to China* (London, 1669).

duras, the Bay of Campeachy, buccaneers, and logwood cutters—places and people poor Captain Gow never knew.

In 1726 appeared another "voyage," usually now attributed to the indefatigable Defoe, *The Four Years Voyages of Capt. George Roberts; being a Series of Uncommon Events Which befell him in a Voyage to the Islands of the Canaries, Cape de Verde, and Barbadoes.* This dull piece has been thought to be by a poor imitator of Defoe or by an actual Captain Roberts whose literary regurgitations Defoe assisted. In the story, Roberts, a Guinea trader, quarrels with his captain at Barbadoes and sails for Guinea in a self-equipped sloop. Pirates plunder him and set him adrift with no sails or food. He is wrecked on the unfrequented and almost inaccessible island of St. John, one of the Cape Verde group. In two years he has supervised the construction of another craft and so returns to England, *anno* 1725. Every voyager must do his describing or get someone who can. Says Roberts, turn to Dampier for a description of the silk cotton tree. He himself (or Defoe) turns to him for "flaws" of wind off the headlands, the harbor at Oratavia, adulterated or fraudulent ambergris like the excrement of animals, and the drying or "kerning" of salt.

DEFOE AND DAMPIER

If the reader has survived to this point, he must feel that either Defoe knew Dampier's *Voyages* almost by heart or he turned to Dampier as occasion arose as one turns to a standard reference work. We know that some such familiarity existed for twenty years (1705 to 1726), and in all probability from the appearance of Dampier's first book in 1697 to Defoe's death in 1731. For routes of travel, for winds and storms, for a thousand nautical and domestic details in far-off places he found Dampier an ever-ready and reliable source. Thus Robinson Crusoe, Friday, Captain

Singleton, and others all have Dampier in their pedigree and are the taller for it.

It is also very probable that Dampier's plain writing did something to Defoe's style. Note how the principle of selection operates in the work of both men, but toward different ends. With Dampier the chief business is exposition. When he is called upon to narrate, he does so not only with simplicity and winning self-effacement but with severe economy. With Defoe the chief business is to tell an interesting tale and a moral one. He, accordingly, has need not so much for exposition as for details of human interest. When Robinson Crusoe builds a hut or canoe, he gives plenty of descriptive and explanatory detail because it is business of human interest: the life of Crusoe depends on it. When Dampier tells how to make a canoe it is to explain to Englishmen at home how West Indian canoes are made. As noted previously, in *Captain Singleton* and the *New Voyage Round the World* Defoe appears to fill in with interesting details the fine openings left by Dampier, who skips over a good story of mutiny. Both authors practice the business of hurrying lightly over non-essential details in similar phrases— "I shall not trouble the reader," and the like.

With these differences of objective, the travels of Dampier and the fictitious travel-narratives of Defoe are composed in kindred spirit. Charles Lamb shrewdly felt this, although Dampier was not in his mind when he wrote the famous letters to Walter Wilson about Defoe. In Defoe's style, he wrote, "there is all the minute detail of a log-book. Dates are painfully pressed upon the memory. Facts are repeated over and over in varying phrases, till you cannot choose but believe them . . . . His style is very beautiful, but plain and *homely*. Robinson Crusoe is delightful to all ranks and classes . . . . it is an especial favourite with seafaring men, poor boys, servant-maids, etc."[2]

[2] *Letters* (Bohn Library, London, 1886), II, 105.

Considered thus, Defoe's simplicity and homeliness seem in themselves to be a reflection of the simplicity and homeliness of the travel-work that he was most familiar with and most influenced by. Merely to make that statement does not, of course, make it true. One should recall that Defoe not only made generous use of Dampier for interesting details but more than once reflects his phrases. Then, too, among the travels that Defoe had read and was reading, Dampier's *Voyages* stood out as the most genuine and at the same time the most carefully composed up to that time, with the possible exception of Rogers' *Cruising Voyage*. I have shown that they were the most interesting since the collections of Hakluyt and Purchas. Biographers of Defoe point to *Robinson Crusoe* as a turning-point in his writing career. He turned from pamphleteering, versifying, and journalism to the composition of long narratives. It is for us to remember that in *Robinson Crusoe* he also first turned to Dampier in any large way, a thing which he did many times thereafter. At least we may say that in Dampier he found a model for his new type of writing: the art of selection practiced to a high degree, a constant striving for novelty, and a confessed appeal to the average reader.

Defoe's journalistic years play their part and should not be minimized in the least. But how different is his sermon on the ways of Providence called *The Storm* from his sermon on the same subject called *Robinson Crusoe?* How different are his arguments on trade and politics in the *Review? The Storm* is but a tedious, dull piece of reporting of the disaster of 1703. The facts are remarkable, but they are dull because there is so much of the same thing. It is clear that Defoe had not at that time observed, or at least did not then observe, the fine sensitiveness he later shows for the attention of the reader. Years later, writing fiction often saturated with the accounts of voyagers (chiefest and freshest of which is Dampier), he adopts the manner and style of Dampier and succeeds as he never did before. His own "natural infirmity of homely plain writing" finds a counterpart in Dampier. The old morality he retains, but reduced. *Robinson Crusoe* and later works are studied performances to inform the reader of strange events and places.

The island experience of Robinson Crusoe has so dominated the whole story that we commonly lose sight of Crusoe the insatiable traveler, Crusoe the trader, and Crusoe the voyager three-quarters round the globe. One forgets that Defoe himself in Volume II called his book the "Travels and Adventures of Robinson Crusoe." It is really a voyage to the South Sea and the East Indies with moral applications. Dampier is a model to Defoe's taste. His resourcefulness he reincarnates in Crusoe. What other details he needs, he takes, or remembers, just as he took from others. Capitalizing on the stream of interest in geography and the general South Sea craze, Defoe was not slow in going immediately to its fountainhead.

Thus eight of Defoe's narratives derive their substance in part from Dampier's *Voyages*. Hakluyt, Purchas, Ides, and Le Comte are Dampier's nearest rivals. But Ides and Le Comte figure in only one or two places and there, because of their subject-matter, in a definitely limited way. Hakluyt and Purchas have been said to provide the broad background of Defoe's geographical knowledge[3] and thus have been accorded first place among works influencing *Robinson Crusoe* and *Captain Singleton*. Yet specific narratives and parts of narratives in them can seldom be definitely cited. One suspects, therefore, that this high place has been granted them out of respect for their classic position in voyage literature and in deference to the fact that Defoe owned copies.

In view of Dampier's extensive and demonstrable influence on Defoe, he must now be placed first in relative impor-

---

[3] Secord, *op. cit.*, pp. 89, 114, 241, 242.

tance. Whereas the events in Hakluyt and Purchas were dim in Defoe's mind, the events of more nearly contemporary and contemporary works to which he turned were often noticeably clear. This study has attempted to show for the first time just how far this is true with regard to Dampier.

On this point it is scarcely possible to emphasize enough the fact that Defoe's geographical knowledge was strictly modern, strictly fresh. It was certainly not a part of the background furnished by the Elizabethans. Being eager all his life to found a colony in South America, he kept himself informed of the coast, climate, and country of Patagonia and Guiana. Several times he was prepared to lay down specific plans for such an enterprise, even to the minute details of soundings of rivers and shore—everything necessary to navigation. His ideas of the distant parts of the world, particularly of unexplored regions, were consistent with the most advanced information of his time. Defoe was progressive in the less dignified sense of the term. The old he felt should give way to the new. He ardently supported trade and the development of colonial business. And for this purpose he seems to have felt that his geography must be the latest and best.

Finally, because of all this we can now see that Defoe was rather closely connected with the "new science." His attitude toward the study of mathematics, the importance of navigation, the colonial expansion of England, and the decided taste for reading travels reveals a definite leaning in that direction. His practical nature and common sense are further appropriate endowments. Yet one student of the effects of the new science upon English literature declares that, whereas Robinson Crusoe himself has "the inventive genius of a virtuoso," Defoe "was doubtless wholly unconscious of the connection with the new science," that on the whole Defoe's attitude was so obscure and his use of new material so slight that he reveals "innate and temperamental indifference."[4] This conclusion is not only hasty but incorrect. Defoe's innate and temperamental zeal for travels reveals the proper frame of mind for "new material." His close relations with William Dampier, who took a definite part in the advance of science, bring him into touch with it. He took from Dampier and others some of the very new material to which he is supposed to have been indifferent. He could hardly have been unaware that he was endowing Robinson Crusoe with the inventive genius of a virtuoso—or a William Dampier.

[4] A. S. Duncan, *The New Science and English Literature in the Classical Period* (Menasha, Wis., 1913), p. 171.

IX

COUSIN GULLIVER

By your great and frequent urgency you prevailed on me to
publish a very loose and incorrect account of my travels, with
direction to hire some young gentleman of either university to
put them in order and correct the style, as my cousin Dampier
did by my advice in his book called "A Voyage Round the
World."

—CAPTAIN GULLIVER to his Cousin Sympson

AMONG the outstanding prose works of the early eighteenth century it is *Gulliver's Travels*, rather than the
fictitious voyages written by Defoe, that most nearly con-
forms to our idea of the literature of travel: an imaginative
work shaped out of the material (or suggestions) in the accounts of real voyages. The sweep of imagination is grander,
the purpose more artfully disguised, the frame on which the
story hangs just as true to real accounts. It is not only one
of the most treasured books in the language; it is the one
most necessary to study closely in connection with the reading tastes for voyages and travels that for thirty years preceded it. Our study is of William Dampier. It is no surprise
to find that the giant intellect of Swift turned to this rugged
old mariner for more than one suggestion.

We shall be concerned almost wholly with the nautical
parts of the narrative. The political significance of *Gulliver's Travels* should never, of course, be forgotten; but we
cannot deal with it here except where it crosses our path in
searching for possible influences of Dampier. The wretched-

ness of the Yahoos, for example, has long been considered to be some reflection of the wretched condition of the Irish people. Yet the realistic details of Swift's descriptions have lately been shown to have derived from books of travel. In the "Letter from Captain Gulliver to his Cousin Sympson written in the year 1727" and inserted then between the address of the publisher to the reader and the beginning of the first voyage, Swift facetiously takes to account the mythical Sympson for persuading him to publish his travels as Dampier did, loosely thrown together and corrected by someone else. This reference not only indicates a knowledge of Dampier's principal book, but it has been taken also to mean that Swift actually modeled his book somewhat after Dampier. Sir Walter Scott, with his customary enthusiasm, remarks about Gulliver: "The character of the imaginary traveller is exactly that of Dampier, or any other sturdy nautical wanderer of the period endowed with courage and common sense."[1]

Further interest in the background of *Gulliver's Travels* has been evinced by scholars who have found apparently all the predecessors of Swift in the tradition of the "extraordinary voyage," philosophic and fantastic things like Cyrano de Bergerac's voyage to the moon. A few German scholars have published their "*Quellen zu Swift's Gulliver.*" They have, however, almost universally omitted any examination of actual voyages and travels and have been reminded of the fact by at least one alert reviewer.[2] Certainly one reader of trav-

[1] *Memoirs of Jonathan Swift, D.D.*, in Swift's *Works* (ed. Walter Scott, 2d ed., Edinburgh, 1824), I, 338–39.

[2] See William A. Eddy, *Gulliver's Travels: A Critical Study* (Princeton, 1923), and articles by E. Hönncher and Theodore Borkowsky in *Anglia* (X, 397–428, XV, 345–99) and by Max Poll in the *Bulletin* of the University of Cincinnati, No. 24. See also the review of Professor Eddy's excellent book by Professor Secord, *Journal of English and Germanic Philology*, XXIII, 461–62.

els has pointed out many accounts of hideous Hottentots and other loathsome aborigines from whom Swift may have gathered suggestions for his Yahoos.[3] Thus the way has been pointed out. Let us pursue it in the direction of Dampier's *Voyages.*

It is not difficult to establish the fact that Swift had read Dampier. The reference to him in *Gulliver's Travels* (just quoted) really indicates that Swift knew one of the later volumes of Dampier as well as the *New Voyage.* For it is in the preface to the *Voyage to New Holland* that he reveals the charges against him of letting others write his books, and it is there that he justifies himself on the grounds that the best authors solicit the corrections of their friends. One may also examine profitably Swift's reading at two very interesting periods of his life. Fortunately a short list of books that he was reading in 1697 and 1698 is preserved.[4] Among the thirty-six titles recorded are six books of travel. This indicates an interest in voyages during his residence at Moor Park in the very years that Dampier's first book appeared. It was also about the time of the composition of *A Tale of a Tub.* In the *Tale* itself there is indication that Swift knew three others. At the very end of the *Travels,* Gulliver (who may or may not represent Swift) remarks, "I have perused several books of travel with great delight in my younger days."

Swift's correspondence with Vanessa shows that he was reading travels in the summer of 1722, during the time of the composition of *Gulliver's Travels.*[5] In August, Swift wrote, "When you are melancholy, read diverting or amus-

[3] R. W. Frantz, "Swift's Yahoos and the Voyagers," in *Modern Philology,* XXIX, 49–57.

[4] Guthkelch and Smith edition of *A Tale of a Tub* (Oxford, 1920), p. liii.

[5] This was begun, declares Professor Eddy, in 1720.

ing books." And we find that on July 13 he had written to her: "The use I have made of it [the bad weather] was to read I know not how many diverting books of history and travels." Swift amused himself, then, by reading voyages, studies congenial to the composition of the *Travels*. He confessed to Mrs. Whiteway that he had borrowed the sea-terms in *Gulliver's Travels* "from the old voyages, which he had fully perused." Furthermore, the sale catalogue of Swift's small library made by George Faulkner in 1745 still exists. While more than half the books in it were in the learned languages, yet English voyages were well represented.

This merely indicates that Swift, like Defoe, was a wide reader of voyages and travels. He caught the contemporary spirit of voyaging, as is demonstrated by some of his other titles, either derived from seamen's lore or creating the atmosphere of a traveler's journal: *A Tale of a Tub*, 1704; his grave, lying two-penny pamphlet, *A Journey to Paris*; and *An Account of the Court and Empire of Japan*, a satire written in 1728. He planned to write still another satire on England, to be called, *A Voyage into England, by a Person of Quality in Terra Australis Incognita, translated from the original*, but Addison, as he complained, took the hint and used it in the *Spectator* (for April 27, 1711) by introducing four Indian kings on a visit to London. "Terra Australis Incognita," or New Holland, was a region that delighted his fancy. He sends Gulliver there on two of his voyages, and in a third causes him to skirt the northern shore en route home. It is this continent that Lord Peter in *A Tale of a Tub* sells over and over again. Swift pretended to write *The Mechanical Operation of the Spirit* from chambers in the Academy of the Beaux Esprits in New Holland. He humorously proposed, at the end of the *Tale of a Tub*, a project of printing a description of Terra Australis Incognita in ninety-six folio volumes.

Although the Antarctic continent was already legend, as evidenced by such tales as James Sadeur's *A New Discovery of Terra Incognita Australis, or the Southern World* (London, 1693), such an interest in New Holland points indirectly to Dampier. The *New Voyage Round the World* provoked the attention of royalty because of its mention of New Holland and the possibility of discoveries to be made there. Dampier's later volumes, which I at least am certain Swift had read, contained the most detailed description of those shores known to the world. Much of the common talk, therefore, about New Holland in the twenty years before *Gulliver's Travels* derived from the captain of the "Roebuck."

We are aided much more by Swift himself, however, who in 1715 made a list of his own books wherein Dampier's *New Voyage Round the World* (3d ed., 1698), autographed by Swift, appeared. This list (now in the possession of Mr. T. P. Le Fanu) is corroborated further by the appearance of the autographed volume itself in 1929 at the sale in New York of Mr. Jerome Kern's library.[6] Although it does not appear to be an annotated volume, we are safe in assuming that Swift knew its contents and probably its author well. Swift did not own useless books.

Considering thus Swift's taste for travels and the works actually in his library, it is no extraordinary thing that *Gulliver's Travels* should be written in a style like Dampier's. The influence of Dampier upon Swift in this way, however, I think has been too hastily assumed because of Swift's own statement. What one must also bear in mind is Swift's style as revealed in his other works. Unless *Gulliver's Travels* is at once different from Swift's other writing and yet much like Dampier's *Voyages*, or unless all of Swift's writing can be shown to be influenced by Dampier, we cannot claim this. Neither of these can be demonstrated

[6] Harold Williams, *Dean Swift's Library* (1932), pp. 3, 7, 72 n.

by argument or diagram. What may be said is that the two styles are in general of the same kind, "clear, masculine, and smooth, but not florid," as Captain Gulliver describes the style of the Brobdingnagians. They both "avoid nothing more than multiplying unnecessary words, or using various expressions." The affinity between them is much the same as that between Defoe and Dampier and between Defoe and Swift. This does not preclude the fact that Swift modeled certain parts of the particular work, *Gulliver's Travels,* upon Dampier. Two minds with so much of the same downrightness, meeting as they surely did, could not fail to be drawn together.

Gulliver's declaration that he was "not so studious of ornament as of truth," his "principal design" being "to inform, and not to amuse thee," is in quite the same mood as Dampier's prefaces in which he refuses "to divert the Reader" with the "Actions of the Company" (the buccaneers), and in which he announces his intention "to give only True Relations" to readers who desire a "Plain and Just Account of the true Nature and State of things described, than of a Polite and Rhetorical Narrative." It takes no stretch of the imagination to conceive that Swift is gently mocking Dampier, so much the same is his language. On the other hand, the idea of simple, unadorned prose in preference to rhetorical prose may be only the common ground of the new scientific prose upon which they both stand.

Again, regarding "Sea-Terms" Dampier early writes that he has steered a middle course, divesting himself of some and including others: "I confess I have not been at all scrupulous in this matter, either as to the one or the other of these; for I am perswaded, that if what I say be intelligible, it matters not greatly in what words it is express'd." So, too, Swift shakes off the responsibility for his famous nautical passage by making the droll Gulliver, addressing his "Cousin Sympson," charge its obscurity to fashions (new words) in sea language. Also, in Richard Sympson's "Publisher to the Reader," Swift extravagantly declares that the editing out of nautical descriptions has reduced the matter one-half. This may seem to have been suggested by Dampier's phrase in his first preface: "I have frequently indeed, divested my self of Sea Phrases, to gratify the Land Reader"; but it unquestionably came from another part of Dampier. The passage from Swift should first be quoted in full. Says Richard Sympson:

> This volume would have been at least twice as large, if I had not made bold to strike out innumerable passages relating to the winds and tides, as well as to the variations and bearings in the several voyages, together with the minute descriptions of the management of the ship in storms, in the style of sailors; wherein I have reason to apprehend that Mr. Gulliver may be a little dissatisfied: but I was resolved to fit the work as much as possible to the general capacity of readers.

Now this is a satire on the tedious character of travel books in general, to which in certain respects Dampier must plead guilty, and against which Defoe also protested. But it is also a clear reflection of Dampier's first preface and his first volume. "I write for my Countrymen," he declared, in justification of his style and spelling. Then he adds:

> The Reader will find as he goes along, some References to an Appendix, which I once designed to this Book; as to a Chapter about the Winds in different parts of the World; to a description of the Bay of Campeachy in the West Indies, where I lived long in a former Voyage; and to a particular Chorographical Description of the South Sea Coast of America. . . . . But such an Appendix would have swelled it too unreasonably: and therefore I chose rather to publish it hereafter by its self, as opportunity shall serve.[7]

The chorographical description never saw the light, but the rest appeared as Dampier's second volume, *Voyages and De-*

---

[7] For these remarks, see *Dampier's Voyages*, I, 20–21.

scriptions, a book four-fifths as large as his first. According to the seventeenth-century meaning of "chorography," the proposed description would have become a South Sea waggoner, or pilot-book, with soundings, bearings, charts, and such nautical information, and would have swelled the second volume to considerably more than the size of the first. As a matter of fact, *Voyages and Descriptions* consisted of three parts as follows: (1) a supplement to the *New Voyage;* (2) a description of several voyages to Campeachy; and (3) "A Discourse of Trade-Winds, Breezes, Storms, Seasons of the Year, Tides and Currents of the Torrid Zone throughout the World." The last of these is important.

Here, then, was a living example of what Cousin Sympson declared he had done to *Gulliver's Travels.* Dampier literally cut down his first material one-half, and in his second volume gave a third of his space to winds, currents, and tides. Unquestionably also Swift was annoyed at Dampier's tables of latitude and approximate longitude for every day's run across the Pacific, inserted with considerable comment in chapter x of the *New Voyage Round the World.* Whether or not Swift had read *Voyages and Descriptions* is not important here. He *did* read the passage just quoted from the first preface, and it contained the idea found in the early pages of *Gulliver's Travels.* Swift's remark is therefore something more than a jibe at all over-nautical accounts. It is certainly in part from Dampier, and, on the basis of cumulative evidence, probably almost entirely so. More than once in the course of his imaginary voyaging he had Dampier in mind, and no traveler whom Swift could have read so accurately supplies the idea as Dampier. One should recall that the "Discourse of Trade-Winds" proved Dampier the most informed English sailor of his day. Nothing like it had been written before. It was one of the chief contributing causes of his fame.

The honesty of Dampier's accounts particularly stands

out, as it naturally would in a day when many real voyages were filled out by the writers' imaginations. As in the case of Defoe, certain phrases may be noted in *Gulliver's Travels* that echo Dampier, such as "I shall not trouble the reader"; and certain satirical thrusts that I shall point out later.

The I-shall-not-trouble-the-reader kind of apology for omission of details we have already seen in connection with Defoe, who appears to have adopted it from Dampier, too. Dampier's phrase was normally as above: "I shall not trouble the Reader with my observations at that Isle" or "But not to trouble the Reader any further with Matters of this Nature." Gulliver, returning from Lilliput, says, "I shall not trouble the reader with a particular account of this voyage." Going out he said, "It would not be proper, for some reasons, to trouble the reader with the particulars of our adventures in those seas." Such a stereotyped phrase is not common outside of Dampier, Defoe, and Swift. It may simply be common to them all. Swift may have caught it from Defoe, and Defoe from Dampier. Or both Defoe and Swift may have borrowed it from Dampier.

In literary finish and vigor the travels of Swift and Dampier are, of course, not comparable. One is the work of an artist great and powerful; the other is the journal of a seaman honest and observing. It is in elements other than style that the influence of Dampier may best be noticed. There is no question that the character of Gulliver is much like that of Dampier. From earliest boyhood Gulliver longed to go to sea. Accordingly, when the first opportunity came he learned "navigation and other parts of mathematics useful to those who intend to travel." He was "condemned by nature and fortune [like Dampier] to an active and restless life." He spent a total of nine and a half years in early voyages to the Levant and the East and West Indies. Dampier spent roughly nine years in early undescribed voyages before he left England on the voyage that eventually carried him around the world. Gulliver was an unusual sailor, being educated beyond the average. "My hours of leisure," says he, "I spent in reading the best authors, ancient and modern, being always provided with a good number of books." Dampier spent his leisure time in observing everything and writing his journals. He found time to read the accounts of former voyages, and carried valuable books and papers with him. Gulliver ashore always observed the manners and dispositions of the people and learned their language, wherein he had "great facility," by strength of memory. Dampier was acute in observing and learning many languages in the course of his voyages. Again, Captain Peacock of Bristol, whom Gulliver meets at Teneriffe on his way out on his last voyage, is clearly a portrait of Dampier.

> On the 14th, we met with Captain Peacock of Bristol, at *Teneriffe*, who was going on to the *Bay of Campeachy to cut logwood* . . . . He was an *honest* man, and a good *sailor*, but a little *too positive* in his own opinions which was the cause of *his destruction*, as it had been of *several others*.[8]

Enough of Dampier's life and character has already been made known in this study to make immediately apparent that every action and characteristic, except one, assigned to Captain Peacock belong also to Dampier, some peculiarly so. On his last and most prosperous voyage he too sailed from Bristol. But Bristol was the second city in England and a great port. It is the mention of logwood-cutting in the Bay of Campeachy, of honesty coupled with good seamanship, and of positive opinions that speak for Dampier. Dampier had once foundered, but escaped alive. Otherwise the description fits him too well to have existed by chance. His journals and reputation at home speak for his honesty. His seamanship was widely recognized as pre-eminent. And his troubles with

[8] Swift, *Works* (ed. Walter Scott, 2d ed., Edinburgh, 1824), XI, 23, 24, 107. "Peacock" is "Pocock" in the early editions.

insubordinate crews on the voyages in the "Roebuck" and the "Saint George," already alluded to, were considered by many to be due to his own stubbornness in command.[9]

No one has ever commented on the fact that Gulliver's entire wandering life, being a series of four long voyages, is strikingly like Dampier's. No figure in Swift's time or before it furnishes so near and interesting a parallel. Drake and Raleigh had made several voyages, it is true; and Drake had been once around the world. But besides this there is little in their characters or their accounts like the character and actions of Gulliver. A tabulation of the voyages of Dampier and Gulliver demonstrates the parallel more plainly than discussion.

It is well known that members of the Scriblerus Club had determined years before that the travels of Martin should be four voyages (to the land of the pygmies, to the land of the giants, to the land of philosophers and mathematicians, and to a fourth land, undetermined, where his contempt for man would be shown). The parallel with Dampier, therefore, is interesting principally for the realistic details which it exhibits. It is, furthermore, the fashion among biographers of Swift to conceive of Gulliver as Swift, and the four voyages as his journeys in England and Ireland. Despite these, the parallel I indicate opposite challenges our attention.

Each of these eight voyages is to a remote region, and Gulliver's are all expediently to places quite unknown, or at least very little known, New Holland being conspicuous. Dampier's part in suggesting this region is made more compelling when we recall not only his remarks in the *New Voyage* and the fame entailed by his later disastrous voyage there but also the fact that his account of New Holland appeared in two distinct volumes several years apart, therefore

[9] Such is the gist of William Funnell's remarks and inferences, and the court-martial of 1702 held Dampier responsible for the trouble with Lieutenant Fisher.

DAMPIER	GULLIVER
I To the South Sea and around the world with the buccaneers in several ships, 1681–1691. (Coasted the northern shore of New Holland.)	
II To New Holland in the "Roebuck," 1699–1701. (Met the "Antelope.")	I To New Holland (Lilliput) in the "Antelope," 1699–1702.
III To the South Sea and around the world in the "St. George," 1703–1707.	II To Alaska (Brobdingnag) in the "Adventure," 1702–1706. (Coasted northern shore of New Holland.)
IV To the South Sea and around the world in the "Duke" and "Dutchess," 1708–1711.	III To Pacific islands near Japan (Laputa, etc.) in the "Hopewell," 1706–1710.
	IV To New Holland (Land of the Houyhnhnms) in the "Adventure," 1710–1715.

easily augmenting Dampier's fame in this connection or even giving the offhand impression that two voyages were made. Further interesting parallels may be seen in the dates of the voyages. Excepting the first of Dampier and the last of Gulliver, there is close correspondence in the length of time spent and the actual dates. Elsewhere in this chapter I have mentioned the similarity of the early years of these wanderers.

It may be to the point to recall that Gulliver progressed, as Dampier did, from a lesser office on shipboard to the captaincy "of several ships." The title-pages of Dampier's several volumes and the two title-pages in the early editions of *Gulliver's Travels* record this rise to rank. On the first of the latter, Gulliver is "LEMUEL GULLIVER, First a SURGEON, and then a CAPTAIN of several Ships." On the second, he is just "*Captain* LEMUEL GULLIVER." This is precisely how Dampier's title-pages follow his career. As a matter of fact, Gulliver was captain in but one ship. He was chief surgeon on his third voyage and merely shared command. The description "then a captain of several ships" applies to Dampier better than to Gulliver. Dampier's *New Voyage* is "By William Dampier." All the later volumes are "By Captain William Dampier." Maps in the *New Voyage* showing "Mr. Dampier's course" around the world eventually also print his name "Captain Dampier." So much for the parallel in their lives.

Gulliver's voyage to Lilliput is made in the "Antelope" from Bristol. He leaves for the East Indies, presumably by way of the Cape of Good Hope, on May 4, 1699. It is difficult to think that this was written by chance when we know that Dampier, sailing for New Holland also in 1699 in the "Roebuck," should meet on the third of June off the Cape of Good Hope the "Antelope" of London bound for the East Indies. Dampier boarded the East Indiaman, exchanged courtesies, and was recognized—a tribute to his fame. Dampier "jog'd on in company with the *Antelope* until the next day" and had sight of her for two more days.

The slender framework of voyaging upon which Swift hangs his satire also owes something to Dampier. The course of Gulliver to Brobdingnag proves to be an adaptation of Dampier's course to New Holland. As far as weather is concerned, both have an easy run to the Cape of Good Hope. Gulliver enjoys "a very prosperous gale," a favorite expression of Dampier. About and beyond the Cape they are both concerned with westerly winds and both comment on them. They are both there in the autumn (May and June). Beyond the Cape, Dampier and the "Antelope" part company, Dampier assuring the reader that the man bound for New

Holland and the East Indies should turn a bit south here. If he heads too far north, Dampier warns, he will be put by his regular easterly course. Gulliver, however, sails north of Madagascar to take advantage of the westerly monsoon. Although this is contrary to the express directions of Dampier, it is in accord with Dampier's map of trade winds in an earlier book (*Voyages and Descriptions*) where an arrow just north of Capricorn marks the westerly monsoon and is labeled "May." The particular use made of these winds, moreover, shows further that Swift was following Dampier's lead in the matter and that he had read Dampier's description of winds and storms in the *Voyage to New Holland*. Gulliver remarks as he turns north,

The winds, which *in those seas are observed* to blow a *constant* equal *gale between the north and west*, from the beginning of *December to the beginning of May*, on the 19th of April began with *much greater violence*, and *more westerly than usual continuing* so for twenty days together.

Gulliver's "constant equal gale" from the west for twenty consecutive days is matched by Dampier's gales from the west, which blew for thirteen consecutive days. Says he:

Having *still* a *Westerly Wind* I jog'd on in company with the *Antelope* . . . . The Wind increased upon us . . . . this *being Winter here*, and the Time for bad Weather, I expected and prepared for a *violent* blast of Wind . . . . The Wind blew extraordinary hard all Wednesday, the 7th of June, but abated of its fierceness before Night; Yet it *continued a brisk Gale* till about the 16th, and still a moderate one till the 19th Day; by which time we had run about 600 Leagues: For the *most part of which time* the Wind was *in some point of the West*. . . . . It blew hardest when at the W. . . . . *This I observed* at other times *in these Seas* . . . . we like them never the worse for being *violent*, for they drive us the faster to the Eastward; and are therefore the only Winds coveted by those who Sail towards such parts of the East-Indies as lye South of the Equator . . . . [these winds] in the *Winter Season* of these Climates they soon meet with; for then the *Winds are generally Westerly at the Cape.*[10]

In both accounts the continued westerly blow is succeeded by violent storms. Gulliver is already beyond the Moluccas. Dampier has traveled 600 leagues to the east. Gulliver's storm then blows him 500 leagues farther, into the Pacific. Dampier works hard to keep the "Roebuck" clear of the shore of New Holland. Both put ashore for water, being desperate for lack of it, but find none. Dampier furthermore notices large "Sampier" and other grasses that grow in tufts as big as a bushel. Gulliver's first surprising observation upon the barren rocky shores of Brobdingnag is the unusual size of the grass, "which, in those grounds that seemed to be kept for hay, was about twenty feet high."

The emphasis in both these passages is noticeably on continued, violent, westerly gales met in the winter season near the Cape of Good Hope. Other accounts of the route by the Cape might have given Swift the mere knowledge of west winds there in the winter, but I have met no other passage that remotely approaches this parallel.[11]

Gulliver's remark to the sea captain who picks him up after his adventures in this land of giants is further to the point. The astonished captain suggests that he publish his travels upon returning, but Gulliver replies: "that I thought we were overstocked with books of travels: that nothing could now pass that was not extraordinary: wherein I doubted some authors less consulted truth than their own

[10] Swift, *op. cit.*, p. 108; *Dampier's Voyages*, II, 416, 417, 418–19. Italics are mine.

[11] Francis Drake found it pleasant enough, contrary to the descriptions circulated by the Portuguese. Misson describes a bad storm at the Cape in his fictitious *Voyage of François Leguat*, but there is no similarity in details with Gulliver's storm.

vanity, or interest, or the diversion of ignorant readers; that my story could contain little beside common events, without those ornamental descriptions of strange plants, trees, birds, and other animals; or, of the barbarous people, with which most writers abound." Here is not only confirmation of the great popularity of travels at this time, but a criticism of a type of voyage of which Dampier's was outstanding, one full of descriptions of natural phenomena. It is one of the products of the Royal Society and the "new science" with which Dampier had close connections. Throughout his books, but particularly in the *Voyage to New Holland,* he emphasizes (with descriptions and plates) plants, birds, trees, fish, and the rest. Sir Hans Sloane's *Natural History of Jamaica* (1707) is more offensive in this regard than possibly any other book of the time and would naturally draw the fire of Swift. It is the association with New Holland, however, that points more directly to Dampier. Gulliver's phrase "wherein I doubted some authors less consulted truth than their own vanity" is completely in accord with some statements of Dampier already discussed in connection with his plainness of style. Swift had read these in the dedication of the *New Voyage.* Writes Dampier, "I have not so much of the Vanity of a Traveller, as to be fond of telling Stories, especially of this kind."

Gulliver's other voyages are all described with greater despatch than the voyage to Brobdingnag, leaving little opportunity for the employment of details from any source whatever, or at least little more than stock and traditional mariners' experiences. Even here, however, certain hasty touches suggest Dampier. On the first voyage, Swift takes Gulliver in a sentence from Bristol to Van Diemen's Land. There is left little to do but wreck him. In the voyage to Laputa, Gulliver is taken quickly to Tonquin but he gives no description of the country. Instead, he is made master of a sloop with fourteen men and sent out to trade. It is while on this mission that he is boarded by pirates and a Dutchman and set adrift in a small canoe. So also part of Dampier's experience in the East Indies on his first voyage around the world was trading out of Achin (on Sumatra) to Fort St. George and Tonquin, but particularly Tonquin. Furthermore, it was by an English captain recently from Tonquin that Gulliver was rescued from the sea at the end of the previous voyage. The ship turned southwest, coasting New Holland, as Dampier had done after his experiences in Tonquin and the East Indies. In both passages there is the association of places prominent in Dampier's first *Voyage* and not to be observed in any other account of travel that Swift might have read.

On his last voyage, the voyage on which he meets Captain Peacock, Gulliver proceeds first to the West Indies, where he recruits more men for his ship, buccaneers from Barbadoes and the Leeward Islands, in the region of much of Dampier's own buccaneering but celebrated in a half-dozen books popular in Swift's day. But, like Dampier, Gulliver is an explorer. "My orders were, that I should trade with the Indians in the South Seas, and make what discoveries I could." It may easily be that Swift had Dampier in mind here, rather than anyone else, because these remarks follow immediately (in sequential paragraphs) the description of Captain Peacock of Bristol, which was certainly meant for Dampier.

One of Gulliver's remarks about maps is also of interest. Robinson Crusoe's correction of errors on existing maps was not necessarily an indication that Defoe was following Dampier. Neither is it true in the case of Gulliver except for certain additional satirical touches. Gulliver, departing from Houyhnhnm-land, which he estimated was in forty-five degrees south latitude southeast of Madagascar, sails east, intending to make "the south-west coast of New Holland, and perhaps some island as I desired, lying westward of it."

From a small island he sights land ahead running from south to north. He continues to sail east and passes *under* New Holland, arriving at the southeastern point on the second day, much sooner than he expected. He remarks then: "This confirmed me in the opinion I have long entertained, that the maps and charts place this country at least three degrees more to the east than it really is; which thought I communicated many years ago to my worthy friend Mr. Herman Moll, and gave him my reasons for it, although he has rather chosen to follow other authors."

Swift is here bringing into his narrative a common point of argument among mariners of the old school—the calculation of distances east and west. There was no exact longitude until after 1735, only differences of longitude. Sea captains logged their ships and kept their records in leagues or "Italian miles" from well-known points. They watched carefully variations north or south from the straight east or west course in a given day's sailing. For the benefit of those who might follow after, they sometimes left charts of long runs with all possible mathematical detail at their command.

Spread on Dampier's pages are two discussions of longitude that will bear examination in connection with Gulliver's remark. Notably, in the volume owned by Swift appear charts of every day's run across the South Sea to Guam. Following the chart he takes up carefully the question of the total distance. If we figure on a basis of "60 Italian miles to an Equinoctial degree," he says, "the South Sea must be of greater breadth by 25 degrees, than it's commonly reckoned by Hydrographers, who make it only about 100, more or less."

For further verification of his point he adds that the breadth of the Indian Sea

must be considerably less than 't is generally calculated to be; if it be true what I have heard over and over, from several able Seamen, whom I have conversed with in these parts, that Ships sailing from the Cape of Good Hope to New Holland, (as many Ships bound to Java, or thereabouts, keep that latitude) find themselves there, (and sometimes to their cost) running aground when they have thought themselves to be a great way off.

Thus the Dutch call it the Land of Indraught, but Dampier prefers to think it is the nearness of the land rather than "any Whirlpool."

When Dampier arrived on the shore of New Holland in the "Roebuck" in 1699, a voyage which we find Swift undoubtedly followed with great interest, he too commented on the wrong location of New Holland. "And here I would note once for all, that the Latitudes mark'd in the Draughts, or Sights here given, are not the Latitude of the Land, but of the Ship when the Sight was taken." Dampier was sailing east by Tasman's chart at the time, and, having sighted land ahead, must have meant observations of distances east and west as well as north and south. Already he had been misguided by his charts, having run to the north of the Abroholo Shoal when he thought he was south of it. "It was laid down wrong in my Sea-Chart." Again, coasting north from Shark's Bay he was confused once more in his bearings east and west, finding himself, like Gulliver, nearer the shore than he should be. "This Morning also when we expected by the Draught we had with us to have been 11 Leagues off Shore, we were but 4; so that either our Draughts were faulty . . . . or also here was a Tide unknown to us that deceived us." This error is further made clear a few pages later on in his account, where he plainly says that Tasman's route was laid down on the chart too near the shore; that is, either the route was too far to the east or the coast was too far to the west. Thus Dampier found the New Holland shore actually farther west than Tasman's chart indicated.

Dampier mentions "Mr. Tasman's Draught" specifically and complains further that the latitudes given were in error by forty minutes, the land being placed too far north. Furthermore, he explains that he found the coast line, not a smooth unbroken line with rivers emptying here and there, but a string of islands lying off the real shore. Gulliver, it should be remembered, was hoping to reach an island lying west of the shore.

Dampier was led to his conclusion partly by the tides. "I had a strong Suspicion that here might be a kind of Archipelago of Islands, and a Passage possibly to the S. of N. Holland and N. Guinea into the great S. Sea Eastward."[12] Gulliver passed under New Holland and came to its southeastern point. He fled from the natives north and spied a sail to the northeast of him, showing that he was on the east coast. The latitude he names would bring him south of Van Dieman's Land, where he probably passed, but it is significant that in this place he specifically calls it New Holland and not Van Dieman's Land as he had done in his first voyage. The map illustrating this voyage clearly indicates that Van Dieman's Land was thought to be a part of New Holland.

In Dampier, then, were all the incidents to prompt a remark like Gulliver's: similar grave errors, pointed out for the same general coast, islands on that coast, and a passage under New Holland to the Pacific.

Another thing, the mention of Herman Moll, ties it to Dampier still more. Swift's playful remark is that he had recommended these changes to Moll but that Moll had "chosen to follow other authors." The Moll maps in Dampier, particularly the map of the world, might easily have suggested this to Swift. Then, too, Moll "followed" Dampier, in changing his maps according to his latest discoveries in the region of Australia. Furthermore, Moll must have been associated with Dampier in Swift's mind, because they

---

[12] For these passages, see *Dampier's Voyages*, I, 300; II, 421, 422, 430–31, 432–33.

are the only contemporaries he mentions in *Gulliver's Travels* by their real names. The whole episode has all the appearance of Dampier's serious records of exploration illustrated by Moll played upon by the flashing genius of Swift. The passage is delightfully ironical, with Dampier and Moll unquestionably the butts of his mock seriousness. And—working backward from these remarks—I take all this as sufficient evidence that Swift knew the *Voyage to New Holland* rather well.

I have studied the maps in the first edition of *Gulliver's Travels* in the hope of finding some further connection between them and their time, perhaps Moll and Dampier. They are unsigned and bear no resemblance to Moll's maps in style. Possibly they were done at the instigation of the printer. They vouch for the reading taste for such things, making the travels of Gulliver at once more real and more strange. Each of the four famous voyages may be seen by them to have been taken to regions then unexplored if not unknown. Lilliput and Houyhnhnm-land are west and southwest of Australia. Brobdingnag is Alaska. And Laputa and the other islands are off the coast of Japan, possibly in the region of the Ladrone Islands. These may easily have been based on Moll's maps. In fact, two of them accord perfectly in outline, place names, etc., with Moll's maps of the same regions found in various works: *Atlas Geographus* (1708–1717), John Harris' *Navigantium* (1705), and Dampier.[13] For the map in Part II, I have found no close parallel. It is like one of Moll's maps but adds new place names. It and the large map in Part III may have been suggested by maps in some other book of travel, or they may have been the product of the drawer's imagination. Plate III, showing

---

[13] For Plate I (Part I, p. 1), see *Atlas Geographus*, III, 818. For Plate VI (Part IV, p. 1), see Harris' *Navigantium*, II, 1. For Plate II (Part II, p. 1), see some suggestions in *Atlas Geographus*, V, 452.

Balnibarbi and the flying island, is copied from a plate in the second volume of Le Comte's *Nouveaux Memoires sur L'Etat present de La Chine* (Amsterdam, 1697), showing a pirate-haunted island that was under the jurisdiction of the province of Canton.

We are not done, however, with New Holland and Dampier. One of the most interesting suggestions that came to Swift from the pages of Dampier concerns the Yahoos, the most horrible product of his savage indignation. Dampier's *Voyages* are prominent among those travel works containing vivid descriptions of monkeys and primitive men in Central America, South Africa, Australia, and the East Indies who, like Swift's Yahoos, live nastily, cohabit bestially, and display no glimmer of reason, who smell foul and eat putrid flesh, who move with ape-like agility, chattering in the branches of trees and flinging down their excrement.

Professor R. W. Frantz, who has summed these all up, declares there is no sure evidence that Swift read any one of the many passages he quotes except one about the Hottentots by Sir Thomas Herbert. He is doubtful of a passage on monkeys from Dampier's second volume (*Voyages and Descriptions*) because the volume which we know definitely Swift owned was Dampier's first (*A New Voyage Round the World*, 3d ed., 1698).

I venture to submit, however, two passages from Swift's copy of Dampier which at least warrant as much attention as any others I have seen. Because of the other connections between Swift and Dampier, they are really of more significance as actual sources.

Let us go back to the unseemly Hottentots. These savages are by no means overlooked by Dampier. In the last chapter of the *New Voyage Round the World* Dampier writes, "These *Hottantots* are People of a middle Stature, with small Limbs and thin Bodies, full of Activity . . . . with great Eye-brows, black Eyes" but not negroid as the New

Guinea natives. "They besmear themselves all over with Grease" and "rub Soot over the greased Parts, especially their Faces, which adds to their natural Beauty, as Painting does in *Europe;* but withal sends from them a strong Smell, which though sufficiently pleasing to themselves, is very unpleasant to others. They are glad of the worst Kitchen-stuff for this purpose, and use it as often as they can get it." Their eating habits are disgustingly Yahoo. The women's "Legs are wrapt around with Sheeps-guts two or three Inches thick, some up as high as to their Calves . . . . These are put on when they are green; and so they grow hard and stiff on their Legs, for they never pull them off again, till they have occasion to eat them; which is when they journey from home, and have no other Food; then these Guts, which have been worn, it may be, six, eight, ten or twelve Months, make them a good Banquet." They never take off their sheepskin garments but to delouse themselves, which they do by sitting in the hot sun for several hours. Their houses are the mean-est possible, shacks made of poles and boughs, like haycocks at a distance. They have no beds, but sprawl about the fire at night. They do "all sorts of servile Work" for the Dutch, about whose doors they squat waiting for "scraps and frag-ments that come from the Table." They run errands for the Dutch but on the whole "are a very lazy sort of People," choosing to live poor and miserable "than be at Pains for Plenty."

Unattractive as the Hottentots were, Dampier yet found something of interest in their customs, strolling forth at night to observe these ill-smelling natives in the heat of their all-night dance at the full of the moon. The natives of New Holland, however, were superlatively the worst of his expe-rience, with absolutely no redeeming feature. In this south-ern land, home of the Yahoo and three times visited by Gulliver, lived, according to Dampier, "the miserablest People in the World. The *Hodmadods* of *Monomatapa*

[Hottentots], though a nasty People, yet for Wealth are Gentlemen to these; who have no Houses, and skin Garments, Sheep, Poultry, and Fruits of the Earth, Ostrich Eggs, &c. as the *Hodmadods* have: And setting aside their Humane Shape, they differ but little from Brutes." They are tall, straight, and thin; "have great Bottle-Noses, pretty full Lips, and wide Mouths." A further unpleasant feature is their eyelids, "always half closed, to keep the Flies out of their Eyes." No fanning keeps the flies away, so that "without the Assistance of both Hands to keep them off, they will creep into ones Nostrils, and Mouth too, if the Lips are not shut very close." They are all "gat-toothed," two front incisors of the upper jaw being out. "They are long-visaged, and of a very unpleasing Aspect, having no one graceful Feature in their Faces." Whereas the Hottentots had huts, these natives have none whatsoever, but lie in the open with only a bough against the wind. They have no God. They speak with a guttural sound "somewhat thro' the Throat," but Dampier, who knew several native languages, could understand no word. Some make a doleful noise. Women snatch their "squeaking and bawling" infants and run away howling. They are supremely lazy and instead of carrying water in return for old clothes "stood like Statues, without motion, but grinn'd like so many Monkeys." Frightened, they run away crying "*Gurry, Gurry,* speaking deep in the Throat."

Here are lines that Swift actually read and although certain features are common to many accounts we can be certain these at least passed before him and sank into his consciousness. Dampier had no morbid curiosity about sex. Having little or no information on this point (concerning the Hottentots especially), he passes it by, though it is a common topic in the works of others. The lecherous nature of the Yahoos, as also their bearded condition, therefore, derived from elsewhere. Their offensive bodily odor, their nearness to brutes, their fondness for decayed ass's flesh, their general uncleanliness and love of filth, the distortion of their features when Gulliver first sees them, their lack of huts or other places of abode except as provided by the Houyhnhnms, and their howling, all come to mind from Dampier's remarks. The Yahoo is a synthesis of characteristics common to many savage nations, as its creator himself declares. Unquestionably Swift had the Hottentots principally in mind and Dampier contributed to the whole repulsive picture.

Thus Swift, under the spell of voyages and travels, felt the sincerity of the extraordinary books of William Dampier. It is true, he could not refrain from poking fun at Dampier, but it is as playful and stingless as the famous passage crammed with nautical terms and lifted from the pages of Sturmy's *Compleat Mariner.* That he was impressed by Dampier's character and the character of his travels there can be no question. From his own remarks we know that he was reading voyages for ideas as he wrote, and from the parts presented here we know one of these must have been Dampier's *Voyages.*

Certain other things in the vague borderland of literary influence have been omitted altogether, despite certain interesting associations. These are such things as the fatiguing public exhibition of Gulliver in Brobdingnag, which suggests Dampier's exhibition of Giolo, the painted South Sea island prince; Swift's habit of mentioning other works he is about to publish, which suggests Dampier's frequent remarks about his other books; the construction of Lilliputian men-of-war in the woods back from the shore, which suggests the difficulties of getting logwood to the sea as described by Dampier. The actual mention of Dampier and Moll, the character of Captain Peacock of Bristol, the parallel between Dampier's four voyages and Gulliver's, the details of Gulliver's voyage to Brobdingnag, his remarks about the errors of the extant maps, his fondness for New Holland, and his general knowledge of it, however, point unmistakably to Dampier.

With *Gulliver's Travels* and *Robinson Crusoe* the influence of Dampier is seen to extend past the smaller excitements of the day and the vogue for voyages into the great and permanent world of highly imaginative literature. With Defoe and Swift he has entered not only into the literature of travel but into the high places of English prose.

X

HONEST COMPLIMENT

The *Histories* of other *Nations,* Accounts of *Voyages* and *Travels,* the Lives of *Heroes* and *Philosophers,* will be both a pleasant and instructive Entertainment. The reading the best Authors on these Subjects, will enlarge and elevate their Souls, and give them a Contempt for the common Amusements of the Sex.

—STEELE, *The Ladies' Library*

A POPULAR success is inevitably followed by a train of imitations that honestly or not profit in some way from the splendor of the original. Such a comet's tail is seen following *Robinson Crusoe,* merging somewhat with the "Gulliveriad" following *Gulliver's Travels.* Desert-island romances have become so numerous and so much alike that they are a type, called by the Germans, *Robinsonaden.* Extended bibliographies of them, with astonishing lists of titles, may be found.[1] Within the period under review, which covers a decade after *Robinson Crusoe,* fictitious narratives like the following appeared:

The Adventures and Surprizing Deliverances of James Dubordieu and his Wife .... Also the Adventures of Alexander Vendchurch .... on an Island in the South Sea. London, 1719.

[1] Hermann Ullrich, *"Robinson und Robinsonaden"* in *Litterarhistorische Forschungen* (1898), Vol. VII. The most imposing list of imitations of *Robinson Crusoe* ever compiled.

The Voyages . . . . *of Captain Richard Falconer*. London, 1720. [By William Rufus Chetwood.]
The Strange Adventures of the Count de Vinevil and his Family. London, 1721. [By Mrs. Penelope Aubin.]
The Strange Adventures and Signal Deliverances of Mr. Philip Ashton, Jun. Boston, 1725. London, 1726.
The Hermit: or, the Unparalled [*sic*] *Sufferings and Surprizing Adventures of Mr. Philip Quarll, an Englishman*. Westminster, 1727. [By Peter Longueville. A very popular tale.]

In the middle of the century came adventures of Peter Wilkins (1751), John Daniel (1751), and William Bingfield (1753). Some of these Robinsoniad flourished on into the nineteenth century as chapbook fare for children and the vulgar. Their connection with *Robinson Crusoe* and the South Sea compels us to examine them also for traces of the influence of Dampier. If Defoe depended on him, what may have been true of lesser, often anonymous, writers of travel fiction? A glance at them shows us that the trails of Dampier and Defoe merge, that their authors lean definitely, at times painfully, upon both great predecessors. Imitation of one has been bolstered by unabashed plagiarism from the other. Let us consider briefly works of William Rufus Chetwood and some of Peter Longueville (author of *The English Hermit*).

CHETWOOD

The immediate circumstances which prompted the writing of William Rufus Chetwood's three books of fictitious voyages appear to have been the South Sea Bubble and the successes of Defoe. Chetwood was a bookseller, dramatist, and a prompter for nearly twenty years at Drury Lane Theatre. The best-known work of his unfortunate career was a *General History of the Stage* (1749), so that he is primarily considered as a figure in the theatrical world. He wrote two dramatic pieces in 1720 that reflect the agitation over the South Sea enterprise: *The Stock Jobbers, or the Humours of Exchange Alley*, a comedy; and *The South Sea, or the Biter Bit*, a farce. Both were published in 1720, though never acted. Chetwood was at this time a bookseller, not becoming a Drury Lane prompter until 1722 or 1723. His name appears on the title-page of Defoe's *King of Pirates*, also of 1720, which was followed immediately by *Captain Singleton*. Thus Chetwood witnessed at once the famous South Sea panic and the appearance of Defoe's successful tales of travel. He, too, took his fling at the subject of greatest momentary interest and wrote, besides the dramatic pieces already mentioned, prose tales of the voyage-and-adventure type.

The Voyages of Captain Richard Falconer.—In this same year, he published *The Voyages, dangerous Adventures and imminent Escapes of Captain Richard Falconer: Containing The Laws, Customs, and Manners of the Indians in America; his Shipwrecks; his marrying an Indian Wife; his narrow Escape from the Island of Dominico &c. Intermix'd with The Voyages and Adventures of Thomas Randal, of Cork, Pilot .... Written by Himself, now alive ....* [quotation from Waller], London, printed for W. Chetwood at Cato's Head, in Russell Street, Covent Garden, and others. 1720. The volume was divided into three Books, paged separately. A second edition, corrected and with additions, appeared in 1724.

This tale is one of the first imitations of *Robinson Crusoe*.[2] It is done in the manner of travel works with a central incident of typical desert-island adventure. The style of travelers is affected in stopping to describe places visited or passed by. Coming to Jamaica, the roaming Falconer halts

---

[2] Ullrich, *op cit.*, VII, 118–19. William Lee says ten had appeared by 1727 (*Daniel Defoe*, London, 1869, I, 300 n.). Falconer's *Voyages* would have been among them, for it was popular enough to be reprinted in 1724.

the narrative in the abruptest manner with, "Jamaica is an Island lying," etc. He affectedly adorns his matter by quotations from the poets: Waller, Milton, Shakespeare, Dryden. A satirical preface in the manner of Swift mentions "Honest Chetwood" who must take responsibility for the sale of the book. It declares, in Defoe's manner, that everything in the story is true. It is signed "Canterbury, Nov. 7, 1719. R. Falconer." It is plain, therefore, before one reads the story, that it is a book made to sell only, and composed by an imitator.

Richard Falconer, without experience of the sea, begins his adventures by sailing to Jamaica as mate to one Captain Wase. From here he goes to Campeachy to trade for logwood, but on the return falls from the stern of the ship and is cast up alone on one of the Alcrane Islands. The island is barren and sandy, affording nothing for his subsistence but a wild fowl called a booby, the eggs of another bird, and a bit of rain water caught in holes dug in the ground. After being here for several weeks he is joined by four men who are cast ashore in a bark. By tedious digging they manage to get the undamaged vessel afloat. Falconer by pure accident leaves the island and his friends when the bark on which he is sleeping alone blows adrift.

After various adventures with Spaniards and pirates, he goes to Cuba, where he sees Indians tortured. Returning to Jamaica he finds his old ship, but his crew run off with it. He then returns to England in his Alcrane bark by way of the Gulf of Florida and Newfoundland. This constitutes what might be called his first voyage, the time being from May 1699 to late 1700.

A second voyage to the West Indies begun in 1701 is more varied but less interesting. The narrative is much broken by descriptions of the Madeiras and the Canaries. An inserted story of Lionel Machin and the beautiful Arabella explains the founding of the city of Funzal. At the

Canaries he takes his reader on an ascent of Teneriffe. Setting out again he is taken by a Turkish galley, but by mutiny overcomes the Turks and is taken up by a Captain Walton bound for the West Indies. He is left by his ship among hostile Indians at the island of Dominico, where he takes an Indian bride. He is finally picked up and is able to join Admiral Benbow's fleet.

In this double dish of conventional adventures served up to the public in 1720 we are interested in tasting only the first part. From the author's own remarks in the first and third books we know that he has used an assortment of travel books and histories for many of his ingredients: Sloane's *Natural History of Jamaica,* Acosta's *History of the West Indies,* Sprat's *History of the Royal Society,* and works of Hugh Linscoten and Peter Martyr. For the adventures between Jamaica and the Bay of Campeachy he has employed Dampier generously, although he nowhere mentions him. In particular, certain descriptions of birds and fish, the details of trading for logwood, and the whole episode on the Alcrane Islands are obviously from Dampier's descriptions of those places and things. Chetwood took little care to conceal the phrases of his source, although these parts are used with more skill than is shown by other imitators of Defoe and Dampier. Dampier's tropic birds as big as pigeons, Dampier's waterspouts, Dampier's Island of Trist and his Logwood Creek, his sucking fish with a "grisly" head and appetite for a bare hook called by "the Antients" the Remora—all figure on Chetwood's page.[3]

No one may say that young Falconer lacks attractiveness as a sailor. Becalmed on the return from Campeachy to Jamaica, he retires astern to the small boat in tow where he enjoys the hushed hours reading Ovid. So wrapt does he

[3] See Dampier (Masefield ed., 1906), I, 55–56, 83, 441–42, and Chetwood, *Voyages of Richard Falconer* (1720), Book I, pp. 11–12, 54–56, 94–95.

become in this unsailorly pastime that he fails to observe the wind rising. In his sudden scramble up the tow line to the ship's stern he falls into the sea and is thus lost to his companions and cast up on the Alcranes.

These islands, he reports, are "five Islands, or rather large Banks of Sand . . . . they lie in the Latitude of twenty two Degrees North, twenty five Leagues from Yucatan" and sixty from the town of Campeachy. His particular island is "about two Miles in Circumference." It is round and has good anchoring on the west side. He finds shelter only under a "Burton-bush," which he spreads over with the abundant "Chicken-weed." There is no water. He lives on boobies and the eggs of another bird, both being plentiful.

This is all clearly from Dampier, who, also en route from Campeachy to Jamaica, ran afoul of the islands and described them thus. They "are 5 or 6 low sandy Islands, lying the Lat. of about 23 d. North and distant from the Coast of Jucatan about 25 Leagues." The largest is not above one or two miles in circuit. "All of them have good Anchoring on the West-Sides . . . . On some there are a few low Bushes of Burton-wood" and some chicken-weed. The fowls there are "Boobies in vast abundance, with Men of War and Egg-Birds."

When Falconer is joined by the four other castaways he fishes with them some distance from the shore on a raft made for the purpose. The first day the catch is only "one *Nurse*, a Fish so called, about two Foot long, something like a Shark, only its Skin is very rough." The next day they catch a small shark about two feet long, and shoot a seal. Dampier describes "Abundance of Fish at some Distance from these Islands," but near them "are Sharks, Sword-Fishes, and Nurses . . . . but of a small Size, the Sword-fish not above a Foot and a half, or two Foot long; neither were the Sharks much longer, and the Nurses about the same Length. The Nurse is just like a Shark only its Skin is

rougher, and is used for making the finest Rasps. Here are
many Seals."

At this point Dampier tells the story of Captain Long,
whose bark was blown ashore here. Long's men wanted to
make a float or raft of her to get off the island with, but he
persuaded them against it. Soon two New England ketches
ran on the reef "and were bulged." He and his men assisted
them in getting their goods to the shore, in return for which
the New Englanders helped him get his bark afloat. He
then sailed away without them.

Chetwood, having employed Dampier so well in order to
wreck his hero and describe his environs, then goes on to
use this story of the sagacious Captain Long. In simple outline it provides the manner of Falconer's escape from the
island. He would surely have died of thirst if the men in a
bark had not been blown ashore. He joins with them and
assists them in getting ashore their provisions. The men had
already lightened their bark of her cargo of logwood, or
"they would have bulg'd in the Sands." When they get the
vessel afloat, he sails off (although unintentionally) without
them. Another West Indian anecdote in Dampier may
easily have suggested being blown off in a moored or
grounded vessel. This is his story of the drunken French
sailors at the island of Aves, when their ship which had
gone ashore there breaks in half, one half floating away with
them still aboard.[4]

These details rather well center in the chief adventure of
Falconer's first voyage and in themselves reveal their source.
One other incident in the third book seems to be from Dampier. An Indian on the island of Dominico, whom Falconer
took for his man Friday, was called Will, and he "was
mighty proud to be call'd so." Dampier's Mosquito Indian

[4] Compare Dampier, *op. cit.*, II, 127–29, 131–32; I, 80–81, and
Chetwood, *op. cit.*, Book I, 57–67, 66–68, 70–71; Book II, 42–43,
respectively.

Will and his comments on the Mosquitoes in general we have already dealt with in connection with *Robinson Crusoe*. But whereas Defoe works freely with such suggestions from Dampier, Chetwood cannot break away, not even from the proper name Will.

The Voyages of Capt. Robert Boyle.—In 1726 William Rufus Chetwood, now a theatrical prompter, published his most popular prose tale of adventure: *The Voyages and Adventures of Capt. Robert Boyle, in several parts of the World, &c. Intermix'd with The Story of Mrs. Villars, an English Lady with whom he made his surprizing Escape from Barbary . . . . To which is added the Voyage, Shipwreck, and Miraculous Preservation of Richard Castleman, gent. With a Description of the City of Philadelphia and the Country of Pennsylvania.*

This enjoyed at least eight reprintings by 1793, besides translation into French, Italian, Dutch, and German.[5] It has been attributed to Benjamin Victor and to Defoe, but is usually assigned now to Chetwood[6] on Chetwood's own statement. On the title-page of a volume of five novels, published in 1741, he prints, "Written by W. R. Chetwood, Prompter to Her Majesty's Company of Comedians at the Theatre Royal in Drury Lane; and author of Faulconer, Boyle and Vaughan's Voyages, &c."

The story is a mixture of the adventures of a traveler and the memoirs of various people encountered on the way. It is more the kind of thing loosely called the roguestory. Not that Boyle, the hero, is a true rogue but that he has a variety of experience in high and low life much in the manner of the heroes in Defoe and certain Continental nov-

[5] J. Sabin, *A Dictionary of Books Relating to America* (1868), IV, 13–14.

[6] See Sabin, *op. cit.*, and Halkett and Laing, *A Dictionary of Anonymous and Pseudonymous Literature* (1926–1932), under "Chetwood" and "*Voyages* of Robt. Boyle," respectively.

elists. Boyle is first apprenticed to a cuckold watch-maker, but is sold by his uncle for a slave and is sent off to Virginia. He is captured by a Sallee rover off the Barbary Coast, the corsair being an Irish renegade. He is kept a prisoner by the Moors at Sallee for a time but escapes with an English lady whom he keeps and treats as his wife. She is, however, stolen back by the Moors. "The History of Mrs. Villars" and "The Story of the Italian Slave" complete this part of the book.

Boyle next sails from Ostia (March 2, 1693) as captain and supercargo of his own ship. He has the satisfaction of retaking the same Sallee rover, after which he touches at the Canaries and stretches over to the coast of Brazil. He makes the Isle of Ascension and then St. Catherine. Going in to the "Bay of Arazatiba" to get water, he is met and entertained by "Captain Dampier." He receives valuable aid from Dampier and asks his advice in escapades with the hostile Indians. Upon being invited to join Dampier's privateering expedition, he refuses (but later rues the fact), and sails away for Buenos Aires and the South Sea. In the Straits of Magellan and the South Sea, he takes prizes, among which is the Manila galleon; and he returns to Ostia on November 1, 1696, "the richest prize that ever came into any port of Italy." After a recital of "The Life of Don Pedro Aquilio," he returns to London to buy an estate in Somersetshire and to find near Bristol the charming Mrs. Villars.

Here is a popular narrative, in which Dampier figures as a character. He is brought into the story as a familiar and well-known person, as though every reader knew that the likeliest person to meet privateering on the Brazilian coast was Dampier. As a matter of fact it is not known where Dampier was in 1693. He may have been in England (having returned from his first great voyage in 1691), or he may have been en route to Corunna. He was certainly not on one of his great privateering voyages. Chetwood may, of course, have selected a time for this meeting from the years in Dampier's life about which the least is known.

But this is of no real importance. Dampier in 1726 and 1727 had still sufficient fame to be introduced into popular works, by Chetwood in the *Voyages of Capt. Robert Boyle* and by Swift in Gulliver's letter to his Cousin Sympson in *Gulliver's Travels*. And I shall soon show that a grand plagiarism from his pages was made in another Crusoe-yarn in 1727.

This meeting of Boyle with Dampier shows more than just the use of Dampier's name. The occasion itself reflects the festive reception of Dampier and Woodes Rogers at the Isle of Grande in 1708, in which the privateers hold festival ashore with music from the ship's company. Their first meeting was like that described by Dampier at the island of Juan Fernandez where one English privateer mistakes another for a Frenchman.

The only other suggestion of Dampier in the book is the citing of many fowls near the Isle of Ascension, by which Boyle knows he is near land.

The Voyages of William Vaughan.—Of voyaging properly speaking there is none whatsoever in *The Voyages, Travels, and Adventures of William Owen Gwin Vaughan, Six Years a Slave in Tunis. Intermix'd with the Histories of Clerimont, Maria Eleanora, and Others. Full of Various Turns of Fortune* . . . . London, MDCCXXXVI, 2 vols. There is no traveling done at all in the first volume, and in the second the hero, a boy, merely takes the usual educational foreign tour with a tutor. "Memoirs" are wrung from nearly every character in the book. In fact, they are what the book was written for. Dampier figures in it not at all. It is worth noting only because the author, proceeding into this his third voyage-narrative, has crowded out voyaging proper completely in order to introduce the more artificial and sophisticated "memoir" or inserted story, which Steele declares in *Tatler* No. 84 "is French for novel." It appears to be a part of the process whereby fiction is made out of fact. The part played in shaping the English novel by such phenomena as the inserted story (of Cervantes and LeSage), the Oriental tale, and the French *memoir* is recognized, although not so clearly as it may yet be. Especially is the relation between English prose fiction and the memoir known. Chetwood's romances display an analogous relation between the voyage and the memoir. And Chetwood was not alone in this. The fictitious voyage is but one step from the real voyage, and the memoir but a step from the fictitious voyage. Part I, for example, of Tom Killigrew's *Miscellanea Aurea: or, the Golden Medley* (London, 1720) is "A Voyage to the Mountains of the Moon." Part II is "The Fortunate Shipwreck." And Part IV is "The Secret History of the Amours of Don Alonzo." The association here of fictitious voyages with "secret history" speaks for itself. In Chetwood may be seen in the work of one man a specific instance of the displacing of rugged homely matter in imitation of the voyages by the shorter inserted tale or memoir. It is an inviting subject for investigation, and it is more than idle speculation to consider whether or not this may be indicative of a general trend in narrative-writing from Defoe to Fielding and Smollett. May not wandering heroes like Tom Jones, Roderick Random, Peregrine Pickle, and their brethren owe much to the heroes of tales of travel (whether authentic or not) as well as to Cervantes and LeSage? Did not Defoe and Swift and their followers and imitators give definite shape and English character to the wandering hero before the spirit of the Continental authors appears in Fielding and Smollett?

LONGUEVILLE'S "ENGLISH HERMIT"

Among the Defoe apocrypha, a work of great popularity at the time and of increasing interest to scholars now is

The English Hermit (Westminster, 1727).[7] Upon the title-page of the first edition the title, as already noted, runs, *The Hermit: or, the Unparalled* [*sic*] *Sufferings and Surprizing Adventures of Mr. Philip Quarll, an Englishman.* Upon the binding, however, is "Quarll's English Hermit," by which it is commonly known. It is clearly an imitation of *Robinson Crusoe* and stands as perhaps the most important English Robinsoniad, chronologically probably the tenth. The preface (signed "P. L.") admits that the aim in publishing is to furnish the world with a performance of the nature of *Robinson Crusoe, Moll Flanders, Colonel Jacque,* and *Gulliver's Travels,* but true and therefore "of more Use to the publick." It was to be the moral and instructive counterpart of Defoe's *"vulgar Stories,"* on the one hand, and the *"Satirical* Vein" of Swift, on the other. As a matter of fact, it is but a dull book full of moral sayings, Christian proverbs, dreams, and Divine Providence intermixed with a typical desert-island story. Yet it sufficed to stir the boyhood imaginations of Crabbe, Coleridge, and probably Wordsworth. Lamb enjoyed Quarll's monkey.[8]

One should note in passing that, only the year before, another story of the Crusoe type had appeared (originally published in Boston in 1725). This was *Ashton's Memorial —An History of the Strange Adventures and Signal Deliverances of Mr. Philip Ashton who, after he had made his Escape from the Pirates liv'd alone on a Desolate Island for about sixteen Months, &c.* This work may have provided the author of *The English Hermit* with the name Philip for a castaway, and itself is reminiscent of Dampier. Ashton's desert island is located in the Bay of Honduras, where, he

---

[7] It went to twelve editions by 1780, and was translated immediately into French, then into German (Dottin, *Daniel Defoe et ses romans,* II, 390–91).

[8] J. L. Lowes, *The Road to Xanadu,* pp. 459–60.

says, there are many sandy islands called "keyes." On one of these the pirate captors of Ashton carouse. Later they load their schooner with "Logwood which the Sloop had brought from the Bay" and send her out on her own account.

The English Hermit is but an obvious slavish imitation of the manner of Defoe, even to the title-page. Philip Quarll, the hero, is attended from childhood by an ill fate. He is of low birth. Early he falls in with a house-breaker. He makes two voyages, marries a whore, lists in the Footguards, marries twice more, is sentenced to death for polygamy, is confined in Newgate, but is pardoned by the King. He is the sole survivor of a shipwreck in the South Sea, where he lives for many years and is finally left by the Bristol merchant who found him, because he prefers solitude to the world of men. His island experience is a perfect parallel of Crusoe's. He has a hut made of stakes and grass. He has an arbor for hot days, clothes and mats of grass, wild animals domesticated, goats, a trained monkey instead of a man Friday, etc.

It is also strongly under the influence of Dampier, and because of that the question of authorship demands a word. It has been attributed to Defoe, but modern opinion is against this. There are certain characteristics of style that suggest Defoe; yet it lacks Defoe's ruggedness. It is furthermore too slovenly in composition and too inaccurate in geographical details.[9] Mr. Arundell Esdaile makes a convincing argument, from a copy the preface of which is different from others and is signed "Peter Longueville," that such was the author's name, an illiterate fellow whose work was done over by hacks and padded by the printer with the memoirs of Edward Dorrington.[10] Nothing else is known about Peter Longueville. The Harvard catalogue attributes *The Eng-*

---

[9] Defoe would never sail icebergs in his tropics!

[10] *The Library*, Series IV, Vol. II, pp. 185–92.

lish Hermit to Longueville or Defoe. I think that, on the grounds of style and the interesting presentation copy found by Mr. Esdaile, it cannot be the work of Defoe. It would be interesting indeed if such authorship could be proved, for then it could be shown that Defoe not only used Dampier but was dominated by him—could not get away from him, plagiarized from him. Whoever the author may have been, he transferred many passages unblushingly from Dampier. Whole phrases are repeated and long passages condensed or poorly concealed. Dampier's East Indian storm with its Corpus-Sanct passage is there. The description of the Cape Verde and Canary Islands is straight copying from Dampier. A single passage will illustrate the crudeness of several pages of this plagiarism:[11]

"THE ENGLISH HERMIT"	DAMPIER
One of them are called *Sall*, it derives its *name from the prodigious Quantity of Salt, that is naturally congeal'd* in *Salt-ponds. There are some poor Goats* on this Island, and *some wild Fowl;* there are Flamingoes, *a large Fowl much like a Heron* but *bigger and of a reddish Colour:* They *feed together* in *muddy Ponds,* or where *there is little Water: They are hard to shoot,* as being *very shy.*	This of *Sall* . . . . hath its name from the *abundance of Salt that is naturally congealed there,* the whole Island being full of *large Salt-ponds* . . . . *there are some poor Goats* on it. . . . . There are *some wild Fowl.* . . . . I saw a few Flamingo's, which is a sort of *large Fowl,* much like a *Heron* in shape, but *bigger, and of a reddish colour.* They delight *to keep together* in great companies, and feed in *Mud or Ponds,* or in such places where there is *not much Water:* They are *very shy,* therefore it is *hard to shoot them.*

[11] *The English Hermit* (1727), p. 63; Dampier (Masefield ed., 1906), I, 99.

Others may be found in the Appendix (pp. 207–214).[12] Other marks of Dampier are not difficult to find. The very island upon which Quarll is cast is one of the Tres Marías off the coast of California, carefully located and described by Dampier, who had careened his ship there and cured himself of dropsy by lying in the sand. From Dampier, Longueville got the fact that the island was uninhabited, and that it contained roots edible when boiled, thick woods, many small animals, many fish, tortoises, seals, etc. Dampier saw the sea red for a mile with tiny lobsters near the Falkland Islands. Quarll's discoverer sees the sea a blood red from fish spawn near the Galápagos Islands. The height of the land, also monkeys and snakes at Gorgona Bay, the description of Juan Fernandez, a brigantine loaded with negroes for the gold mines, and a description of the sloth seem all to be from the same dependable source.[13]

To end the painful disclosure, I might add that this abject dependence upon Dampier argues well for authorship by an ignorant Peter Longueville rather than by an experienced journalist like Defoe, who borrowed matter freely from a dozen sources but who always used his material intelligently. Dampier's *Voyages* not only got favor among the great but won the honest compliment of imitation from lesser writers.

[12] I am indebted to Professor Lowes for three references (*The Road to Xanadu*, p. 459).

[13] Compare *The English Hermit* (1727), pp. 55–56, 47, 58, 61, 48, and Dampier, *op. cit.*, I, 289–90, 109, 193, 114–19.

XI

UNWITTINGLY HE CARVED A NICHE

Parcere paucorum *diffundere crimen in* omnes. And it is a
generous kind of civility to report alwayes the best.
                                        —HOWELL, *Forraine Travell*

After I . . . . had waded on still farther and farther in the
sweet studie of the historie of Cosmographie, I began at length
to conceive, that with diligent observation, some thing might
be gathered which might commend our nation for their high
courage and singular activitie in the Search and Discoverie of
the most unknowen quarters of the world.
               —RICHARD HAKLUYT, Epistle Dedicatorie,
                              Vol. I, *Principall Navigations*

IN THE preceding chapters we have seen what kind of
works William Dampier wrote, what impression they
made upon a world already familiar with such things, and
especially what part they played in the composition of fictitious travel narratives immediately following, the highest
examples of which are *Robinson Crusoe* and *Gulliver's
Travels.* We may now look into a few more corners and
some out-of-the-way places where readers in the early years
of the eighteenth century came upon Dampier.
    Journalism of the day naturally reflected the principal
events of Dampier's life, or at least those that caught the
fancy of the public. Thus we have seen that Tutchin, Dunton, Steele, and Addison refer familiarly to Dampier. Remarks of Steele and Addison should naturally be of especial
interest. In *Spectator* No. 121 Addison refers to him on the

subject of the sagacity of birds and animals. In *Tatler* No. 62 Steele tells an amusing story supposedly from Dampier to illustrate his theme: that those who profess to serve mankind should honestly admit that they seek only to serve themselves. "Of all the disinterested professors I have ever heard of," he writes, "I take the boatswain of Dampier's ship to be the most impudent, but the most excusable." He then proceeds to tell how, far at sea and out of provisions, the crew cast hungry eyes upon the boatswain, "a fat, healthy, fresh fellow." They unanimously agreed to eat him, the captain and lieutenant being safe "only by being carrion." The boatswain perceived their intentions, and addressed them as follows:

"Gentlemen Sailors,

"Far be it that I should speak it for any private interest of my own, but I take it, that I should not die with a good conscience, if I did not confess to you that I am not sound. I say, gentlemen, justice, and the testimony of a good conscience as well as love of my country, to which I hope you will all return, oblige me to own, that Black Kate of Deptford has made me very unsafe to eat; and (I speak it with shame) I am afraid, gentlemen, I should poison you."

Now this story does not happen to be in Dampier at all— a fact which increases rather than lessens its significance. It may have been confused in Steele's mind with Captain Swan's remark to Dampier when it was learned that the crew planned to eat them if the provisions gave out. "Ah! Dampier, *you would have made them but a poor Meal;* for I was as lean as the Captain was lusty and fleshy."[1] Legend grew about the name of Dampier and his adventures. Here, some seamen's tale or some anecdote from another narrative has been attributed to Dampier. If it be a mere tale told for amusement and referred to Dampier only in jest, it indicates

---

[1] *Dampier's Voyages* (Masefield ed., 1906), I, 296.

still that Steele knew he was dealing with a name well known to his audience. It shows in a small way what Defoe, Swift, and Chetwood show in a larger way, that Dampier passed well enough into English tradition to be used as the material of literature.

Historical, geographical, and scientific works pay respect to Dampier's opinions and descriptions, not to say anything of succeeding accounts of travel. Herman Moll, Oldmixon, Jeremy Collier, Woodes Rogers, Frezier, Shelvocke, and others support their writings by reference to or quotation from Dampier.

Some of the lesser satirists use him. Tom Brown pictures a bookseller in a fury because Dampier's last unsuccessful voyage has brought down his sales. William King, whose *Art of Cookery* is outweighed in volume by the number of his satires done in the manner of the voyagers, takes pains in *The Transactioneer* (a satire on the *Transactions* of the Royal Society)[2] to correct the scientific knowledge of Dampier and in so doing to ridicule the style of Sir Hans Sloane.

Ned Ward, although familiar with contemporary works of travel and fond of satirizing them, nowhere mentions Dampier specifically. He does, however, know of the log-wood trade so carefully explained by Dampier. Says *Snap* (a sharper) to *Log* (a mariner), "Then, I suppose, you have heard some of the *New-England* Saints Sing Psalms, whilst they've been stealing of *Log-wood?*"[3] He satirizes those who encouraged explorations of the passages to the Indies, in the character of a Scots pedlar who reports to the Lying Club that he was let down in a bottomless well till he came to the Indies. The Scotsman offered this new-found passage to the East India Company.[4]

[2] William King, *Original Works* (1776), II, 10.
[3] "The Humours of A Coffee-House," in *Works* (fourth ed.), II, 310.
[4] *A Compleat and Humourous Account of all . . . . Clubs and Societies* (1745), pp. 218–20.

Dampier's relations with the Royal Society and its members have been pointed out in part already. Samuel Pepys, John Evelyn, Sir Hans Sloane, and Dr. John Woodward had personal contact with him. The chapter-by-chapter digest of his first volume in the *Philosophical Transactions* mildly compliments his style as "very Intelligible and Expressive." A letter to William Dampier from his brother published in the *Transactions*[5] shows not only his interest in botany but that of his family as well, particularly his "Uncle Dampier." At the request of the Royal Society, Dampier placed his collection of Australian plants in the hands of Dr. Woodward, geologist and physician. Dampier's connection with the new science was therefore close.

Sir Hans Sloane, more than anyone else, seems to have had a personal interest in Dampier. He not only engaged Thomas Murray to paint his portrait, but he acquired Dampier's manuscripts and journals. At least, the only extant manuscript came into the possession of the British Museum through the Sloane collection. Physician, collector, author, and president of the Royal Society for many years, Sir Hans was one of the most eminent scientists in England in his day. A great part of his reputation was made by his two-volume *Voyage to the Islands of Madera, Barbadoes . . . . and Jamaica, with the Natural History of the last* (1707 and 1725). In the long introduction to this work there are passages that indicate Dampier's influence upon him.

He describes, for example, with considerable detail the logwood trade between Campeachy and Jamaica. He mentions the town of Campeachy, Logwood-River, two hundred English cutters living in huts, two creeks or lagunas several leagues from where the ships ride, the trade to Jamaica in sloops for three pounds per ton, or for half the profits, beef cattle on an island near by and deer near the river, and

---

[5] *Philosophical Transactions of the Royal Society*, XX, 49–52.

several molestations of the trade by the Spaniards. These are all prominent in Dampier's well-known account in *Voyages and Descriptions*. Sloane declares that he had been informed by "Several Persons who used the Logwood Trade, or who were employed in cutting that Wood." I take this to mean Dampier principally and others with whom he had talked during his fifteen months' residence at Jamaica. A further connection with Dampier here seems to be his description of the treatment for Guinea worm, which infests the human skin. This is to roll it round a stick a little each day and at the same time to apply a plaster. "I was told," he writes, "that this was the only remedy." In the midst of Dampier's account of Campeachy and logwood-cutting he describes two kinds of leg worms, one of them the Guinea worm. Being troubled with one of the latter while in Virginia, he "kept a Plaister to it to bring it to a Head" and rolled two inches of it each day on a stick until he "strained it out gently" to the length of two feet. Then he solemnly relates how a negro horse-doctor cured it by a powder and a charm.[6]

Thus science paid its respects to the great English navigator.

What of poetry? My remarks earlier, that the prose of the day rather than verse took notice of marine affairs, are well borne out here. Dampier was not sung.

It is strange that Matthew Prior, at one time Commissioner of Trade and Plantations, should leave no remark about him. From his "Essay upon Learning" in *Dialogues of the Dead*, it would seem that he held books of history and travel in no high regard. From reading them, he declares, one may become only "a Mere Story Teller." It is strange, also, that a poem like the *Court of Neptune* (1699) by John Hughes, which employs for its principal theme the return of

[6] Dampier, *op. cit.*, II, 187–88.

William and the supremacy of Britain on the sea, should not speak of Dampier. It is full of the sea. "Rais'd sublime on Contemplation's wings," he perceives the beauty and power of the sea; he sees Newton's soul and calls it "the great Columbus of the skies"; he would still explore "fresh wonders"; he sees Jamaica a prize more than Spain's whole fleet from Peru or Chile's golden coast; but he fails to see Dampier. Dampier's name is not among the long list in William Walsh's *The Golden Age Restored* (1703). Gay does not mention him in *Trivia;* and Pope is quite silent. One may surmise that, because the members of the Scriblerus Club talked together regarding the projected travels of Martin (who turned out to be Gulliver), they all knew and discussed works of travel, perhaps including Dampier because of the mention of him in *Gulliver's Travels.* On the other hand, his influence upon Swift's satire may have been purely through the mind of Swift. Pope's four poems *Occasioned by Reading the Travels of Captain Lemuel Gulliver* (1727) are his closest approach to Dampier. Young's odes on the ocean, the merchant, and Britain's fame upon the sea provide the proper atmosphere but fail to mention specific voyagers, certainly not Dampier.

The attitude of the Queen Anne and early Georgian poets toward voyages was for the most part purely conventional, being either romantic or satirical. Voyagers themselves were either liars or chroniclers of dull facts. South Sea islands were of the typical romantic kind described by Bishop Berkeley or Sir Samuel Garth.[7] There no high winds blow. In the midst of luxuriant growth flow gentle streams graced by swans. All is innocent, pure, natural, Edenlike. In *Sweet William's Farewell to Black Eyed Susan,* Gay gives a romantic picture of a sailor embarking on a voyage. But Defoe and Ned Ward in prose give quite another kind of picture.

[7] *Proposal for a College in the Summer Islands* (1726), and *The Dispensary,* Canto IV.

The poetry of the time, largely satirical, dealt with the town (the streets, rakes, prominent literary and political persons) and nature viewed artificially. A recent survey of the poetry of John Gay's lifetime (1685–1732) presents a picture of London through this single medium.[8] In hundreds of quotations, among which many deal with the South Sea Bubble and travelers about the town, the name of Dampier and the subject of voyages do not appear. Dampier simply belonged to a sphere of life that the poetry of the time failed in any real way to touch. Many years were yet to pass before Falconer was to write *The Shipwreck*, and Cowper "I am monarch of all I survey," or Coleridge *The Ancient Mariner*.

Books of voyages and travel, though published extensively and read by many, still enjoyed their popularity with only the mild interest, perhaps the indifference, of polite poetical circles in London. The traveler, except the great Elizabethan heroes, was still under suspicion. He found his audience in the readers of romances and adventures, those less critical minds that in all ages ask little to be wafted away to strange lands, and that ordinarily respect poetry but read prose. This difference between the attitude of high and middle classes can be well illustrated in the attitudes of Defoe and Pope to the same individual, Alexander Selkirk. Defoe read about him, and others, and wrote *Robinson Crusoe*. Pope mentions him but once, in a letter to Lord Bathurst in 1719.[9]

One should not forget, furthermore, that this prejudice against travelers' tales extended throughout the eighteenth century, although less noticeably after Anson and Cook. In 1784 Dr. Johnson made a famous and characteristic remark. "These Voyages . . . . [pointing to three large volumes of

[8] W. H. Irving, *John Gay's London* (Cambridge, 1928).

[9] *Works* (Elwin and Courthope edition, 1871–1886), VIII, 327.

Cook's *Voyages to the South Seas,* which had just come out] who will read them through? A man had better work his way before the mast, than read them through; they will be eaten by rats and mice, before they are read through. There can be little entertainment in such books; one set of Savages is like another." This from a man who was deceived by Psalmanaazaar, who could not distinguish Omai from Lord Mulgrave against the light, and who himself wrote an account of travel. "No man was more incredulous," wrote Boswell, "as to particular facts, which were at all extraordinary."[10]

Dampier was at once the heritage and the product of the growing middle class, away from which the silver age of poetry was turning. Pope and the other followers of reason were simply not concerned with him or his kind. The only ones among the great to feel his influence or to have an interest in him were Swift and the scientists whom Swift hated, the Greshamites and the fellows of the Royal Society. Dampier's relations with the literary world of the early eighteenth century, therefore, are relations with prose—prose narratives both real and fictitious, with which is also concerned a considerable stir in the publishing of voyages and travels.

In perspective then, Captain William Dampier stands as the principal begetter of voyages and travels for a thirty-year period. He himself wrote the most outstanding accounts in this time of actual voyages and so stimulated other accounts that, with the excitement of the South Sea Bubble and some more recent spectacular expeditions, built up a background of interest in geography and travel against which Defoe and Swift and their imitators projected their popular fictions of the sea. Any comprehension of the prose narrative of this time cannot be complete without considering the great influence of Dampier. Landsmen who wrote of the

[10] Boswell, *Life of Samuel Johnson* (Birkbeck Hill edition), IV, 308; II, 247.

sea felt safe in utilizing *Dampier's Voyages*. Defoe, the liar who lies like the truth, is dead. Defoe of the quick imagination lives. In Dampier lay embryonic bits that developed under Defoe's hand into many significant parts of the character and adventures of a great figure in world-literature. In varying degrees this is true of six other narratives of Defoe. Dampier, by comparison with other sources of Defoe, is by far the most important. In *Gulliver's Travels* Dampier's person, as well as his experience, is forever fixed in another classic. Captain Peacock is Captain Dampier and Gulliver's routes are often those of Dampier. *Robinson Crusoe* and *Gulliver's Travels* might have been written had there been no *Dampier's Voyages*. But they would not have been the same. Yet had Dampier never set the fashion for voyages and travels in these years it is not improbable or far-fetched to think they might never have been written at all. The complex fibers of the literary, the scientific, the lay world were definitely stimulated or changed by the interesting and daring life of this buccaneer and the calm record of his adventures. And if Defoe and Swift, Steele, Addison, Chetwood, Longueville, Evelyn, Tutchin, and Dunton, Knapton, Harris, and the Churchills, and all the others so belabored in these pages were to be set aside, the travel-literature of England would still be enriched by four rugged narratives, that in sincerity and clearness of expression form a document of great human interest, the descriptive parts of which frequently border upon the finer regions of literature far above those of the usual mariner's journal.

APPENDIX

Page references are to Peter Longueville's *The English Hermit* (1727) and Masefield's edition of Dampier (1906). Italics are mine. The language of the storm described in the first few passages (*The English Hermit*, p. 56) is repeated in a later description (p. 153).

The English Hermit	DAMPIER
P. 56	I, 409
Before we had sail'd six Leagues, the *Wind freshen'd upon us*, and the *Sky look'd extraordinary black at North-East*, and *mov'd towards us*, that *made us take in our Topsails*, and *afterwards to rief our Mainsail*, and *Mizen; at which Time it began to rain*, and *pour'd down, as if through a Sive;*	about 4 a clock in the afternoon, the Wind came to *N.E.* and *freshened upon us* and the *Sky look'd very black* in that quarter, and the black Clouds began to rise apace and *mov'd towards us* . . . . *This made us take in our Topsails,* . . . . about 9 a clock *we rift our Main-sail* and Foresail . . . . at 11 a clock we furl'd our *Main-sail and ballasted* [reefed] *our Mizen; at which time it began to rain,* and by 12 a clock at night it blew exceeding hard, and the Rain *poured down as through a Sieve.*
P. 56	I, 409
the *Sea seem'd as if it had been all on Fire*, by the *prodigious Thunder and Lightning.*	It *thundered and lightened prodigiously,* and the Sea *seemed all of a Fire* about us; for every Sea that broke *sparkled like lightning.*

207

The English Hermit	DAMPIER
P. 56	I, 409
(It then being Night,)	It was 12.
P. 56	I, 409
the Waves, that seem'd to dash against the clouds, by the Wind, *sparkled like Lightning.*	The violent Wind raised the Sea presently to a great heighth.
P. 56	I, 409
At last, *breaking in upon our Deck*, it *carried away one of our Anchors.*	it ran very short and began *to break in on our Deck.* One Sea struck away the Rails of our Head, and our Sheet-Anchor . . . . was violently washt off.
Pp. 56–57	I, 409
and we *durst not bring our Ship to the Wind, for Fear of her Foundering,* it *being dangerous in a Storm to turn a Ship backward and forward;* so were obliged to ly in the Trough of the Sea.	afterwards *we durst not adventure to bring our Ship to the Wind* again, *for fear of foundring, for the turning the Ship to or fro from the Wind is dangerous insuch violent Storms.*
P. 57	I, 409–10
But the Wind and Rain abating, we observ'd, to our great Joy, a Corpus Sanct at the Top of our Spindle:* These *Corpus Sanct's* are good Signs, *when seen aloft,* but a bad Omen, and denotes a great Storm, *when seen on our Decks.*	After four a clock *the Thunder and the* Rain abated, and then *we saw a Corpus Sant* at our Main-top-mast head, *on the very top of the truck of the Spindle.* This sight rejoyced our Men exceedingly; for the height of the Storm is commonly over when the Corpus Sant *is seen aloft* but *when they are seen lying on the Deck,* it is generally accounted a bad Sign.

The English Hermit	DAMPIER

P. 57

I, 410

It *is a small glimmering Light like a Star, when aloft, but, when on the Deck, appears like a Glow-worm.* It is the Opinion of Mariners, that it is a *Sort of a Jelly,* incorporated by the Wind, Rain, and Sea Vapours, and Air, because it is never observ'd, unless in stormy weather.

A Corpus Sant *is a certain small glittering light; when it appears as this did* . . . . *it is like a Star; but when it appears on the Deck, it resembles a great Glow-worm.* . . . . I have heard some ignorant Seamen discoursing how they have seen them creep . . . . but I did never see any one stir . . . . except upon the Deck . . . . Neither did I ever see any but when we have had hard Rain as well as Wind; and therefore do believe it is *some Jelly.*

P. 57

I, 411

We sailed right before the Wind, which was Southwest.

We continued scudding right before Wind and Sea. [Later on, after a calm, the wind sprang up at S.W.]

P. 62

I, 98

[Before coming to Cape Verde Is.,] a heavy Turnado, attended with Lightning, which fell as if the Element had been on Fire.

[Sailing from Achomack, Virginia, Dampier passes through a terrible storm, going to Cape Verde Islands.]

P. 63

I, 99

These islands are called so from *Cape Verd* in Africa and *are mostly inhabited by Portuguese.*

they lie several degrees off from Cape Verde in Africk, whence they receive that Appellation. . . . . *They are mostly inhabited by Portuguese Banditti.*

The English Hermit   DAMPIER

P. 63   I, 101–102

In St. Nicholas we traded with [Dampier describes ambergris
some of the *Spaniards* for *Am-* and trading for it at Sall and the
bergreece: but they were very Nicobar Islands, where] as I
fraudulent, *having very much* have been . . . . informed, [there
counterfeited it. Here are *some* are] great quantities of very
Vineyards and Plantations be- good Ambergreece. Yet the In-
longing to the Portuguese: Here habitants are so subtle that they
is Wine much like Madera, also will *counterfeit it,* both there and
of a *pale Colour and thick:* The here. . . . .
People are *swarthy,* and the *In-*
habitants live scattering in the I, 102
Vallies.   We went from this Island of
                                    Sall, to St. Nicholas . . . . in the
                                    Heart of it there are Valleys,
                                    where the Portuguese, which in-
                                    habit here, *have Vineyards and*
                                    Plantations, and Wood for fewel.
                                    . . . .

                                    I, 103
                                    The Gouvennour brought aboard
                                    some wine made in the Island,
                                    which tasted *much like Madera*
                                    Wine: It was *of a pale colour,*
                                    and lookt thick . . . . *other in-*
                                    habitants . . . . *lived in scatter-*
                                    ing Valleys more remote. They
                                    were all *very swarthy.*

P. 63   I, 103

While we was *at this Island we* *At this Island we scrubb'd the*
scrub'd our Ship's Bottom, and *bottom of our Ship,* and here
dug some Wells on shore, where also we *dug Wells ashore* on the
we got some Water.   Bay, and filled all our Water
                                    . . . .

The English Hermit

P. 64

On the Eighth we went to the Isle of *Mayo, another of the Cape Verd Islands,* but made no Stay.

I, 103

we went from hence to *Mayo, another of the Cape Verd Islands.*

P. 64

We saw at Southwest the Island of *del Togo,* which *is remarkable for being a Vulcano* or burning Mountain, which *issues out Flames of Fire; yet they are only discern'd in the Night,* and *then are seen a great Way at Sea:* Yet there are inhabitants on this Island (*as I have been inform'd* by the *Portuguese* of the Island of St. *Nicholas*) *that live at the Foot of the Mountain, near the Sea:* There is also *Cocoa Nuts, Plantins, Goats and Fowls.*

I, 105

Fogo and Brava are two small Islands lying to the Westward of St. Iago, but of little note; only Fogo *is remarkable for its being a Vulcano:* . . . . out of the top whereof *issue Flames of Fire, yet only discerned in the night:* and then *it may be seen a great way at Sea.* Yet this Island is not without Inhabitants, who *live at the foot of the Mountain near the Sea:* Their substance is much the same as in the other Islands: they have some *Goats, Fowls, Plantains, Coco-Nuts, &c., as I am informed.*

P. 65

We sail'd all Night with a small easy Gale, and at Break of Day made the *Canaries.* . . . . about three Leagues; we crouded all our Sail, and came to an Anchor in the Harbour of *Sancta Cruz,* in the Island Teneriffe . . . . in *about thirty Fathom Water, black slimy Ground, about half a Mile from the Shore:* It being generally pretty high Land, it is

II, 351

[He stood away for the Island of Teneriffe and put in at Santa Cruz.] So there I come to an Anchor Jan. 30th, *in 33 Fathom-water, black slimy Ground; about half a Mile from the Shore* . . . . The Shore is generally high Land, and in most Places steep too. *This Road lies so open to the East,* that Winds from that

The English Hermit	DAMPIER
very bad going a-shore here in Boats, and Ships riding here *are often forc'd to put to Sea, or slip their Anchors,* by reason the *Road lies so open to the* East. Ships are here *supply'd with good Water* between the *Coves,* where the Ships generally water.	Side make a great Swell, and *very bad going ashore in Boats:* The Ships that ride here are then *often forced to put to Sea,* and sometimes to cut or *slip their Anchors,* not being able to weigh them. The best and smoothest Landing is in *a small sandy Cove,* about a Mile to the N.E. of the Road, where there is *good Water,* with which Ships that lade *here are supply'd* . . . .
Pp. 65–66	II, 351–52
Sancta Cruz, a small Town fronting the Sea, has two Forts to secure the Road:	Between this Watering-place and Santa Cruz are two little Forts; which with some Batteries scatter'd along the Coast command the Road. *Santa Cruz its self is a small unwalled Town fronting the Sea, guarded with two other Forts to secure the Road.*
P. 65	II, 352
Here some *English* Merchants reside. Their Houses are low and uniform, *cover'd with Pantile:*	There are about 200 Houses in the Town, all two Stories high, strongly built with Stone, and *covered with Pantile.*
Pp. 65–66	II, 353
They have *Oranges, Lemons, and other Fruits, Flowers, and Salading,* also Abundance of pleasant Gardens.	The Laguna, near Santa Cruz have many Gardens which are set round with *Oranges, Limes, and other Fruits:* In the middle of which are Pot-herbs, *Sallading, Flowers, &c.*

The English Hermit	DAMPIER
P. 66	II, 355
At Orotavia . . . . *are many Convents.* Ships are forc'd *to slip their Cables* perhaps *three or four times,* by reason of the Winds, and put to Sea before they can take in all their Loading.	I was told that that Town [Oratavia] is bigger than Laguna; that it has but one Church, *but many Convents:* That the Port is but ordinary at best, and is very bad when the N.W. Winds blow. . . . . Upon these Signs Ships either get up their Anchors or *slip their Cables and put to Sea,* and ply off and on till the Weather is over. Sometimes they *are forced to do so 2 or 3 Times before they can take in their Lading.*
P. 66	II, 355–56
Here is *Wheat, Barley, and Maize, also Beans and Peas; Apples, Pears, Plumbs, Cherries, Pomegranites, Citrons, Oranges, Lemons, and several other Fruits* excellently good; *also Horses, Asses, Mules, Cows, Goats, Hogs, Deer and Fowl,* both tame and wild, very plenty. *Provisions are dear on the trading Islands, but cheap on the other.*	here is Store of Grain, as *Wheat, Barly and Maiz* . . . . They have also *some Beans and Peas* . . . . *Apples, Pears, Plumbs, Cherries, and excellent* Peaches, Apricocks, Guava's, *Pomegranates, Citrons, Oranges, Lemons, Limes* . . . . They are also well stocked with *Horses, Cows, Asses, Mules, Sheep, Goats, Hogs,* Conies, and Plenty of Deer . . . . Lastly, here *are many Fowls,* as . . . . *Fowls and other Eatables are dear on the Trading Islands, but very plentiful and cheap on the other.*
P. 57	I, 123–24
We . . . . anchor'd [at Lobos] at twenty Fathom Water, in	This Lobos consists indeed of *two little Islands,* . . . . a small

The English Hermit

DAMPIER

clean Ground, between *the two Islands.* Here we resolv'd to careen our Ship; accordingly, observing the Time of high Water, we *put her into a Cove,* in the *southermost* Island, where we hall'd her up as far as we could on the Land . . . . *The Island is barren, and without fresh Water.* Here we kill'd several *Seals, Sea Lyons, Boobies and Penguins, a Sea-Foul about as big as a Duck, whose Flesh is very ordinary Food, but their Eggs extremely good.* Here also we found a *small black Fowl, that makes Holes in the Ground to roost in at Nights,* whose *Flesh is* very good . . . .

Channel between, fit for Boats only . . . . There is a *small sandy Cove* or Sandy Bay sheltred from the Winds, at the West end of the *Eastermost* Island, where Ships may careen . . . . Within Land they are both of them partly Rocky, and partly Sandy, *Barren, without any fresh Water,* Tree, Shrub, Grass, or Herbs: or any Land Animals (for the *Seals and Sea-Lions* come ashore here) but Fowls, of which there are great multitudes; as *Boobies, but mostly Penguins . . . .* Penguins *are a Sea-Fowl, about as big as a Duck . . . . Their Flesh is but ordinary Food; but their Eggs are good Meat.* There is another sort of *small black Fowl,* that make holes in the *Sand for their Night Habitations,* whose *Flesh is good sweet Meat.*

BIBLIOGRAPHY

A LIST OF THE MOST USEFUL WORKS CONSULTED

ARBER, EDWARD. *Term Catalogues, 1668–1709* (London, 1903–1906). 3 vols. An invaluable bibliographical aid.
ATKINSON, GEOFFREY. *The Extraordinary Voyage in French Literature* (New York and Paris, 1920–1922). 2 vols. Volume I, "Before 1700"; and Volume II, "From 1700–1720."
BLAIR, EMMA HELEN, and ROBERTSON, JAMES A. *The Philippine Islands, 1493–1803* (Cleveland, 1906). 55 vols. Shows how Dampier figured in the early history of the Philippines.
CAMPBELL, JOHN. *Lives of the . . . . British Admirals . . . .* (London, 1817). 8 vols. Continued down to 1779 by Dr. Birkenhout, to 1780 by Henry R. Yorke, and to 1816 by W. Stevenson (who wrote the life of Dampier).
CHETWOOD, WILLIAM RUFUS. *The Voyages, dangerous Adventures and imminent Escapes of Captain Richard Falconer . . . .* (London, 1720). Divided into three books, paged separately.
————. *The Voyages and Adventures of Capt. Robert Boyle, in Several Parts of the World, &c.* (London, 1726).
————. *The Voyages, Travels, and Adventures of William Owen Gwin Vaughan, Six Years a Slave in Tunis* (London, MDCCXXXVI).
CLOWES, WILLIAM LAIRD [editor]. *The Royal Navy. A History from the Earliest Times to the Present* (London and Boston, 1898). 5 vols.
CHURCHILL, AWNSHAM and JOHN. *A Collection of Voyages and Travels* (London, 1704). 4 vols., folio. References are to this edition unless otherwise stated. Later editions are 1732, 8 vols., folio, and 1744–1747, 8 vols., folio. A classic collection, second only to Hakluyt and Purchas.

COOKE, CAPT. EDWARD. *A Voyage to the South-Sea and Round the World, performed in the years 1708, 1709, 1710 and 1711* (London, 1712). 2 vols. Contains a long account of Alexander Selkirk.

DAMPIER, WILLIAM. *Works.*
Original editions (not always accessible; bibliography and titles often confused):
New Voyage Round the World (London, 1697).
Voyages and Descriptions (London, 1699).
Voyage to New Holland (First Part, London, 1703; Supplement, London, 1709).
Collection of Voyages (London, 1729). 4 vols. Collected edition made by Knapton.
Reprints (see Churchill, Harris, Kerr, and Pinkerton in this list for Dampier in the large collections of voyages):
Dampier's Voyages (London, 1906). 2 vols. Ed. John Masefield. The best modern edition. Referred to in my notes as *Dampier's Voyages* or "Dampier." Generally accessible in libraries but out of print and getting expensive because Masefield's name makes it a collector's item.
A New Voyage Round the World (London, 1927). Ed. N. M. Penzer. A limited edition, on vellum paper, of Dampier's first book in the Argonaut Press Series.

DAMPIER, WILLIAM. *Biographies.*
Campbell. (See Campbell, *Lives of the British Admirals.*)
Cooke. (See Cooke, *A Voyage to the South-Sea.*)
Funnell. (See Funnell, *A Voyage Round the World.*)
Gosse. (See Gosse, *The Pirates' Who's Who,* and *History of Piracy.*)
Gray, Sir Albert. "Introduction" to Dampier's *New Voyage Round the World* (London, 1927). Brief and authoritative.
Markham, Clements R. *The Sea Fathers* (London, 1884). Popular biography, brief, old-fashioned, eulogistic.
Masefield, John. *On the Spanish Main* (New York, 1906). Romantic relation of one of Dampier's voyages.
Russell, W. Clark. *William Dampier* (London and New York, 1889). Men of Action Series. No longer authoritative.
Smyth, W. H. "Life of William Dampier" in the *United Service Journal.* July–November, 1837. No longer authoritative.

Verbeek, Paul. *William Dampier's Leben und Werke,* Nach den Quellen bearb. In *Deutsche Geographische Blätter,* Vols. XXII–XXIII. Bremen, 1899–1900. An abstract of this was published separately under the same title at Bremen, 1899. Painstaking, dull, from geographico-commercial point of view.

Wilkinson, Clennel. *William Dampier* (London and New York, 1929). In the Golden Hind Series. An authoritative life, well written.

DEFOE, DANIEL. *Works.*

The Novels and Miscellaneous Works of Daniel Defoe (Oxford, 1840). 20 vols.

The Romances and Narratives of Daniel Defoe (London, 1895–1896). 16 vols. Ed. George A. Aitken. Good critical introductions and new material including *Captain Gow* and the *King of Pirates.*

The Compleat English Gentleman (London, 1890). Ed. Karl D. Bülbrig.

An Account of the Conduct and Proceedings of the Pirate Gow. Reprinted from the original edition, with Preface and Notes (London, [1890]).

The Four Years Voyages of Capt. George Roberts; being a Series of Uncommon Events Which befell him in a Voyage to the Islands of the Canaries, Cape de Verde, and Barbadoes . . . . Written by Himself (London, 1726).

A General History of Trade (London, 1713). Four parts in one volume, being the bound numbers of a serial issued monthly for four months: [?] to September. Each part has separate title-page.

An Historical Account of the Voyages and Adventures of Sir Walter Raleigh (London, 1719).

The History of the Principal Discoveries and Improvements, In the Several Arts and Sciences: Particularly the great Branches of Commerce, Navigation, and Plantation, In all Parts of the known World (London, MDCCXXVII). A "monthly Undertaking," issued for four months: October, November, December, January, 1726–1727.

DEFOE, DANIEL. *Works* (*continued*).

Letters to Harley, July 1711, submitting a plan of trade, *British Manuscripts Commission Reports, Report on the Portland MSS,* V, 50–52, 58–61, 67.

A Plan of the English Commerce being a Compleat Prospect of the Trade of this Nation, as well the Home Trade as the Foreign. Humbly offered to the Consideration of the King and Parliament (London, 1728).

A Tour thro' the Whole Island of Great Britain, Divided into Circuits of Journies. Giving a Particular Account of whatever is Curious and worth Observation . . . . (London, 1724–1725). 2 vols.

A Weekly Review of the Affairs of France and of all Europe as affected by that nation with an entertaining part in every sheet being the Advice from the Scandalous Club (London, 1704–1712). Vols. 1, 2, 3, 6, 7. Only eight of the original nine volumes are known to exist.

DEFOE, DANIEL. *Biography and Criticism.*

Aitken, George A. "Defoe's Library," in the *Athenaeum* (June 1, 1895), Vol. I for 1895, pp. 706–707.

Dottin, Paul. *Daniel De Foe et ses romans* (Paris and Oxford University Press, 1924). A thesis written in the University of Paris.

———. *The Life and Strange and Surprising Adventures of Daniel Defoe* (New York, 1929). Good life, excellent bibliography.

Lee, William. *Daniel Defoe: His Life, and recently discovered Writings: extending from 1716 to 1729* (London, 1869). 3 vols. Helpful bibliography, but superseded by Trent.

Masefield, John. *Masters of Literature: Defoe* (London, 1909).

Minto, William. *Daniel Defoe* (London, 1885). English Men of Letters Series. Not authoritative.

Secord, Arthur W. *Studies in the Narrative Method of Defoe* (Urbana, Illinois, 1924). A doctoral dissertation at the University of Illinois, being Vol. IX, No. 1, in the *University of Illinois Studies in Language and Literature.* Contains the only serious study of Dampier's literary influence heretofore made.

Trent, William Peterfield. *Defoe, How to Know Him* (Indianapolis, 1916).

———. Bibliography of Defoe in *Cambridge History of English Literature*, Vol. IX. Best Defoe bibliography.

Ullrich, Hermann. "Robinson und Robinsonaden," in *Litterarhistorische Forschungen* (1898). Vols. 6–10 (Heft VII). A list to amaze one who is unaware of the number of desert-isle imitations of *Robinson Crusoe*.

Wackwitz, F. *Enstehungsgeschichte von D. Defoes Robinson Crusoe* (Berlin, 1909).

Wilson, Walter. *Memoirs of the Life and Times of Daniel Defoe containing a Review of his Writing* (London, 1830). 3 vols.

Wright, Thomas. *The Life of Daniel Defoe* (New York, 1894). New edition, 1931, with little new in it.

DE LA ROCHE, MICHAEL. *Memoirs of Literature* (London, 1722). 8 vols. This is the second edition, revised and corrected, of the serial that originally ran from March 1710 to September 1714. Continued as *New Memoirs of Literature*, published from 1725 to 1727.

DUNTON, JOHN. *The Life and Errors of John Dunton, late a Citizen of London* (London, 1705).

English Hermit, The. (See Longueville.)

EVELYN, JOHN. *Diary.* Edition Wheatley (London, 1906). 4 vols.

EXQUEMELIN, JOHN (modern spelling, ESQUEMELING). *The History of the Bucaniers of America* (third edition, London, 1704). Recent ed., with introductory essay by Andrew Lang (New York, 1923).

FORBES, W. CAMERON. *The Philippine Islands* (New York, 1928). 2 vols.

FUNNELL, WILLIAM. *A Voyage Round the World. Containing an Account of Captain Dampier's Expedition into the South-seas in the Ship St. George, in the Years 1703 and 1704* (London, 1707). An apologia, hostile to Dampier.

GIOLO. *An Account of the Famous Prince Giolo, son of the King of Gilolo, Now in England: With an Account of his Life, Parentage and his Strange and Wonderful Adventures . . . . Written from His Own Mouth . . . .* (London, 1692). A chapbook, thought to be written by T. Hyde, thoroughly fictitious.

GOSSE, PHILIP. *The Pirates' Who's Who. Giving Particulars of the Lives and Deaths of the Pirates and Buccaneers* (Boston, 1924).

————. *The History of Piracy* (New York, 1932).

HACKE, WILLIAM. *A Collection of Original Voyages* (London, 1699).

HARRIS, JOHN. *Navigantium atque Itinerantium Bibliotheca or, A Compleat Collection of Voyages and Travels . . . .* (London, 1705). 2 vols., folio. Revised and enlarged by Dr. John Campbell, 1744 and 1764, 2 vols., folio. A classic collection, second only to Hakluyt and Purchas.

HATTON CORRESPONDENCE. Edited by Sir Edward Maunde Thompson for the Camden Society under the title of *Correspondence of the Family of Hatton, being chiefly Letters addressed to Christopher, first viscount Hatton, A.D. 1601–1704.* 2 vols. ([Westminster], 1878). In the Camden Society Publications, n.s., XXII–XXIII.

HEAWOOD, E. *A History of Geographical Discovery in the Seventeenth and Eighteenth Centuries* (Cambridge, 1912).

History of the Works of the Learned. Edited by de la Crose (London, 1699–1711). A monthly serial in which the reviews consist chiefly of digests. "Trifling" books omitted.

JOHNSON, CAPTAIN CHARLES. *A General History of the Robberies and Murders of the Most Notorious Pyrates* (London, 1724). The third edition (1725) reprinted in two volumes (Kensington, 1925 and 1927), edited by Philip Gosse.

KERR, ROBERT. *A General History and Collection of Voyages and Travels arranged in systematic order: forming a complete History of . . . . Navigation . . . . to the present time* (Edinburgh, 1811–1824). 18 vols.

LE FANU, T. P. (See Swift.)

[LONGUEVILLE, PETER]. *The Hermit: or, the Unparalled* [*sic*] *Sufferings and Surprizing Adventures of Mr. Philip Quarll, an Englishman* (Westminster, 1727). Page references are to this edition, described by Esdaile as issue "I" of the first edition.

————. Esdaile, Arundell. "Author and Publisher in 1727. 'The English Hermit,' " in *The Library*, 4th series, II, 185–92 (London and New York, 1922). The issue is that of 1 December 1921.

————. Jones, W. A. *Characters and Criticisms* (New York, 1857). 2 vols. Chapter on Longueville's *English Hermit*, attributing it to Defoe. Not carefully written.

LOWES, JOHN LIVINGSTON. *The Road to Xanadu. A Study in the Ways of the Imagination* (Boston and New York, 1927). Some spicy remarks about *The English Hermit* and Dampier.

Memoirs of Literature. (See de la Roche.)

MOLL, HERMAN. *Atlas Geographus, or a Compleat System of Geography* (London, 1717). 5 vols. The bound volumes of Moll's serial which ran from 1708 to 1717.

NIEUHOFF, JAN. *An Embassy from the East India Company of the United Provinces to China.* Englished by John Ogilby (London, 1669). Folio.

Philosophical Transactions: giving some Accompt of the Present Undertakings, Studies, and Labours in many Considerable Parts of the World (London, 1665–   ).

PINKERTON, JOHN. *A General Collection of the Best and Most Interesting Voyages and Travels* (London, 1808–1814). 17 vols.

RAY, JOHN. *A Collection of Curious Travels and Voyages* (London, 1693). 2 vols. Reprinted in 1707.

ROGERS, CAPTAIN WOODES. *A Cruising Voyage Round the World: First to the South-Seas, thence to the East-Indies, and homewards by the Cape of Good Hope. Begun in 1708, and finish'd in 1711* (London, 1712). New edition, 1928. One of the most popular voyages in Queen Anne's age.

SABIN, JOSEPH. *A Dictionary of Books Relating to America from its Discovery to the Present Time* (New York, 1868–1881). 13 vols.

SELKIRK, ALEXANDER. *Providence Displayed.* An anonymous contemporary account reprinted in the fifth volume of the *Harleian Miscellany* (London, 1810). Vol. V.

SLOANE, SIR HANS. *A Voyage to the Islands Madera . . . . and Jamaica with the Natural History of the last of those Islands . . . .* (London, 1707).

STEELE, SIR RICHARD. *The Englishman.* Original numbers, especially No. 26, containing an account of Alexander Selkirk.

———. *The Ladies' Library. Written by a Lady* (London, 1714). 3 vols.

———. *Tatler.* Edited by George Aitken (London, 1898–1899).

[STEVENS, CAPTAIN JOHN.] *A New Collection of Voyages and Travels* (London, 1711). 2 vols.

SWIFT, JONATHAN. *Works.*

The Works of Jonathan Swift, D.D. . . . . with Notes and a Life of the Author, by Sir Walter Scott. Second edition (London and Edinburgh, 1824). 19 vols. Page references to *Gulliver's Travels* are to Vol. XI of this edition.

Works (London, 1897–1907). 12 vols. Edited by Temple Scott.

Gulliver's Travels (London, 1926). Edited by Harold Williams. Reprint of the first edition including maps. Excellent bibliographical notes.

A Tale of a Tub (Oxford, 1920). Edited by A. C. Guthkelch and D. Nichol Smith.

SWIFT, JONATHAN. *Letters.*

Ball, F. Elrington. *The Correspondence of Jonathan Swift, D.D.* (London, 1910–1914). 6 vols.

Hill, George Birkbeck. *Unpublished Letters of Dean Swift* (London, 1899).

SWIFT, JONATHAN. *Criticism.*

Borkowsky, Theodore. "Quellen zu Swift's Gulliver," in *Anglia,* XV, 345–99.

Eddy, William A. *Gulliver's Travels: A Critical Study* (Princeton Press, 1923).

Frantz, Ray William. "Swift's Yahoo's and the Voyagers," *Modern Philology,* XXIX, 49–57.

Hönncher, E. "Quellen zu Dean Swift's Gulliver's Travels," in *Anglia,* X, 397–428.

Le Fanu, T. P. "Dean Swift's Library," in the *Proceedings of the Royal Society of Antiquaries of Ireland* (Dublin, 1896). Poll, Max. *The Sources of Gulliver's Travels.* In the *Bulletin* of the University of Cincinnati. Number 24, 1909.

Williams, Harold. *Dean Swift's Library* (Cambridge, 1932).

TAVERNIER, JEAN BAPTISTE. *The Six Voyages of John Baptista Tavernier, A Noble Man of France now living, through Turkey into Persia and the East-Indies. Finished in the Year 1670 . . . . made English by J. P.* (London, 1678).

——. *A New and Particular Relation of the Kingdom of Tunquin* (London, 1680). In Tavernier's *Six Voyages* near the end as part of "A Collection of Several Relations and Travels . . . . not printed among his first Six."

TEIXEIRA, PEDRO (also TEIXERA). *The Travels of Pedro Teixera* (London, 1902). Edited by Sinclair and Ferguson, printed for the Hakluyt Society, Series II, Vol. IX. First appeared in Knapton's geographical serial, *A View of the Universe* (London, 1708–1711).

ULLRICH, HERMANN. (See Defoe.)

WAFER, LIONEL. *A New Voyage and Description of the Isthmus of America . . . .* (London, 1699).

INDEX

A

Acapulco, 20, 42, 129, 130

Achin, 16, 20, 89, 91, 92, 105, 109

Acosta's *History of the West Indies*, 186

Addison, Joseph, 3, 37, 66, 159, 197, 205

"Adventure," 167

Adventures and Surprizing Deliverances of James Dubordieu and his Wife, 182

Aitken, George, 96, 101, 111, 217, 218

Alcrane Islands, 185, 186, 187

Aleppo, 90

Aleutian Islands, 4

Amusements Serious and Comical (Brown), 43, 66 n.

Ancient Mariner, 107, 203

Annus Mirabilis, 2

Anson, Admiral, 4, 5, 203

"Antelope," 167, 168

Arabian Sea, 42

Arber, Edward, 35, 50, 215

Archangel, 90, 144

Argensola, 132

Ascension, Island of, 22, 190

Atalantis Major (Defoe), 63

Atlas Geographus (Moll), 35, 42, 55, 60, 176, 221

Atlas Maritimus & Commercialis, 61

Avery, Captain John, 67, 93, 94, 95 ff., 102; *see also* Defoe

B

Bahia, *see* Bay of All Saints

Bantam, 7

Barbadoes, 110, 172

Bathurst, Lord, 203

Bay of All Saints, 23, 100, 120, 121, 122, 123, 128

Behring Strait, 4

Benbow, Admiral, 3, 99 n., 186

Bencoulen, 18

Bengal, 63, 89, 90, 91, 92

Berkeley, Bishop, 202

Bermuda, 112

Beunting, Henry, 62

Bonny, Anne, woman pirate, 94 n.

Borneo, 91

Bosman's *New and Accurate Description . . . . of Guinea*, 60

Bristol privateers, 26 ff., 39, 66, 96, 99

Brown, Tom, 43, 66 n., 199

Buenos Aires, 120, 122, 190

C

California, 42, 142, 143, 144, 196

Campbell, John, 41, 44, 59, 215, 216, 220

Campeachy, Bay of, 8 ff., 19, 33, 42, 78, 97, 98, 110, 162, 185, 186, 187, 200

Canada, 143

Canary Islands, 113, 117, 120, 121, 122, 185, 186, 190, 195

Cape Catoch, 9, 78

Cape of Good Hope, 18–19, 21, 22, 29, 89, 100, 104 and n., 117, 119, 120, 121, 122, 123, 127, 128, 129

Cape St. Augustine, 120

Cape Verde Islands, 113, 120, 121, 123, 195, 209, 211

Captain Singleton, 72, 86, 94, 100 ff., 116, 138, 146, 151, 153, 184; influence of Dampier shown in, 102 ff., 105 f., 107 ff.; sources of, 94, 102

Careri, Gamelli, 132

Cavendish, 51

Celebes Islands, 11

Cervantes, 192

Ceylon, 121

Chaucer, Geoffrey, 2

Cheapo River, 15

Chetwood, William Rufus, 183–92, 199, 205, 215; use of Dampier by, 186, 187 ff.

China, 63, 68, 90, 91, 92, 144, 149

Churchill, Awnsham, 35, 41, 54, 60, 205, 215

Churchill, John, 35, 41, 54, 60, 205, 215

"Cinque Ports," 24, 26

Cockburn, John, 63

Coleridge, Samuel Taylor, 2, 6, 107, 193, 203

Collection of Original Voyages (Hacke), 35, 37, 38, 53, 56 and n., 57, 58, 220

Collection of Voyages and Travels (Churchill), 35, 41, 54, 60, 215

Collier, Jeremy, 38, 199

Colonel Jacque, 110–14, 116, 138, 146, 193; influence of Dampier shown in, 111 ff.

Comical Pilgrim (Defoe), 63

Compleat English Gentleman, 73

Compleat Geographer (Moll), 43, 61

Congreve, William, 3, 67

Construction of Maps and Globes, 61

Cook, Captain James, 203, 204

Cook, Captain John, 12, 113, 133, 134

Cooke, Captain Edward, 39, 71, 216

Corea, 144

Corpus Sanct, or St. Elmo's fire, 46, 107, 108, 195, 208 f.

Cowley, Captain, 38, 57

Cowper, William, 4 n., 203

Coxon, Captain, 11, 98

Crabbe, George, 4 n., 193

Cruising Voyage (Rogers), 39 f., 87, 99, 221

Cuba, 100, 185

Cyrano de Bergerac, 157

D

D'Acugna, C., *Voyages*, 53

Dampier, William, vii, viii, 5, 6, 7– 8, 20 f., 29 f., 32 f., 36 f., 41, 126, 132 n., 140; with the Bristol privateers, 26–29, 39; the buccaneer, 6 f., 11 ff., 16, 38, 39, 136 ff.; the Campeachy voyages, 8 ff., 21; Chetwood and, 186, 187 ff.; Defoe's use of, 68 f., 70, 72 and n., 73, 74 ff., 90 ff., 97 ff., 102 ff., 105 f., 107 ff., 111 ff., 116, 119, 120 ff., 126 ff., 130 ff., 133 ff., 136, 138 ff., 147, 148, 149, 150 ff., 153 ff., 164, 189, 199, 205; his "Discourse of Trade-Winds," 21, 34, 113, 163; editions of the

Voyages, 29, 32, 33 f., 56, 57, 58, 73, 216; and *The English Hermit*, 192 ff., 207 ff.; and Herman Moll, 29, 42, 65, 126, 175 f.; influence upon Swift, 156, 157, 158, 159–81; his journals, vii, 14, 19 f., 20 n., 22, 47, 91, 124, 165; literary influence of, vii, 35, 38 ff., 53 ff., 151 ff., 181, 183 ff., 194, 195 f., 197 ff., 204 f.; his *New Voyage Round the World*, 7, 11 ff., 20 f., 31 f., 41, 47, 48, 56, 73, 80, 84, 128, 158, 160, 163, 171, 172, 177 ff.; popularity of the *Voyages*, 31 f., 33, 34, 35, 37 ff., 43, 50, 53, 55, 57, 59, 68, 107, 148, 196; his publisher Knapton, 20, 21, 33, 35, 43, 55 ff.; his style, 43–49, 126, 151, 152, 153, 160, 161, 162, 164, 171; his *Voyage to New Holland*, 7, 22, 23, 28, 34 f., 41, 48, 126, 128, 141, 158, 169, 171, 176; voyage in the "Roebuck," 20–23, 174; voyage in the "Saint George," 23–26, 99; his *Voyages and Descriptions*, 7, 8 ff., 21, 33 f., 48, 49, 163, 169
Dampier's Passage, 22, 42
Darien, Isthmus of, 13, 21, 38, 42, 97, 98
Davis, Captain, 19, 140
Defoe, Daniel, vii, 3 and n., 6, 37, 44, 51, 63, 64, 66, 67, 69 ff., 93, 94, 148, 154 f., 159, 184, 192, 193, 194 f., 196, 202, 203, 204; *Captain Singleton*, 72, 86, 94, 100–110, 116, 138, 146, 151, 153, 184; *Colonel Jacque*, 110–14, 146; *The Consolidator*,

149; Dampier used by, 68 f., 70, 72 and n., 73, 74 ff., 90 ff., 97 ff., 102 ff., 105 f., 107 ff., 111 ff., 116, 119, 120 ff., 126 ff., 130 ff., 133 ff., 136, 138 ff., 147, 148, 149, 150 ff., 153 ff., 164, 189, 199, 205; interest in trade, 144 ff., 154; *King of Pirates*, 94, 95 ff., 116, 184; his *New Voyage Round the World*, 115–47; *Robinson Crusoe*, vii, 32, 35, 65, 70, 71, 72–92, 93, 94, 107, 109, 115, 116, 120, 126, 146, 152 f., 181, 182 ff., 197, 203, 205; his style, 151 ff., 161, 162
de la Roche, Michael, 63, 219
de Mandelslo, J. Albert, 102, 105
de Renneville, R. A. C., *Voyages*, 54
Dialogues of the Dead (Prior), 202
Diaper, William, 3 n.
Dibdin, Charles, 3 n.
"Discourse of Trade-Winds" (Dampier), 21, 34, 104 n., 113, 163
Dominico, Island of, 186
Donne, John, 2
Dorrington, Edward, 194
Drake, Sir Francis, 3, 41, 51, 119
Drury Lane, 67
Dryden, John, 2, 185
"Duke," 27, 28, 167; *see* Bristol privateers
Dunton, John, 55, 205, 219
"Dutchess," 27, 28, 167; *see* Bristol privateers

E

Eaton, Captain, 12, 133, 134
Editions of Dampier's *Voyages* to 1729, 58
Eddy, William A., viii

Elford's Coffee-house, 66
English Hermit (Longueville), 183,
192 ff., 207 ff., 221
Englishman (Steele), 65, 71
Esdaile, Arundell, 194, 195
Esquemeling (or Exquemelin), 6 n.,
32, 38, 52, 53, 54, 71, 87, 93,
97, 98
Essay on Projects (Defoe), 145
Essex, Earl of, 2
Evelyn, John, 7, 21, 33, 36, 37,
200, 205, 219
Exquemelin, *see* Esquemeling

F

Falconer, William, 2, 3–4 n., 203
Falkland Islands, 4, 128, 196
Fielding, Henry, 192
Fisher, George, 123
Florida, Gulf of, 185
Formosa, Island of, 11, 90, 101,
107
Fort St. George, 130
Foyer, Archibald, 38
Frantz, R. W., 177
Frezier, Captain, 40, 41, 199
Friday, *see Robinson Crusoe*
Frobisher, Sir Martin, 119, 125,
144
Fryke and Schewitzer, *Relation of
Two Several Voyages*, 61
Funnell, William, 24, 25, 39, 57,
59; his *Voyage Round the World*,
25 and n., 39, 57, 59, 60, 65,
99, 216, 219

G

Galápagos Islands, 13, 140, 196
Garrick, David, 3 n.
Garth, Samuel, 202

Gay, John, 3 n., 64, 66, 67, 202,
203
*General History of the....Most
Notorious Pyrates* (Johnson), 67,
71, 93, 96, 220
General History of the Stage (Chet-
wood), 183
General History of Trade (Defoe),
63
Giolo, 31, 180, 220; *see* Jeoly
Goa, 103
Golden Island, 21, 38
Gorgona Bay, 196
Gow, Captain, 67, 93, 110, 149,
150
Grand, Isle of, 191
*Great Historical, Geographical,
Genealogical and Poetical Dic-
tionary* (Collier), 38
Great Lakes, 144
Guanchaquo, 11, 12, 13
Guayaquil, 11, 40, 99, 100
Guiana, 74, 145, 154
Gulliver's Travels, vii, 35, 37, 46,
149, 156–81, 182, 197; Dam-
pier's influence shown in, 156 ff.,
164 ff., 177 ff., 191, 202, 205;
the Yahoos, 157, 158, 178 ff.

H

Hacke, Captain William, 35, 37,
38, 53, 56 and n., 57, 58, 60,
220
Hakluyt, Richard, 50, 59, 71, 74,
152, 153, 154
Hakluytus Posthumous (Purchas),
51, 71
Harris, John, 25 n., 35, 41, 42, 44,
54, 59, 60, 205, 220
Hatton, Charles, 32 f., 46, 52

Hatton Correspondence, 32–33 and n., 52 and n., 220
Havana, 111
Hawaiian Islands, 4
Hawkins, Sir John, 51
Henley, Anthony, 66
Herbert, Sir Thomas, 177
Hermit, The, see *English Hermit*
Historical Account of the Voyages and Adventures of Sir Walter Raleigh (Defoe), 74, 145
Historical Relation of Ceylon (Knox), 70, 85, 102
History of the Buccaneers [Bucaniers] of America (Esquemeling), 6 n., 38, 52, 53, 71
History of the Principal Discoveries and Improvements.... (Defoe), 63, 147
History of the Royal Society (Sprat), 186
History and Strange Adventures of Philip Ashton, 193
History of the Works of the Learned, 34 f., 57
Hobby, Captain, 11
Honduras, 7, 83, 193
"Hopewell," 167
Hottentots, as a source of the Yahoos, 158, 178 ff.
Hudson's Bay, 51, 143, 144
Huet, P. D., 62
Hughes, John, 3 n., 201 f.

I

Ides, E. Ysbrants, 70, 71, 153
Imitations of *Robinson Crusoe*, 182 ff., 193
Indian Sea, 42
Indo-China, 149
Isthmus of America, 11; *see* Darien

J

Jamaica, 8, 9, 10, 11, 13, 98, 110, 135, 184, 186, 187, 200, 202
James, Captain, 9
Japan, 144
Java, 7, 103
Jeoly (Giolo), Dampier's "Painted Prince," 20, 31, 36, 180, 220
"John and Martha," 7
Johnson, Captain Charles, 67, 71, 220
Johnson, Samuel, 3, 203 f.
Jones, Tom, 192
Journey over Land from the Gulf of Honduras to the Great South-Sea, 63
Journey to London (King), 66 n.
Journey to Paris (Swift), 159
Juan Fernandez, 20, 23, 24, 26, 28, 41, 43, 71, 75, 80 ff., 86, 88, 89, 100, 133, 134, 135, 191, 196

K

Kern, Jerome, 160
Kidd, Captain, 67, 93
Killigrew, Tom, 192
King, William, 64 and n., 66 n., 199 and n.
King of Pirates (Defoe), 94, 95 ff., 116, 184; *see* Avery, Captain
Knapton, James, 20, 21, 33, 35, 37, 43, 56, 60 ff., 205; relations with Dampier, 55 ff.
Knox, Robert, 70, 77 n., 85, 102

L

Ladies' Library, 63, 222
Ladrone Islands, 140, 176
Lamb, Charles, 151, 193

Lang, Andrew, 6
Le Comte, Louis, 70, 71, 153, 177
Lee, William, 110, 184 n., 218
Leeward Islands, 172
Le Fanu, T. P., 160, 223
Le Maire, 140, 141
Le Maire, Straits of, 127, 128
Le Sage, 192
Lima, 12, 13, 133
Linscoten, Hugh, 186
Lloyd's, 5
Lobos Islands, 11, 134, 213 f.
Logwood industry, 8 ff., 30, 33, 78 f., 97, 98
London Journal, 64
Longueville, Peter, 183, 196, 205; *The English Hermit*, 192–96, 207–14, 221
Love for Love (Congreve), 3
Lowes, J. L., 46 and n.
Luttrell, Narcissus, 36

M

Macheath, Captain, 67
Madagascar, 89, 90, 100 f., 102, 105, 110, 117 f., 121, 129, 130, 133, 169, 172; pirates there, 21, 69, 93, 95, 96, 99 f., 118, 119, 138 f.
Madeira Islands, 185
Magellan, Straits of, 4, 127, 128, 134, 147, 190
Malacca, Straits of, 90, 120
Manila, 130, 131, 137
Markham, Clements R., 19 n., 22–23
Martyr, Peter, 186
Marvel, Andrew, 2
Masefield, John, 6 and n., 22; his edition of Dampier, 19 n., 216
Mayo, Island of, 211

Mechanical Operation of the Spirit, 159
Memoirs of Literature (de la Roche), 63
Mercator (Defoe), 78
Merry Travelers (Ward), 66 n.
Milton, John, 2, 185
Mindanao, *see* Philippine Islands
Miscellanea Aurea (Killigrew), 192
Misson, Maximilien, 66, 102, 105, 170 n.
Moll, Herman, 4, 29, 42 ff., 55, 60, 61, 63, 65, 73, 126, 173, 175, 176, 180, 199, 221
Moll Flanders, 93, 110, 116
Moll Flanders (Defoe), 193
Montague, Charles, 21, 32, 48
Morgan, Sir Henry, 52
Mosquito Indian of Juan Fernandez, 20, 38, 43, 80, 84, 88 ff., 135 and n., 188; source of Defoe's Friday, 80 ff.
Mosquito Indians, 12, 83, 84
Mulgrave, Lord, 204
Murray, Thomas, 200
Muscovy, 90

N

Narborough, Sir John, 52, 116, 119, 125, 126
Narrative Method of Defoe (Secord), 70 n., 72 n., 77 n., 218 f.
Natural History of Jamaica (Sloane), 171, 186, 200, 222
Navigantium atque Itinerantium (Harris), 25 n., 42, 44, 54, 59, 220
Nelson, Admiral, 3
New Britain, Island of, 22, 42
New Collection of Voyages and Travels (Knapton), 54, 60

New Collection of Voyages and Travels (Stevens), 55, 222
New Discovery of Terra Incognita Australis (Sadeur), 160
Newfoundland, 7, 102, 185
New Guinea, 21, 22, 42, 140, 141
New Holland, 21, 22, 30, 34, 35, 41, 42, 121, 129, 140, 167, 168, 170, 171, 172, 173, 174, 175, 177, 178, 180
New Voyage and Description of the Isthmus of America (Wafer), 56, 58, 223
New Voyage Round the World (Dampier), *see* Dampier
New Voyage Round the World (Defoe), 72, 115–47, 115 n., 151; Dampier's influence shown in, 115 ff., 119 ff., 122 ff., 126 ff., 130 ff., 136 ff.; and Defoe's interest in trade, 144 ff.
Nicaragua, 83
Nicobar Islands, 11, 16, 90, 105, 106, 109
Northeast Passage, 144
Northwest Passage, 4, 140, 144
Nova Zembla, 143, 144
Numismata: A Discourse of Medals (Evelyn), 37

O

Occasioned by Reading the Travels of Captain Lemuel Gulliver (Pope), 202
Oldmixon, *History of England*, 38, 199
Oldys, William, 59 and n.
Olearius' *Voyages and Travels of the Ambassadors*, 51, 71, 102
Omai, 204
Oratavia, 150, 213

Orford, Earl of, 21, 32, 34
Orinoco River, 74 and n.
Orkney Islands, 149
Osborne's *Collection of Voyages*, 42
Ostia, 190
Oxford, Earl of, 146

P

"Painted Prince," 20, 36, 180; *see* Jeoly
Panama, 12, 13, 133
Patagonia, 52, 118, 119, 136 and n., 154
Paterson, William, 21, 37
Pembroke, Earl of, 41, 48
Penzer, N. M., viii, 58, 216
Pepys, Samuel, 21, 200
Pernambuco, 120, 121, 122
Perry, Henry Ten Eyck, viii
Persia, Gulf of, 89
Philippine Islands, 11, 19, 20, 30, 42, 68, 69, 90, 101, 107 f., 118, 119, 120, 129, 130 ff., 133, 136 f., 139, 142
Philosophical Transactions, 199, 200
Pickering, Captain, 24
Pickle, Peregrine, 192
Pinkerton's *Voyages*, 50 n.
Plate River (Rio de la Plata), 122, 126, 127, 147
Pope, Alexander, 3, 202, 203, 204
Porto Bello, 11, 21
Port Royal, 8
Port Saint Julian, 127
Principall Navigations (Hakluyt), 51, 71
Prior, Matthew, 201
Providence Displayed, 43, 66, 71, 88, 221; *see* Selkirk

Psalmanaazaar, George, his *Island of Formosa*, 64 n., 66
Puná, 97, 98 ff.
Purchas, Samuel, 51, 59, 71, 152, 153, 154

Q

Quarll, *see* Longueville
Quito, 40

R

Raleigh, Sir Walter, 51, 145
Random, Roderick, 192
Ray, John, 52, 54
Read, Captain, 106
Read, Mary, woman pirate, 94 n.
Remarks on Several Parts of Italy (Addison), 66
Review (Defoe), 145, 146, 148, 149, 152
Ringrose, Basil, 37, 38, 49, 98, 137
Rio de la Plata, *see* Plate River
Rio Janeiro, 122
Roberts, Captain George, 150; his *Voyages and Cruising*, 56
Robinson Crusoe, vii, 32, 65, 69–92, 93, 94, 109, 115, 116, 126, 146, 153, 197, 203, 205; Crusoe's man Friday, 74, 79 ff.; Dampier's influence shown in, 35, 68 f., 70, 71, 72, 73, 74 ff., 84 ff., 90 ff., 107, 120, 150 f., 152, 181, 189; imitations of, 182 ff., 193; origin of name, 84 ff.
Robinsoniad, *see* Imitations of *Robinson Crusoe*
"Roebuck," 21 f., 166, 167, 168, 170, 174

Rogers, Captain Woodes, 5, 27, 28, 29, 39 f., 45, 66, 70, 88, 95 n., 96, 99, 152, 191, 199, 221
Roxana, 93
"Royal Prince," 7
Royal Society, 22, 32, 48, 171, 199, 200, 204

S

Sadeur, James, 160
"Saint George," 23 ff., 37, 99, 166, 167
Saint Helena, island of, 19, 20
St. Iago (Cape Verde Islands), 211
St. John, island of, 150
St. Lawrence River, 144
St. Matthias Island, 87
St. Nicholas, island of, 210, 211
Sall, island of, 195, 210
Sallee, 190
Santa Cruz (Cape Verde Islands), 211, 212
Santa Maria, 24
Santa Maria River, 15
Sawkins, Captain, 11, 97
Scanderoon, 90
Scotch East India Company, 21
Scott, Sir Walter, vii, 6, 157
Scriblerus Club, 166, 202
Secord, Arthur W., viii, 70 and n., 72 n., 77 n., 218 f.
Seitz, Robert W., viii
Selkirk, Alexander, 26, 28, 29, 30, 43, 65, 70, 71, 79 ff., 82, 84, 88, 89, 106, 203, 221, 222; connection with Dampier's Mosquito Indian, 87 ff.
Serial publication of travels, 50, 55, 61, 63
Shakespeare, 2, 185

Sharp, Captain, 11, 13, 57, 97, 137
Shelvocke, Captain, 40 f., 199
Sheppard, History of John, 116
Siam, 90, 91
Sir Harry Wildair, 67 n.
Six Voyages of John Baptista Tavernier, 223
Sloane, Sir Hans, 37, 171, 186, 199, 200, 201, 222
Smollett, Tobias, 3, 192
South Sea, 11, 26, 27, 41, 98, 127, 133, 136, 140, 145, 173, 183, 190
South Sea, or the Biter Bit, The (Chetwood), 184
South Sea Bubble, 5, 67, 69, 183, 203
Spectator, 37, 159, 197
Spenser, Edmund, 2
Spice Islands, 20, 68, 90, 91, 101, 107, 108, 121, 130
Spragge, Sir Edward, 7
Sprat, *History of Royal Society*, 186
Steele, Richard, 37, 63, 65 f., 192, 197, 198, 205, 222
Stevens, Captain John, *View of the Universe*, 55, 60, 222
Stock Jobbers, or the Humours of Exchange Alley (Chetwood), 184
Stradling, Captain, 24, 26
Strange Adventures of the Count de Vinevil (Aubin), 183
Strange Adventures and Signal Deliverances of Mr. Philip Ashton, Jun., 183, 193 f.
Sturmy's *Compleat Mariner*, 180
Successful Pyrate (Johnson), 67
Sumatra, island of, 11, 16, 18, 89, 92, 106

Surkan, 91
Swan, Captain, 13, 19, 47, 136, 137, 198
Swift, Jonathan, vii, 3, 37, 44, 46, 64, 66, 140, 158 ff., 185, 191, 192, 193, 199, 202, 204, 205; bibliography of works, letters, and criticism, 222–23; *Gulliver's Travels*, 156–81; *see also Gulliver's Travels, Tale of a Tub*, etc.
System of Geography (Moll), 55

T

Taboga, Island of, 24
Tahiti, 4
Tale of a Tub (Swift), 158, 159
Tartary, 90, 144
Tasmen, Janszoon, 52, 174
Tatler, 37, 192, 198
Tavernier, Jean Baptiste, 223
Teixeira, Pedro (also Teixera), 132 and n., 223
Tellez, Balthazar, *A New View of the Universe*, 54, 61
Tempest, The, 2
Teneriffe, 186, 211
Term Catalogues, 1668–1709 (Arber), 35, 56, 64, 215
Terra Australis Incognita, 139, 140, 159
Terra del Fuego, 140
Thomson, James, 3 and n.
Timor, Island of, 22
Tinker, Chauncey Brewster, viii
Togo, Island of, 211
Tonquin, 20, 30, 49, 91, 92, 149 and n., 171, 172
Tour thro' the Whole Island of Great Britain (Defoe), 126
Trade, Defoe's interest in, 144 ff.

Transactioneer (King), 199
Travels of the Holy Patriarchs, Prophets, Judges, Kings, our Saviour Christ, and his Apostles, 62
Travels of the Jesuits, 61
Treatise of Both Globes, 63
Tres Marías Islands, 196
Trivia (Gay), 66, 202
Truxillo, 11, 13, 134
Tutchin, John, 37, 51, 205

U

Ullrich, Hermann, 182 n., 219

V

Valdivia, 13, 133, 147
Van Diemen's Land, 171, 175
Vanessa, 158
van Schouten, William, 41, 118, 140
Vera Cruz, 111
Victor, Benjamin, 189
Virginia, 11, 20, 49, 134, 209
Voyage to Cajamai (King), 64, 66 n.
Voyage into England (Swift), 159
Voyage to New Holland, see Dampier
Voyage Round the World (Funnell), 25 and n., 39, 57, 59, 60, 65, 99, 219
Voyage to the South-Sea (Cooke), 71, 216
Voyages, collections of: before Dampier, 50 ff.; following Dampier's *New Voyage,* 35, 41, 53 ff., 59, 60; need for bibliography of, 50 n.

Voyages and Adventures of Capt. Robert Boyle (Chetwood), 189–91, 215
Voyages . . . . of Captain Richard Falconer (Chetwood), 183, 184–89, 215
Voyages and Descriptions, see Dampier
Voyages to the South Seas (James Cook), 204
Voyages of William Vaughan (Chetwood), 191–92, 215

W

Wafer, Lionel, 21, 37, 38, 47, 56, 60, 65, 93, 223
Waller, Edmund, 184, 185
Walsh, William, 3 n., 202
Walton, Captain, 186
Ward, Ned, 3 n., 66 n., 199, 202
Wase, Captain, 185
Wells, Edward, *An Historical Geography of the Old and New Testaments,* 62
West Sea, 143
Whiteway, Mrs., 159
Wilkinson, Clennel, vii, 217
William III, King, 93, 146, 202
Wilson, Walter, 151
Wood, Captain, 144
Wood, Sir John, 119, 125
Woodward, Dr. John, 22, 200
Wordsworth, William, 193

Y

Yahoos, *see Gulliver's Travels*
Young, Edward, 3 n., 202

Z

Zana, 11